THE REFLEXIVE NATURE OF AWARENESS

The Reflexive Nature of Awareness

A Tibetan Madhyamaka Defence

PAUL WILLIAMS

MOTILAL BANARSIDASS PUBLISHERS
PRIVATE LIMITED • DELHI

First Indian Edition: Delhi, 2000
First Published: Britain, 1998

Published in association with
Curzon Press, Britain

ISBN: 81-208-1714-1

Also available at:

MOTILAL BANARSIDASS
236, 9th Main III Block, Jayanagar, Bangalore 560 001
41 U.A. Bungalow Road, Jawahar Nagar, Delhi 110 007
8 Mahalaxmi Chamber, Warden Road, Mumbai 400 026
120 Royapettah High Road, Mylapore, Chennai 600 004
Sanas Plaza, 1302, Baji Rao Road, Pune 411 002
8 Camac Street, Calcutta 700 017
Ashok Rajpath, Patna 800 004
Chowk, Varanasi 221 001

British Library Cataloguing in Publication Data
A catalogue record of this book is available from the British Library

FOR SALE IN SOUTH ASIA ONLY

Printed in India
BY JAINENDRA PRAKASH JAIN AT SHRI JAINENDRA PRESS,
A-45 NARAINA, PHASE I, NEW DELHI 110 028
AND PUBLISHED BY NARENDRA PRAKASH JAIN FOR
MOTILAL BANARSIDASS PUBLISHERS PRIVATE LIMITED,
BUNGALOW ROAD, DELHI 110 007

Contents

EDITOR'S PREFACE

This volume inaugurates a series of monographs on Buddhism as a part of the cultural and intellectual life and history of Tibet and the Tibetan cultural area, an area encompassing lands from the Himalayas to the far reaches of Mongolian civilisation. The Dharma Vajra Series will include works exploring the diversity of these traditions through a variety of approaches, including not only philosophical analyses, but also historical, sociological, and anthropological studies, textual and literary studies, bibliographic works, and studies of Buddhist arts and music.

We are fortunate indeed to have Paul Williams' work on self-awareness *(rang rig/svasaṃvedana)* as our lead volume both for its subject matter and its author. Self-awareness is a topic that is central to the practice of Tibetan Buddhism—especially the rDzogs chen tradition of the rNying ma school—as well being one of the doctrinal points essential to Tibetan doxographic analyses of the Buddhist philosophies of Indian Mahāyāna. It is one of the notable issues in the dialogue between Yogācāra and Madhyamaka Buddhism in India and later, in Tibet, between the dGe lugs tradition initiated by Tsong kha pa and writers such as Mi pham 'Jam dbyangs rnam rgyal rgya mtsho, dialogues that shed light not only on Buddhist views about the nature of the mind and of spiritual experience, but also on the primary ontological distinction made in Mahāyāna Buddhism, that between conventional and ultimate truth.

These are subjects that Paul Williams has explored for some time, beginning with his presentation to the Csoma de Kőrös Symposium held in Austria in 1981—a paper subsequently published as "On *Rang Rig*" and included in its entirety as an appendix to the present work. The author has written prolifically on Madhyamaka in Tibet—introducing us to thinkers and ideas outside of the dGe lugs pa orthodoxy and, in so doing, giving voice to Tibetan philosophical interpretations that have not received as much attention as they should from modern Western scholars. His 1989 book *Mahāyāna Buddhism: The Doctrinal Foundations* (London and New York: Routledge) is well known for its lucid overview of the Mahāyāna texts and their philosophies not only in India and Tibet but throughout Asia. The present work is a continuation of what he has given us in the past: clear, but closely argued, expositions and analyses of Tibetan interpretations of Indian Buddhism, illuminated by a fine insight into the historical context of Tibetan Buddhist philosophising.

Joe Bransford Wilson
The University of North Carolina at Wilmington

ACKNOWLEDGMENTS

This monograph began as an article for a collection of my papers on the Indo-Tibetan interpretation of verses from the *Bodhicaryāvatāra*. That book is forthcoming as *Studies in the Philosophy of the Bodhicaryāvatāra*. The article simply outgrew its paper format and has become an academic monograph, although it really belongs with those other papers. Research on the present work and most of the writing was completed during my tenure of the Numata Chair of Buddhist Studies at the University of Calgary, Winter 1994. I remain extremely grateful to the University of Calgary, its library, and the Department of Religious Studies for the wonderful facilities and hospitality they extended to me during that visit. I have developed a great affection for Calgary and its university, and the department showed itself a model of how to treat a visiting professor. In particular, I should like to thank my colleagues in Buddhist Studies at Calgary, Leslie Kawamura and A.W. Barber, together with their families, for their warm friendship, the stimulating discussions, and willingness to help and offer whatever might be needed for my research. I am grateful also to Ernst Steinkellner for permission to reprint as Appendix 2 my 1983 article 'On *rang rig*', and to my research student Ornan Rotem for covering some of my teaching while I was in Canada, and for his computing talents, patience and humor. A particular debt of gratitude is due to Joe Wilson, who not only accepted this book for inclusion in his series but also went over it minutely, helped with the preparation of the manuscript, and made a number of helpful suggestions. I should also like to record my appreciation of Ursula King for her encouragement and support, including financial support, for Buddhist Studies and the Centre for Buddhist Studies at the University of Bristol.

I am delighted to be able to dedicate this small book to Leslie Kawamura, a meticulous scholar who I am sure will not agree with much that I have written, a great enthusiast for Mi pham and one of the first to introduce Mi pham to Western scholarship.

PREFACE

Those with an interest in these things are now familiar with the idea that the philosophical and meditative tradition called rDzogs chen, known most notably from the rNying ma pa school of Tibetan Buddhism, teaches a primordial substratum *(gdod ma'i gzhi)* which while beyond all conceptuality is commonly referred to using terms which have a primary mentalistic significance. For example, this primordial substratum is spoken of as 'mind-as-such' or 'the very nature of mind' *(sems nyid/sems kyi chos nyid* or *sems kyi rang bzhin)*. Another important term is *rang gi rig pa*, 'awareness of itself' or 'reflexive awareness', sometimes referred to as 'a mere gnosis which is reflexive awareness' (*so so rang rig pa'i ye shes tsam)*. This reflexivity of the primordial substratum is one of its most important characteristics, indicated in the use of such metaphors as 'luminosity' *(gsal ba)* or 'clear light' *('od gsal)*, and the use sometimes of the mirror-image in trying to give some analogous understanding of that which is held to be beyond all conceptuality. Common to many of these metaphorical images is the idea of something which renders itself known in the very act of referring beyond itself to others. Thus, to use a common image, the lamp makes known objects in a dark room and in so doing makes itself known too. It is not necessary to bring another lamp *ad infinitum* in order to illuminate the first lamp. The mirror is known in its reflectivity, in reflecting an image it also makes itself known as a mirror. We can speak of this quality found in mirrors and lamps—but, in Buddhist thought, most clearly and notoriously in lamps—as reflexivity. The lamp is reflexive, it illuminates itself *in the very act* of illuminating others.

The primordial substratum in rDzogs chen (and Mahāmudrā too for that matter) is of the very nature of mind-as-such, and it is characterised by reflexivity. This primordial substratum, however, while in some sense ultimate, is not thought of as something completely other than the relative, the conventional. The nature of mind-as-such could not be divorced from mind, whatever that mind may be including everyday consciousness *(rnam shes)*. Tibetan systems always strive to show how the two truths, ultimate and conventional, are finally integrated. The ultimate nature of mind (= *ye shes*, 'gnosis'), mind-as-such *(sems nyid)*, while completely undefiled, always pure, is necessarily the ultimate nature of all mind (indeed all things). Thus if mind-as-such is fundamentally characterised by reflexivity, it could not be that this reflexivity comes into existence when mind-as-such is realized in the enlightened understanding. Rather, reflexivity is the very characteristic of all mind, it is what mind is—mind, consciousness makes itself known in the very act of knowing things which are other than it. Indeed the very presence of reflexivity in all consciousness is closely integrated with the realization of the presence of mind-as-such in all consciousness.

There is no problem in seeing that all this is indeed the rDzogs chen perspective.[1] The idea that all consciousness is in its very nature characterised by self-awareness *(rang rig/svasaṃvedana)* is also a view held widely in Indian Mahāyāna thought. It is an essential feature of Cittamātra (Yogācāra), and is defended with epistemological sophistication by Dharmakīrti. As we shall see, it plays an important role in the formation by Śāntarakṣita of what Tibetan doxographers call 'Yogācāra-Svātantrika Madhyamaka'. On the other hand the self-awareness of consciousness is attacked with vigor as part of their criticisms of Yogācāra Cittamātra by the Svātantrika Bhāvaviveka and also by Candrakīrti and Śāntideva. Candrakīrti and Śāntideva are both spoken of in the Tibetan tradition as 'Prāsaṅgika Mādhyamikas'. Thus it would seem *prima facie* that the rDzogs chen perspective on self-awareness has some affinities with the Cittamātra trend of Indian thought, but definitely not with Prāsaṅgika Madhyamaka. On the other hand no Tibetan tradition and few thinkers from the eleventh century onwards would be prepared to admit to holding anything other than a form of Madhyamaka, usually Prāsaṅgika Madhyamaka, as the highest philosophical viewpoint *(lta ba)*. No one would want to admit to holding Yogācāra Cittamātra as the highest viewpoint.

There is no doubt that any view of an ultimate reality—whether mentalistic or not—could have problems in integrating with a Prāsaṅgika Madhyamaka perspective which clearly criticizes all ultimate, inherently existent, entities. Nevertheless, there are various strategies by which they could be reconciled.

---

[1] For a good and authoritative survey of rDzogs chen thought and history see Karmay (1988), esp. ch. 7.

For example, it is possible to argue that Prāsaṅgika Madhyamaka is correct as far as it goes, but yet does not have the finally final word. Perhaps it simply clears away that which does not exist, without treating a true Ultimate Reality which in fact does exist. Or Prāsaṅgika could be held to be correct as far as anything which can be conceptualized is concerned, although our putative Ultimate Reality is nonconceptual and therefore not touched by the Prāsaṅgika negations of inherent existence. This might be related to a strategy whereby Prāsaṅgika becomes correct as far as philosophical analysis is concerned, although when we enter into direct nonconceptual absorption in meditation we find a true Ultimate Reality. Or it might even be possible to argue with the hermeneutical ingenuity not uncommon among Tibetans that Prāsaṅgika Madhyamaka does indeed teach a true Ultimate Reality, or even that the ultimate reality is not really an inherently existent Ultimate Reality at all. Thus there are strategies by which an adherent of rDzogs chen might attempt to reconcile a Prāsaṅgika perspective with his or her approach to the ultimate reality.

A problem arises, however, with what is held to be a Prāsaṅgika approach to the conventional. We have seen that while reflexivity ('self-awareness') is a feature of the rDzogs chen ultimate reality, it is important that this reflexivity is also present in all mental states, in all states of consciousness. Consciousness *qua* consciousness is reflexive.[2] While a follower of

2 Unless otherwise indicated, I shall use the term 'consciousness' with reference to any mental event and not simply as a translation for *vijñāna/rnam shes*. Thus in this usage *jñāna/ye shes* would also be included under the scope of the term 'consciousness'. It is important to bear this in mind, since the

rDzogs chen might be able to accommodate the Prāsaṅgika denial of any putative Ultimate Reality, what of the Prāsaṅgika denial of what are in fact essential *features* of the rDzogs chen ultimate reality? What of the denial of *svasaṃvedana*? One response would be to suggest that while the Prāsaṅgika does indeed deny self-awareness, that denial is of an ultimate self-awareness (which we could then cope with, in fact neutralize, using the suggested strategies above), but does not deny that consciousness *qua* consciousness, in other words consciousness as known in the world, is self-aware. In other words, the Prāsaṅgika denial is of only the ultimate status of *svasaṃvedana*, and does not include its conventional existence as indeed an essential feature of what we know and accept conventionally as consciousness. The problem here, however, is that from at least the time of Tsong kha pa and the foundation of the dGe lugs tradition of Tibetan Buddhism in the early years of the fifteenth century it has been strongly urged that the Prāsaṅgika denial of *svasaṃvedana* is a refutation of the existence of self-awareness or reflexivity *both ultimately and conventionally*. Indeed so strongly did Tsong kha pa hold this view that he saw it as one of the eight difficult points which serve to distinguish Prāsaṅgika Madhyamaka from other Buddhist tenet systems. Thus it is central to Tsong kha pa's understanding of the view of Prāsaṅgikas like Candrakīrti and Śāntideva that no consciousness at all can be characterised by this feature of self-awareness or reflexivity.

If Tsong kha pa is right, then it would have obvious and severe repercussions for the rDzogs chen perspective. Even if the ultimate reality were reflexive in

rDzogs chen tradition commonly distinguishes between *rnam shes* and *ye shes*.

nature, for anyone who wished to accept Prāsaṅgika Madhyamaka as the highest tenet system it would not be possible to integrate that ultimate into the conventional through the presence of reflexivity in all consciousness. It might be possible to argue against Tsong kha pa, however, that the Prāsaṅgika critique of *svasaṃvedana* is not at all of its conventional existence but only of its ultimate, inherently existent, status. Strategies could then subsequently be employed to rescue reflexivity as a feature of nonconceptual ultimate reality realized in nondual absorption. The first exercise is one of hermeneutics. It has to be argued that to interpret the Prāsaṅgika critique as a refutation of the conventional existence of *svasaṃvedana* is a misunderstanding of Prāsaṅgika sources. The next exercise is one of philosophical reconstruction. It has to be shown that whether or not it is a concern of the Prāsaṅgika, nevertheless consciousness *qua* consciousness is indeed characterised by self-awareness, and this does not in fact *contradict* the Prāsaṅgika perspective. The rDzogs chen ultimate reality can wait for the time being.

There were those prior to Mi pham who argued that the Prāsaṅgika critique of *svasaṃvedana* is of only its ultimate, inherently existent, reality and not its conventional status. But in his commentary to Śāntideva's *Bodhicaryāvatāra* 9, and his reply to his critics, 'Ju Mi pham 'Jam dbyangs rnam rgyal rgya mtsho (1846-1912) made perhaps the longest and most sophisticated attempt to explain in terms understandable to dGe lugs scholars why Śāntideva and Prāsaṅgika Madhyamaka should not be taken as negating the conventional existence of *svasaṃvedana*. Mi pham was strongly opposed by the dGe lugs scholars, for apart from anything else if Mi pham were right then it would undermine an essential aspect of dGe lugs doxography and orthodoxy. One of the eight characteristics of Prāsaṅgika Madhyamaka as discerned by Tsong kha pa—who is said to have received direct instruction on Madhyamaka from Mañjuśrī himself, and indeed to have been an emanation of Mañjuśrī—would be wrong.

The present monograph is very much an introduction to this dispute, an attempt to identify some of the issues and arguments and to draw the attention of other scholars to their interest. In common with some of my previous work it is also an attempt to indicate the diversity of interpretation in Tibetan Madhyamaka, and some of the strategies by which Tibetan Mādhyamikas integrated Madhyamaka into their wider system-building. This monograph is definitely not the, or even a, final word on its subject. It is perhaps not even a complete work. Mi pham replied to his Mādhyamika critics principally in two texts. The one, the *Sher 'grel brgal lan nyin byed snang ba* which Mi pham wrote in reply to criticisms by the dGe lugs lama bLo bzang dpal ldan bstan 'dzin specifically of his commentary to *Bodhicaryāvatāra* 9, forms a major source for the present study. His other reply, the *gZhan gyis brtsad pa'i lan mdor bsdus pa Rigs lam rab gsal de nyid snang phyed*, was written in reply to criticisms from another dGe lugs lama, Pa ri bLo bzang rab gsal. Unfortunately, although I have been able to use a number of Mi pham's other works in order to supplement the present study, I have not had access to the *Rigs lam rab gsal de nyid snang phyed*. This is particularly unfortunate as bLo bzang dpal ldan bstan 'dzin's attack on Mi pham's treatment of *svasaṃvedana* is not particularly sophisticated, and in his day it seems that Pa ri bLo bzang rab gsal was Mi pham's principal dGe lugs adversary.[3] On the other hand I have looked through Pa ri bLo bzang rab gsal's *'Ju lan ga bur chu rgyun* (1969). While there are many interesting topics in this collection of three refutations of Mi pham's thought, the issue of *svasaṃvedana* does not appear to have been a notably important theme in their debate. It seems that perhaps Mi pham's most extensive discussion of *svasaṃvedana* can be found in his reply to bLo bzang dpal ldan bstan 'dzin. At any rate, it is *an* extensive discussion, giving a series of interesting arguments, and does not appear to differ in treatment of our theme from shorter discussions found in other accessible works by Mi pham.

My approach to the treatment of self-awareness in Mi pham's texts and that of his critic has been through contextualization in Buddhist intellectual history, and philosophical unpacking, unraveling, and paraphrase. It will be obvious to anyone who reads Tibetan that I have followed my original sources very closely, although in unpacking I have tended to elaborate critically in the hope of clarification and understanding. I have included the Tibetan and Sanskrit sources for my discussion directly in the footnotes, with the intention of immediate accessibility, and of course I have striven to be faithful to my sources although I am not sure I have always succeeded. At points the textual

---

[3] I have also not had access to E. Gene Smith's introduction to an edition of Mi pham's reply to his critics, which is one of the most frequently used secondary sources on Mi pham's debates with dGe lugs lamas. I think this must be in volume 5 of the Ngagyur Nyingmay Sungrab series, published in Gangtok, although I am not sure. I have not seen as well K. Lipman 1981. 'A controversial topic from Mi pham's analysis of Śāntarakṣita's *Madhyamakālaṃkāra*', *Windhorse I*, Berkeley (Asian Humanities Press), which may have something of relevance.

arguments have been so compressed that I am uncertain whether I have understood them properly. I have indicated when I am unsure in the footnotes. Academic scholarship is, or should be, a collaborative venture and I am quite sure that there are those who know a great deal more about this sort of thing than I do. Even if they do not, a fresh approach may yet yield new understandings and I look forward to further clarification of this material in the future.

It could be argued that rather than paraphrase and philosophical unraveling I should have presented a straightforward translation, perhaps with commentarial notes. Or perhaps someone will detect an omission in that I should have offered some discussion of my hermeneutical strategy (Is there such a thing as a 'straightforward translation'? How do I feel about Gadamer or Derrida?), rather than naively plunging straight into the texts. I accept the point. My background is in the history of philosophical ideas, and I dislike the constraints of formal translation, even with a commentary. On the other hand I like naively plunging straight into the primary sources. I do what I do, and approach my material in the way I approach it. My justification is that I do not aim for any ultimate, any perfection, but simply to say something that might be of some interest to others. Those who wish for a formal translation are very welcome to wish for one, and perhaps even to do one. Those who wish to discuss methodology and hermeneutical strategies are also very welcome to do so. In my naiveté I prefer to do something else.

Centre for Buddhist Studies
University of Bristol
July 1994

CHAPTER ONE

Introducing *Svasaṃvedana* — and Its Two Types

In a paper 'On *rang rig*' published over ten years ago I noted an observation made by the Eighth Karma pa Mi bskyod rdo rje that there were many earlier commentators to the *Madhyamakāvatāra* who understood Candrakīrti's refutation of *inter alia* self-awareness (*svasaṃvedana* or *svasaṃvitti;* Tibetan: *rang rig*) to be a refutation solely from the ultimate, and not the conventional, point of view. Mi bskyod rdo rje refers in particular to the infamous (from a dGe lugs point of view) Sa skya pair Go ram pa bSod nams seng ge and Shākya mchog ldan, and in my earlier paper I briefly discussed among other things the defense of this way of reading the Prāsaṅgika refutation of self-awareness found in a commentary to the *Madhyamakāvatāra* by Go ram pa bSod nams seng ge.[1] An approach that sees the refutation of *svasaṃvedana* as occurring on only the ultimate level and not conventionally is also known to Tsong kha pa's pupil and suc-

---

1 See Williams (1983), reprinted below as Appendix 2.

cessor rGyal tshab rje, for he mentions it disparagingly in the context of a discussion of the other great source for the Prāsaṅgika treatment of *svasaṃvedana,* Śāntideva's *Bodhicaryāvatāra.*[2] Not surprisingly, given his context, here rGyal tshab rje specifically mentions previous commentators to the *Bodhicaryāvatāra* as not properly understanding Śāntideva's purport on this issue. For Tsong kha pa the nonexistence of self-awareness *even conventionally* is one of the 'eight great difficult points' *(dka' gnas chen po brgyad)* of the Madhyamaka which serve to distinguish the correct understanding of Nāgārjuna, and therefore in fact Prāsaṅgika Madhyamaka, from other Buddhist philosophical traditions (see Tsong kha pa 1970). For Tsong kha pa and rGyal tshab rje the simple nonexistence on any level of *svasaṃvedana* is a particular feature of Prāsaṅgika Madhyamaka, and the two great Prāsaṅgika refutations are contained in the *Madhyamakāvatāra* and *Bodhicaryāvatāra* of Candrakīrti and Śāntideva respectively, both members (the principal members) of an identifiable (sub-)school of Buddhist thought, identified through their correct understanding of the eight great difficult points.[3] As one of Mi

---

[2] See rGyal tshab rje (1973), p. 222: 'di ni rang rig med par dran pa skye ba'i rigs pa mkhas pa'i dbang pos mdzad pa phul du byung ba zhig snang ste spyod 'jug gi bshad pa byed pa rnams kyis ji bzhin du ma thon pa 'dra'o //...spyod 'jug gi dgongs pa ni tha snyad du rang rig 'gog pa min zhes pa ni rgyal sras chen po'i bzhed pa gtan min zhes gsung ngo //.

[3] Cf. the *Spyod 'jug shes rab le'u'i spyi don rim par phye ba Zab mo rten 'byung gi de kho na nyid yang gsal sgron me* by Thub bstan chos kyi grags pa (1990b), p. 756: gzhung 'di dang dbu ma 'jug pa gnyis kar don dam du ma zad tha snyad du'ang rang rig bkag pa yin te /. This text was recently published in China together with two other texts on the *Bodhicaryāvatāra* by Thub bstan chos kyi grags pa (= Mi nyag Kun bzang bsod nams), who although

pham's vigorous dGe lugs pa critics, the 'Bras spungs lama bLo bzang dpal ldan bstan 'dzin (Tre bo brag dkar sprul sku), put it in an attack on Mi pham's own defense of the conventional status of self-awareness, it is necessary to be able to explain the issue of *svasaṃvedana* without conflating the higher and lower tenet-systems.[4]

In order not to beg any questions, I have chosen at this stage to translate *svasaṃvedana/rang rig* by the reasonably literal 'self-awareness', understood here as consciousness aware *in some sense* of itself rather than consciousness aware of *a Self,* an *ātman,* which would of course be unacceptable to a Buddhist. We shall see, however, that the use of '*rang rig*' by Mi pham—affirmed by him as existing conventionally and acceptable as such even for the Prāsaṅgika Mādhyamika—corresponds to a particular emphasis found in the interpretation given by Śāntarakṣita, and in that context I shall sometimes translate it, where I give a translation at all, more precisely by 'reflexive awareness' or 'the reflexive nature of awareness'. This switch in transla-

---

clearly a dGe lugs pa was a pupil of several 19th century rNying ma pa lamas associated with the *ris med* movement and appears to be a favorite writer on the *Bodhicaryāvatāra* with the present Dalai Lama. See Dalai Lama (1994), pp. 7-8. For a recent translation of his *Spyod 'jug shes rab le'u'i gzhung 'grel Zab mo rten 'byung gi de kho na nyid gsal ba'i sgron me* see Khenchen Kunzang Palden and Minyak Kunzang Sōnam (1993).

[4] bLo bzang dpal ldan bstan 'dzin's attack is contained in his *Zab mo dbu ma'i gnad brjod pa blo gsal dga' ba'i gtam.* It is a rather impatient criticism of Mi pham's commentary (1975a) to the ninth chapter of the *Bodhicaryāvatāra,* and is quoted extensively by Mi pham in his reply (1975b). For the names of bLo bzang dpal ldan bstan 'dzin and his text see *ibid.* p. 101. On not mixing up higher and lower tenet systems see his comment on pp. 199-200: grub mtha' gong 'og gi lugs [200] rnams so so nas ma 'dres par 'chad dgos pa'i phyir ro //.

tion in the light of Śāntarakṣita's understanding corresponds, I suggest, to an ambiguity (or at least a systematic lack of clarity) in the use of the concept of *svasaṃvedana* in Buddhist writings.

This ambiguity can be seen reflected in a convenient explanation given by the dGe lugs lama Thub bstan chos kyi grags pa (Mi nyag Kun bzang bsod nams) in his *Spyi don* to the ninth chapter of the *Bodhicaryāvatāra*. It takes as its starting point an exposition of the *pūrvapakṣa* by the Svātantrika Mādhyamika Bhāvaviveka:

> As it is said in [Bhāvaviveka's] *Tarkajvālā:* 'According to the Cittamātrin, consciousness has a twofold appearance. It appears to itself and it appears as the object. The consciousness which appears as the object—having taken on the aspect of an external object—becomes an object for the consciousness which appears to itself.' Thus is set forth the position of the *pūrvapakṣa*.
>
> (i) That which is spoken of as appearing to itself is the subjective aspect. That which is spoken of as appearing as the object is the objective aspect. That very objective aspect which has taken on the aspect of the object is explained as the object of the subjective aspect. Therefore, the experience of the objective aspect by the subjective aspect is explained as the meaning of 'self-awareness'. Thus what is called self-awareness is a separate subjective aspect.[5]

---

[5] Is the self-awareness the result of the cognition by the subjective aspect–the ***experience*** of the objective aspect by the subjective aspect–or identical with the subjective aspect itself? This lack of clarity is reflected also in other sources. Dignāga states that the self-awareness is the result of the perceptual situation, the

> (ii) Accompanying all the consciousnesses that are aware of others there is also a mere luminosity, a mere awareness, of its own nature, turned solely inwards, without dependence on the external object, and [here] all the dual-appearances of object and subject are posited as a mistake.[6]

Thus in an experience of seeing blue (a) the eye-consciousness takes on the aspect *(ākāra/rnam pa)* of blue. This eye-consciousness with the aspect of blue is the objective aspect *(grāhyākāra/gzung rnam)*.[7] Such might

---

pramāṇaphala, and Dharmapāla appears to have taken Dignāga as distinguishing between the subjective aspect and the resultant self-awareness. See Hattori (1968), p. 28 (*Pramāṇasamuccaya* 1:9a and 10) and relevant notes, particularly 1:67. But other sources (as here, admittedly dGe lugs) are clear that the self-awareness *is* the subjective aspect itself. See, for example, lCang skya rol pa'i rdo rje cited in Klein (1991), p. 164 and text p. 119, and Phur bu lcog in Newland (1992), p.203.

6 Thub bstan chos kyi grags pa (1990b), p. 752: rtog ge 'bar ba las / sems tsam pas rnam shes ni gnyis su snang ste / rang snang ba dang yul du snang ba'o // yul du snang ba'i rnam shes ni phyi rol gyi yul gyi rnam par gyur nas rang snang ba'i rnam shes kyi yul du 'gyur ro zhes phyogs snga'i 'dod pa bkod pa ste / rang snang ba zhes pa 'dzin rnam dang / yul du snang ba zhes pa gzung rnam dang / yul gyi rnam par gyur pa'i gzung rnam de nyid 'dzin rnam gyi yul du bshad pas 'dzin rnam gyis gzung rnam myong ba rang rig gi don du bshad do // des na rang rig ces pa ni 'dzin rnam yan gar ba ste gzhan rig gi shes pa thams cad kyi steng na rang nyid gsal tsam dang rig tsam pa phyi rol gyi yul la ltos med du kha nang kho nar phyogs shing yul yul can gyi gnyis snang thams cad log pa zhig la 'jog go //. Thub bstan chos kyi grags pa has taken most of this from mKhas grub rje's *sTong thun chen mo.* See mKhas grub rje (1972), pp. 418-9, and Cabezón (1992), pp. 345-6.

7 According to Dignāga the objective aspect itself has two aspects, those of blue and cognition. See *Pramāṇasamuccaya* 1:11ab and *vṛtti*, and Hattori's note 1:70. See also Matilal (1986), pp. 151-2, and Klein (1986), p. 113. For Cittamātra (*pace* certain

be called 'seeing blue', but if it is only seeing blue then clearly its object is blue and it is not *conscious of* seeing blue, a mental act for which the object would be not blue but 'seeing blue'. That is, it is not seeing that one sees blue, it is not knowing that one knows. If consciousness of blue is 'seeing blue', then consciousness of seeing blue is 'seeing {seeing blue}', i.e., seeing *that* one sees blue. If it is seeing blue but it is not conscious of seeing blue then, it is argued, there is no real seeing blue at all. As Śāntarakṣita put it in his *Tattvasaṃgraha,* if one does not know that one knows then the consciousness itself is unknown. If the consciousness itself is unknown then it could not know other objects.[8]

contemporary interpretations) it seems that the eye-consciousness with the aspect of (in this case) blue is *all* there is. There is no external object causing the eye-consciousness with the aspect of blue. The causes are internal 'seeds'. Thus the 'object' is in reality the objective aspect (at least for *sākāravāda* Cittamātra). For Sautrāntika there is still an external object acting as a cause for the eye-consciousness with the aspect of blue, although we know from the history of Western philosophy that once an 'objective aspect' (perception? sense-datum?) has been introduced between the perceptual object and its cognition some form of idealism becomes a strong temptation.

[8] See *Tattvasaṃgraha* (Dwarikadas Shastri ed.) 2020-2021. For an extensive account drawing on the Nyāya critique of the Buddhist position see Matilal (1986), ch. 5. Śāntarakṣita is going to use this point to show how in fact the only coherent real sense of 'self-awareness' is not a result of the subjective aspect experiencing the objective aspect, but is that inherent self-knowing, i.e., not being known by anything else, which is necessary at some point (and the sooner the better) in order to prevent an infinite regress here (knowing that one knows that one knows...etc.). That is obviously a different sense of 'self-awareness' from the subjective aspect experiencing the objective aspect. I shall be using 'self-awareness (i)' for the self-awareness we are discussing at the moment, a result of the subjective aspect taking the objective aspect as its object. I shall use 'self-aware-

In order for knowing that one knows to occur and therefore, it is maintained, for a proper perceptual act to take place, it is argued here that (b) the eye-consciousness with the aspect of blue has to become the object of an awareness *that* it is an eye-consciousness with an aspect of blue. This second awareness is said to be the result of a separate subjective aspect *(grāhakākāra/'dzin rnam)* which accompanies and experiences the eye-consciousness with the aspect of blue. Thus far it appears to be an awareness which takes an object, although that object is a simultaneous consciousness in the same person's mental continuum. Therefore, *this* model of self-awareness is patterned on an awareness of others *(gzhan rig)*, those things normally posited as outside the consciousness continuum. It is similar to, although apart from anything else because of its posited universality (it is always occurring wherever there is consciousness) it is not the same as, introspective awareness, an awareness which can sometimes be employed in order to observe one's own mental acts. Thus far also this form of self-awareness is dualistic in the sense that if this is what occurs then the subjective aspect and the objective aspect are not literally and in all respects the *same*, nor are they experienced as the same, even if they oc-

ness (ii)' or 'reflexive awareness' or 'the reflexive nature of awareness' for the sense of inherent self-knowing, i.e. not requiring a further knower, which terminates any tendency towards infinite regress. It seems that self-awareness (i) requires self-awareness (ii) but the latter is logically independent of it, for not all traditions accept self-awareness (i), although (Śāntarakṣita and Mi pham are going to maintain) *any* explanation of consciousness–including crucially explanations even by Mādhyamikas of consciousness as a conventional phenomenon–will require self-awareness (ii).

cur in the same consciousness continuum.[9] This point is made quite strongly in referring to a separate *(yan gar ba)* subjective aspect. Therefore, the subjective aspect here results in '*self*-awareness (i)' in the sense that there is not as such an awareness of something outside its own mental continuum (the present stage of person *x*'s own aggregate continuum of *cittacaitta*).

---

9 As we shall see, in the technical language of later dGe lugs exegesis, they are one entity but different isolates *(ngo bo gcig ldog pa tha dad)*. That is to say, the self-awareness is not a different consciousness from the (object-) perceiving consciousness, but they are not the same in the sense that their names have the same meaning (i.e., mean literally the same thing and their referents cannot be distinguished even by a conceptual consciousness). They are separable by thought. Although it is not difficult to see what the device of *ngo bo gcig ldog pa tha dad* is getting at, unraveling the exact logic of this much-used dGe lugs strategy (particularly with reference to explaining the relationship between the two truths–see Newland (1992), ch. 4) may not easy. It is clearly not a case of Frege's distinction between sense and reference. To use Frege's example, it is not like 'the morning star' and 'the evening star', which are two expressions with different meanings that can occur in propositions with different truth values, and yet they have the same referent. Perhaps the matter is more one of psychology—an ability to make an often perfectly real mental distinction between two things versus the actual physical ability to separate them. Anyway, this dGe lugs device for explaining the relationship between self-awareness and the objective aspect is the result of a long consideration of the problem, and rests partly on further factors of reflexivity which I shall discuss subsequently. At this point in our discussion it also has problems given the reference to the subjective aspect as *separate* from the objective aspect. Clearly, the subjective aspect *does* take the objective aspect as an object, and if *x* takes *y* as an object their difference would appear *prima facie* to be more than just a difference for thought. What this means, and whether it is coherent, relates to some of the Prāsaṅgika criticisms of the notion of *svasaṃvedana* (see here, for example, Klein (1986), p. 113).

What self-awareness, self-consciousness, is aware of here is its own (object-taking) consciousness. But it is not said *here* to be nondualistically aware of *itself*, i.e. reflexive in a way which would render it meaningless to speak of its taking itself as an *object*. Rather, it is the result of a subject(ive aspect) aware of a conceptually (and also phenomenologically?) different object(ive aspect).

The principal argument for self-awareness—in fact what I have called self-awareness (i)—is said by Thub bstan chos kyi grags pa to be the argument from memory (1990b, pp. 752-3). It is an argument which appears to have originated with Dignāga (*Pramāṇasamuccaya* 1:11d), and is widely referred to both by those who advocate *svasaṃvedana* and those like Candrakīrti (*Madhyamakāvatāra* 6:74-5) and Śāntideva (*Bodhicaryāvatāra* 9:23) who would deny it. I have dealt with this argument elsewhere, mainly with reference to its treatment in Candrakīrti's *Madhyamakāvatāra* and Tsong kha pa's comments (see Appendix 2 below). I do not intend further to discuss the argument as such here. It is relevant to our current concerns, however, just to note its broad structure.

Dignāga tells us that 'one does not see the recollection of that object which has not been experienced' *(nyams su ma myong bar don dran pa ni mthong ba med de)*.[10] To quote from my previous description of the argument:

[10] From Kanakavarman and Dad pa'i shes rab's version of the *Vṛtti* on *Pramāṇasamuccaya* 1:11d (Hattori (1968), p. 185). Hattori (pp. 110-1) explains 1:11d with reference also to other sources as meaning that 'Whatsoever is recollected has been experienced before. The recollection is an effect (*kārya*) of the previous experience (*anubhava*). Thus the reason "*smṛteḥ*" [from recollection] (k. 11c) is *kārya-hetu*..., and effectively proves that the cognition itself has been experienced or self-cognised before...'.

> When I remember that I sensed blue at a former time the sensation is a cause, although not the only cause, of the memory. In remembering—and in the Buddhist discussion of memory I think we can see an example of a particular case of *reflective* awareness, awareness taking as its object another awareness which occurred previously—the awareness which serves as the referent of the memory act is seen to have both subjective and objective elements. That is, Tsong kha pa explains, when we remember, the memory image is seen to be composed of 'formerly *this* was seen' and 'it was seen *by me*'. Or, as Tsong kha pa expressed it elsewhere, when I remember that I truly saw blue there is a memory of blue and a memory of seeing blue. Thus in the original act there must have been the sensation of blue and also the sensation of seeing blue.[11]

The argument is, therefore, an argument for two elements in the original experience irreducible to each other. There is an eye-consciousness of blue and there is another element in the consciousness experience which is taking that eye-consciousness of blue as an object. This is shown by the two elements in recollection. One can remember *that* one experienced blue because one not only experienced blue but also *knew that* one experienced blue. If a person did not know that he or she experienced blue, then how could that person remember *experiencing* blue, and therefore remember blue?

---

11 Williams (1983) pp. 324-5; Appendix 2 below. The references to Tsong kha pa are to Tsong kha pa (1973), p. 175 and Tsong kha pa (1970), p. 25.

I have suggested that the model for self-awareness (i) is awareness of others, awareness of external referents. In Cittamātra the external referent as a cause for the eye-consciousness taking on the aspect of blue is simply eliminated, and one is left with only the subjective aspect taking as its referent the objective aspect in a resultant experience which is really simply *svasaṃvedana*. There is thus really a nondual flow of self-aware consciousness (the *paratantrasvabhāva*) experienced *as if* divided into subject and object.[12] Inasmuch as we unenlightened beings mistakenly think that there is a subject polarized against an external object (the *parikalpitasvabhāva*) this can be related to the structure of consciousness as subjective aspect (*grāhakākāra*) polarized against the objective aspect (*grāhyākāra*). In other words not only is the model used to explain self-awareness (i) based on awareness of external others, it actually is indeed the Cittamātra explanation of the awareness of others as if external.

I have argued elsewhere (Williams 1994) for seeing the ontological opposition of Cittamātra to Madhyamaka as based on the (intuitively quite convincing) Abhidharma claim that there must be a real substance *(dravya)* in order for there to be conceptual constructs *(prajñapti)*. To claim, as Madhyamaka clearly does, that literally everything is simply a conceptual construct (*prajñaptimātra*, i.e. all *dharmas* are lacking in inherent existence *(niḥsvabhāva))* is in Vaibhāṣika Abhidharma terms and, I suggest, Citta-

---

[12] This point is made quite clear by Dignāga in *Pramāṇasamuccaya* 1:10: yadābhāsaṃ prameyaṃ tatpramāṇaphalate punaḥ / grāhakākārasaṃvittī trayaṃ nātaḥ pṛthakkṛtam // = Tib. (Kanakavarman and Dad pa'i shes rab): gang ltar snang ba de gsal bya / tshad ma dang de'i 'bras bu ni / 'dzin rnam rig pa'o de yi phyir / de gsum tha dad du ma byas //. See also Hattori's note 1:65.

mātra terms also, quite incoherent. No matter how clever the Madhyamaka arguments are, they must involve misusing the concept *'prajñapti'*, and if taken literally would amount to nihilism in spite of the Madhyamaka claim to deny nihilism in favor of an equation of emptiness and dependent origination. To say that all things are conceptual constructs is to say that *all* things are constructed but patently are not constructed out of anything. Ontologically in opposing a nihilism which it was sure resulted from complete *niḥsvabhāvatā* Cittamātra had to involve a *dravya,* and this meant the inherent existence of something. Given the Abhidharma framework, not to mention the requirements of rationality, this was thought to be coherent and sensible.[13]

[13] I want to dwell a bit further on these points, because they seem to me important. There has been a tendency in recent scholarship in both Japan and the West to portray the history of Buddhist thought as a series of footnotes to Nāgārjuna. I suggest this has seriously distorted our assessment of the material. It used to be common to portray Buddhism as divided into two 'schools', Hīnayāna and Mahāyāna. Fortunately we are now beginning to appreciate that in its Indian origins, and probably always in India, Mahāyāna was a minority vision with multifarious associated practices within what could better be termed 'Mainstream Buddhism'. Those (almost certainly by far the majority) who failed to adopt the Mahāyāna vision were said polemically by the Mahāyāna to be followers of a 'Hīnayāna'. In fact what we have is simply Buddhism, with Mahāyāna within it as a minority aspiration. Likewise I suspect it is wrong (even if, for example, it is done by Tibetans) to portray Buddhist thought as divided into equal rival schools of, for example, Vaibhāṣika Abhidharma, Sautrāntika, Madhyamaka and Yogācāra. Rather, Sautrāntika, Madhyamaka and Yogācāra occur in different ways within a framework supplied by the Abhidharmas. In a sense, Buddhist philosophical thought *is* Abhidharma, and it is to the Abhidharma framework that we must go if we are to understand what is

really going on. The history of Buddhist philosophical thought is actually a series of footnotes to the Abhidharma. The Abhidharma is an elaboration of a basic Buddhist division between the ways things are and the ways things seem to be, with the way things seem to be constructed through mental imputation, reification and conceptualization out of the way things are. In Vaibhāṣika Abhidharma the constructs are referred to as conceptualized existents *(prajñaptisat)*, what I call 'secondary existents', and those reals out of which things are constructed are substantial existents *(dravyasat)*, my 'primary existents'. In Vaibhāṣika Abhidharma at least, entities which have primary existence are also *dharmas*, and said to have a *svabhāva*. Secondary existents, conceptual constructs, are not *dharmas* and are *niḥsvabhāva*. Thus the Madhyamaka claim that all is *niḥsvabhāva* is equivalent to a claim that all is *prajñaptisat*, that there are no *dravyas*, and even *dharmas* are not *dharmas* in the (Vaibhāṣika) Abhidharma sense. As is well-known, the Madhyamaka seems to see an implied incompatibility between having a *svabhāva* and dependent origination. This is an argument derived within Madhyamaka. It would not be acceptable to a Vaibhāṣika. It is self-evidently absurd from an Abhidharma point of view to argue that *all* things are conceptual constructs, for that would mean that they are constructs but not constructed out of or upon anything. Madhyamaka reasoning must be at fault somewhere, and the place to look is in the equation of *niḥsvabhāva*—if the term *svabhāva* is being used in the Vaibhāṣika sense—with dependent origination. One reason why some modern scholars have wanted to argue that there is no fundamental ontological difference between Madhyamaka and Yogācāra Cittamātra, I suspect, is that the nondual consciousness stream *(= paratantrasvabhāva)* in Cittamātra is a stream, a continuum, and therefore in Madhyamaka terms must be *niḥsvabhāva* and should therefore have the weakest possible rather than strongest possible ontological status. Each moment of that continuum is the result of causes and therefore impermanent. Thus each moment too must be *niḥsvabhāva*. Therefore, Cittamātra could not be teaching an inherently existent *(sasvabhāva)* nondual consciousness continuum. These, however, are precisely *Mādhyamika* arguments, resting on an equation of dependent origination and emptiness, *niḥsvabhāvatā*. Once this equation is granted, of course, the argument follows and we soon find that all things have only *prajñaptisat*. If we return the debate to the Abhidharma framework, however, and look at Cittamātra ontology within that context then the issues begin to appear a little different. Within the Abhidharma framework, quite reasonably, it is absurd for all things to have only *prajñaptisat,* for all things to be constructs. If literally all things were constructs this would indeed be quite simply equivalent to saying that nothing exists at all. I was once asked why it was, since the Madhyamaka arguments seem so clear and to some so compelling, all Buddhists did not adopt Madhyamaka? The answer is that for an Ābhidharmika—and, I suggest, a follower of Yogācāra—the conclusion that Madhyamaka amounted to nihilism did not rest on a misunderstanding of Madhyamaka (a failure to understand that emptiness does not equal nothing at all, but is an equivalent of dependent origination). It rested rather on an understanding that there is something very strange in maintaining that *all* is a conceptual construct (i.e., *niḥsvabhāva)*. Even if the Mādhyamika says he or she is a not a nihilist, in fact, if the Mādhyamika does not accept any *dravya* at all, then he or she is playing with words and must be a nihilist nevertheless. The Buddhist opponents of Madhyamaka knew their Madhyamaka perfectly well, including the equation of emptiness and dependent origination. They just felt (with at least arguably good reason) that it was all absurd. Thus the crucial opposition for understanding the relationship between Madhyamaka and Cittamātra ontology is not *svabhāva::niḥsvabhāva* (= dependent origination), which loads the dice in Madhyamaka terms, but the central Abhidharma opposition between *dravyasat* and *prajñaptisat.* In terms of *this* opposition, whoever says that it is not the case that all things have *prajñaptisat* must be saying that at least one thing is a *dravya.* This is a crucial ontological opposition, for *dravyasat* is the strongest sort of ontological status. Thus if any tradition says that not all things are *prajñaptis* (because this amounts to nihilism) that tradition is marking the strongest sort of ontological difference with Madhyamaka. We do not need to focus on the issue of *svabhāva* as such in order to identify strong ontological opposition. Nevertheless, *in Abhidharma terms* this *dravya* must have a *svabhāva,* whether it is dependently originated or not. It is clear that early Yogācāra Cittamātra texts were attacking a

What we are seeing now in the argument for self-awareness (i) is an epistemological theory showing that the one *dravya* which serves as a substratum for conceptual construction in Cittamātra is, as a matter of fact, nondual self-aware consciousness, self-aware because there is no other thing for it to be aware of, and therefore self-aware in that a subjective aspect of consciousness takes an objective aspect of consciousness as its object. The argument for *svasaṃvedana* in this Cittamātra context is intimately involved with the argument for nondual consciousness-only, and combines with the need for a *dravya* to give what seems to me to be the characteristically Cittamātra perspective of an inherently-existing nondual consciousness continuum which is the substratum for that polarization into postulated inherently separate subjects and objects, a polarization which forms the root delusion, the illusion of duality. In arguing for *svasaṃvedana* in this

tradition which held that all things have only *prajñaptisat* (See my paper 'An argument for Cittamātra'. See also Williams (1989), ch. 4). Thus they can only be attacking Madhyamaka, for Madhyamaka was the only Buddhist system which maintained that all things have only *prajñaptisat* (= *niḥsvabhāva*). In holding that at least one thing is not *prajñaptisat* the Yogācāra clearly marked the strongest possible ontological difference from Madhyamaka. Alternatively, if Yogācāra also held that all things are *prajñaptisat* (note that the question here is whether they hold that all things are *prajñaptisat*, not *niḥsvabhāva* which is a term 'contaminated' by Madhyamaka associations), then Yogācāra is not a complementary philosophical tradition to Madhyamaka. It actually *is* Madhyamaka. What we find in Yogācāra Cittamātra, therefore, is a reassertion of the Abhidharma *prajñaptisat::dravyasat* opposition which had been overruled (through *dravyasat* as a null category) by Madhyamaka in a way which in Abhidharma (= 'Mainstream' Buddhist philosophical) terms must equal nihilism. It is perhaps not entirely surprising, therefore, that we have also a Yogācāra Abhidharma.

sense of self-awareness (i) one is thus close to arguing for *cittamātra,* and an argument for *cittamātra* involves a vision of ontology in opposition to Madhyamaka which (with the exception of Śāntarakṣita and his followers) usually led to a view of the ultimate and inherent existence of *citta* when correctly understood in its nondual sense. Therefore, in opposing *svasaṃvedana* in general, and the memory argument in particular inasmuch as it is involved with this vision of *svasaṃvedana* (self awareness (i)), Mādhyamika writers like Candrakīrti and Śāntideva were opposing both something which could serve as an example in the reasoning proving *cittamātra* (an example where consciousness takes as its referent not an external object but itself, consciousness), and also an element closely involved in the demonstration of one inherently-existing ultimate nondual self-aware consciousness.[14] It is important to appreciate this point

[14] See, for example, *Bodhicaryāvatāra* 9:16-17: yadā māyaiva te nāsti tadā kim upalabhyate / cittasyaiva sa ākāro yady apy anyo'sti tattvataḥ // cittam eva yadā māyā tadā kiṃ kena dṛṣyate / uktaṃ ca lokanāthena cittaṃ cittaṃ na paśyati //. The reference in this context to the Buddha's saying that the mind cannot see the mind is a critique of the view that the mind can take a cognitive object in a subject-object relationship, where the object itself is also the very same mind. In other words it is a critique of a situation where there *is* (as it were) a subject-object relationship and both subject and object in that relationship are consciousness. It is an argument directed at self-awareness (i). As we shall see, the sense in which mind sees mind in self-awareness (ii) is not really a subject-object relationship at all, and is therefore not a relationship of mind seeing mind. This sort of language is at most metaphorical. This difference is at the root of appreciating that there is a difference between self-awareness (i) and self-awareness (ii). That this difference was rarely appreciated explains the move from the Cittamātra argument that subject and object are both consciousness and therefore there is self-awareness, to the exis-

early in our analysis, since Mi pham is going to argue that Candrakīrti's and in particular Śāntideva's arguments against *svasaṃvedana* are directed against *svasaṃvedana* as inherently-existing, in other words an ultimate reality, and not against the conventional everyday existence of *svasaṃvedana*. Mi pham's principal influence is Śāntarakṣita, and in accepting the Prāsaṅgika Mādhyamika critique of the memory argument Mi pham is going to suggest that it is directed against an argument for an inherently-existing separate self-awareness (through inherently-existing experiences and memories) which clearly does not exist even conventionally. Since in Prāsaṅgika Madhyamaka to exist inherently is to exist ultimately, and is equivalent to being found as the terminating point of a critical analysis which searches for ultimates, Mi pham is going to argue that the memory argument does not work as an argument for *svasaṃvedana* in the context of a critical analysis of Cittamātra, which is precisely a critical analysis searching for ultimates, an inherently-existing nondual *svasaṃvedana* which is intimately involved in the specific Cittamātra ontological and epistemological project. And Mi pham is going to want to suggest that it simply does not follow from this Mādhyamika critique of *svasaṃvedana* in general and the memory argument in particular in the context of a debate with the Cittamātrin, that the Mādhyamika is also committed to saying that there is no such thing as *svasaṃvedana*

tence of self-awareness of consciousness on the model of a lamp illuminating itself as well as others (as will become clear, a 'self-awareness (ii)'-type example of reflexivity). See, for example, this move in the *Bodhicaryāvatāra* discussion. The example of the lamp occurs in the Sanskrit text at verses 22-3. We are back to the memory argument (a 'self-awareness (i)'-type argument) at verse 24.

even on an everyday conventional level. Mi pham is helped in his argument by what seem to me to be the elements of an alternative perspective on *svasaṃvedana* which I shall call for the time being 'self-awareness (ii)', an alternative perspective that, while helping Mi pham (in this context a Mādhyamika), is arguably, and certainly for Mi pham, separable from the Cittamātra ontological and epistemological project, an alternative perspective which is initially and usually mixed in with self-awareness (i) but comes into its own in certain innovations in the theory of *svasaṃvedana* which were stressed by and probably originated with Śāntarakṣita. Self-awareness (ii) is one of reflexivity as the defining characteristic of consciousness. Consciousness is in its own essential or inherent nature as consciousness reflexive.[15]

[15] My use of 'essential or inherent nature' here is to be distinguished from inherent existence *(svabhāva)* in a sense not acceptable to a Mādhyamika like Śāntarakṣita. It is rather like the uniquely-defining characteristic *(svalakṣaṇa)* found in the Abhidharma but understood in an everyday conventional sense (the 'quiddity' of *x*) as it would have been acceptable I think to Śāntarakṣita or even Nāgārjuna.

CHAPTER TWO

Śāntarakṣita on the Reflexive Nature Of Consciousness

I want now to return to our quotation from Thub bstan chos kyi grags pa (pp. 4-5 above) in which I separated into two paragraphs his description of *svasaṃvedana* after his citation of Bhāvaviveka's *Tarkajvālā*. In terms of our analysis so far, there appears to be some problem, or at least unclarity, with the second of these paragraphs. The 'mere luminosity' or 'mere awareness' which accompanies consciousnesses that are aware of others would seem to be itself a form of *svasaṃvedana,* a form of consciousness accompanying the objective aspect but characterized by self-awareness in the sense of reflexivity, rather than taking the objective aspect as an object. It is not obvious that what is being referred to here with 'mere luminosity' and so on is the subjective aspect, or even a result of the subjective aspect. The subjective aspect experiences (and is, therefore, aware of) the objective aspect. Here, however, we have a 'mere awareness' said to be aware of its own nature 'turned solely inwards'. The objective aspect which is experienced by the subjective aspect is dependent upon an object which, if not actually external, is at least (more often than not) *as if* external. The subjective aspect in experiencing the objective aspect is involved in a situation of at least some sort of duality, and inasmuch as it depends on an objective aspect which depends upon an 'external' object, it can itself be said to be dependent upon the external object insofar as there is one. But here the mere luminosity is said to be without any dependence on an external object, and completely uninvolved in any dualistic appearances of subject/object. Thus even if the 'mere luminosity' and 'mere awareness' here were connected to the subjective aspect, they could not be identical with it. Rather, 'mere luminosity' (a common image used in Indian philosophy for reflexivity—a light illuminates itself at the same time as it illuminates others) must relate to Śāntarakṣita's discussion from the *Tattvasaṃgraha* mentioned earlier (esp. ch. 1, n. 8 above), which would see in the self-validating factor of reflexivity an answer to the problem of an epistemological infinite regress. Consciousness validates its own existence because to validate its own existence is constitutive of its very being as consciousness. That is, consciousness is self-referring in a non-objectifying way, just as a lamp illuminates itself not as one object among others to be illuminated, but through the very act of *being* a lamp, an illuminator of others. This is reflexivity—to be conscious of others *is* to be conscious of oneself as well, because otherwise it would not be consciousness and therefore not consciousness of others. That is just what consciousness is.

'Mere luminosity' here, I suggest, is reflexivity and this is patently a different sense of 'self-awareness' from 'self-awareness (i)'. Self-awareness (i) *in some sense* takes an object, and in some sense that object is itself. The issue of an object is not relevant to reflexivity *qua* reflexivity. What the object of consciousness is, is an additional issue to the nature of consciousness itself. For example, in the case of an eye-consciousness seeing blue, we know that since it is a consciousness it must be reflexive. That it takes as its object blue, or indeed anything else (including itself as an object, if that were possible) is completely irrelevant to the issue of reflexivity.[1] I have, therefore, called reflexivity when applied to consciousness 'self-awareness (ii)'.

In his *Madhyamakālaṃkāra,* and again with the same verses in his *Tattvasaṃgraha,* Śāntarakṣita introduces *svasaṃvedana* not through argument—through recourse to, say, the memory argument—but through assertion, an appeal to its fundamental obviousness. Consciousness is to be understood structurally as 'not-insentience' (that is, as not *jaḍa/bems po*), and the issue is what defines consciousness as not-insentience for, Śāntarakṣita comments, 'consciousness occurs as the very opposite of that the nature of which is insentience'. In actual fact, Śāntarakṣita explains, the very quality of not being insentient is something's self-consciousness or self-awareness.[2] That is what

---

1 From which it should follow, incidentally, that in the case of self-awareness (i) the objective aspect as a consciousness has self-awareness (ii) as reflexivity, and the subjective aspect as that which experiences the objective aspect also has self-awareness (ii) as reflexivity ('experiences' is a consciousness-term), and these two reflexivities are the same *qua* reflexivity of consciousness, but not the same *qua* the same consciousness-instant. This again makes it quite clear also that self-awareness (i) cannot be the same as self-awareness (ii).

2 *Madhyamakālaṃkāra* 16, ed. Masamichi Ichigo (1989): rnam shes bems po'i rang bzhin las // bzlog pa rab tu skye ba ste //

self-awareness is—it is the consciousness-quality of consciousness; it is the very quality which makes consciousness not unconsciousness. According to the elaboration in Śāntarakṣita's *Madhyamakālaṃkāravṛtti*, consciousness is posited as being of the nature of self-awareness because it is essentially luminous by nature. This in turn is because it is the very opposite from that the nature of which is absence of awareness, such as a chariot and so on.[3] Elsewhere, Prajñākaragupta has observed that some things require something else to illuminate them, that is, to render them knowable. Some, such as a pot (or here, a chariot), require both a lamp (light) and the visual organ. The lamp itself, on the other hand, requires only the visual organ. But there are other things—consciousnesses—which do not require anything else to render them knowable. They are accordingly self-aware. They are known (their existence is known) by their very occurrence. Thus consciousnesses are the opposite of things which require something else to render them knowable, and this quality of oppositeness lies in their self-

---

bems min rang bzhin gang yin pa //de di'i bdag nyid shes pa yin//. This equals *Tattvasaṃgraha* 1999: vijñānaṃ jaḍarūpebhyo vyāvṛttam upajāyate / iyam evātmasaṃvittir asya yā'jaḍarūpatā //.

3 *Madhyamakālaṃkāravṛtti* (Taipei Derge edition) p. 120: 'di rang rig pa'i rang bzhin du rnam par gzhag pa ni rang bzhin gyis gsal ba'i bdag nyid yin pa'i phyir te / shing rta la sogs pa la rig pa med pa'i rang bzhin las bzlog pa'i phyir ro //. Unless noted otherwise, all bsTan 'gyur references in this monograph will be to the Taipei Derge edition (SMC Publishing Inc., 1991). Note here, incidentally, the close connection between luminosity and awareness. Since consciousness is in its very being as consciousness not {not-aware} it is luminous by nature, and this luminosity by nature is what we mean by 'self-awareness'. See below, note 10, and cf. also Dharmakīrti's *Pramāṇaviniścaya* (Vetter ed. p. 98).

awareness.[4] The appeal here is not to an epistemological theory, but to the obviousness of this for everyone. As Kamalaśīla puts it, the quality of not needing to depend on another possessed of illumination (i.e., the fact that illumination by consciousness is self-validating) occurs in accordance with the everyday way of

---

[4] On Prajñākaragupta see his *Pramāṇavārttikālaṃkāra* (R. Sankrityayana ed.), p. 353, as discussed in Matilal (1986), p. 156. Matilal points out that in reply Bhāsarvajña accuses Prajñākaragupta with the fallacy of *asiddhi,* essentially in this context question-begging. Perhaps Prajñākaragupta is not putting forward a formal argument here, but is rather appealing to an obvious self-givenness. It is interesting also that the Naiyāyikas argue against the Buddhist position that consciousness is distinguished from insentience, not through *self*-awareness but through the fact that consciousness, unlike insentient entities, illuminates (i.e., renders known) *others.* Cf. Tsong kha pa's response to the memory argument, discussed in Williams (1983), pp. 325-6 (and Appendix 2 below): 'Tsong kha pa points out that one can infer simple sensation from memory, but one is unable to infer self-consciousness. On the basis of sensing blue one can conclude in memory that formerly there was the awareness of blue, but this only allows the establishment of simple awareness, not self-awareness. On the other hand if there is a memory of simple awareness of blue it is unnecessary to postulate self-consciousness.' The reference is to Tsong kha pa's *dKa' gnas chen po brgyad,* pp. 26-7. Saying I am conscious of seeing blue, Tsong kha pa wants to argue, does not add anything to saying that I see blue. But Śāntarakṣita might respond that while he does not deny the points made by the Naiyāyika and Tsong kha pa, the question still remains concerning what makes consciousness different from insentience? Against the Naiyāyika, what enables consciousness to be aware of others when pots are not? The answer, Śāntarakṣita wants to say, is that quite patently consciousness (unlike pots) is the sort of thing the existence of which is known in the very act of knowing others. This is simply patently the case, obvious to anyone, and this is what we mean by *svasaṃvedana.*

things.[5] And elsewhere Kamalaśīla comments that it is not fitting to criticize this self-awareness, since it is established even for cowherders.[6] Mokṣākaragupta makes the essentially same point in claiming in his *Tarkabhāṣā* that *svasaṃvedana* is established on the strength of our own experience.[7] This appeal to *svasaṃvedana* in a pre-reflective sense, a self-awareness which is felt to be obvious even to peasants (G.E. Moore's 'man-in-the-street'), shows the difference between this sense of 'self-awareness' (self-awareness (ii)) and the previous sense (self-awareness (i)) which is bound-in with a particular philosophers' epistemology. It will also show for Mi pham the possibility of separating *svasaṃvedana* in *this* sense from its Cittamātra origins and connotations and arguing for its obviousness in conventional terms in a way which it

---

5 *Madhyamakālaṃkārapañjikā*, p. 188: gsal ba gzhan la mi ltos pa nyid du tha snyad kyi lam la 'jug pa yin no //. Of course, 'illumination' here refers to illumination by consciousness, for which the illumination of a lamp serves as a metaphorical example. We have seen that even the illumination of a lamp depends on consciousness in order to render it knowable, in a way that consciousness itself does not. Also there should be no confusion between the self-validating nature of consciousness (i.e., that one cannot be in doubt whether one is conscious or not, whether one is experiencing at all), and a claim that experiences are self-verifying (i.e., that all or certain experiences are indubitable). The categories may overlap, but we are not concerned here with claims of self-verification.

6 rang rig pa yang gnag rdzi yan chad la grub pa'i phyir klan kar yang mi rung ngo //. Cited from the *M.A. Pañjikā* by Ichigo (1989), p. 234 n. 64.

7 Mokṣākaragupta (1988), p. 24: anubhavaprasiddhaṃ ca svasaṃvedanatvaṃ katham apahnūyeta? See too the translation by Yuichi Kajiyama p. 51 (1989 reprint, p. 238), who also gives a reference to Vidyākaraśānti's *Tarkasopāna*.

is felt will not conflict with even Prāsaṅgika Madhyamaka.

The idea of portraying self-awareness as the quality of consciousness understood as the reverse of insentience *(bems po)* may well have originated with Śāntarakṣita.[8] Mi pham wrote a detailed commentary to the *Madhyamakālaṃkāra,* and its influence on his discussions of the status of *svasaṃvedana* can be seen also every time Mi pham refers to self-awareness in his other works, and defends its acceptability conventionally as the defining quality of consciousness understood as the opposite of insentience (*bems po'i rang bzhin las bzlog pa*).[9] Mi pham expands *Madhya-*

---

[8] It may have been influenced by the comment of Dharmakīrti in *Pramāṇaviniścaya* 1:38cd: grāhyagrāhakavaidhuryāt svayaṃ saiva prakāśate (cited by Ichigo, *ibid.*, p. 235 n. 71. Cf. p. 175). It is noticeable, though, that when Prajñākaramati (on *Bodhicaryāvatāra* 9:21) and Mokṣākaragupta (1988, p. 23) want to refer to this way of seeing *svasaṃvedana,* as the reverse of insentience *(jaḍa/bems po),* it is Śāntarakṣita they quote.

[9] See for example Mi pham's *Madhyamakālaṃkāra* commentary (Mi pham 1976a), p. 143: shes pa 'di ni rang gi ngo bo bem po lta bu ma yin pas rang gi ngo bo rig par bya ba rkyen gzhan la ltos mi dgos pa de phyir rang rig ces bzhag pa tha snyad ches 'thad de /. And his commentary to the *Bodhicaryāvatāra* (Mi pham 1975a), pp. 21-2: mdor na rang rig pa 'gog pa ni don dam par 'gog pa yin gyi bem po las log tsam la [22] tha snyad du rang rig par 'dogs pa'i tshul de 'gog pa ma yin te / Mi pham cites *Madhyamakālaṃkāra* 16-17 in his reply to Blo bzang dpal ldan bstan 'dzin (Mi pham 1975b), p. 203, and also the *bDe mchog 'byung ba sogs sngags kyi rgyud* to the same effect (p. 212): bems po min phyir bdag nyid rig //. The tantra's use of this expression, incidentally, strongly suggests its influence either directly or indirectly by Śāntarakṣita's tradition (had it been the other way round, Śāntarakṣita or Kamalaśīla would surely have quoted the tantra (as *buddhavacana*) in their support). Also, in an independent work on Madhyamaka (Mi pham 1976b), p. 795, he says: de phyir shes pa ni shing rta dang rtsigs pa sogs

makālaṃkāra 16 with reference to the developed Tibetan psychology familiar also in the dGe lugs monasteries where he had spent some time. Actually, he says, whatever is a consciousness occurs as having the defining characteristic of luminosity and awareness, and is the opposite of those things which are free from luminosity and awareness and have the nature of insentience, such as a chariot, a wall and so on. Thus what is by nature not insentient is thereby said to be conscious of its very own self, or to be self-aware, self-luminous.[10]

---

las bzlog ste /. The additional example of a wall *(rtsig(s) pa)* comes from Kamalaśīla's *Madhyamakālaṃkārapañjikā*, p. 188, and is again used by Mi pham in his *Madhyamakālaṃkāra* commentary, p. 142.

[10] Mi pham (1976a), p. 142: don la rnam par shes pa gang zhig shing rta dang rtsig pa la sogs pa bem po'i rang bzhin gsal rigs dang bral ba dag las bzlog pa gsal zhing rig pa'i mtshan nyid can du rab tu skye ba ste / de ltar bem po min pa'i rang bzhin gang yin pa de lta bu 'di ni bdag rang nyid shes pa'am rang rig rang gsal zhes pa yin no //. The definition of consciousness as luminosity and awareness is common in dGe lugs texts. See, for example, Geshe Kelsang Gyatso (1993), p. 16. But luminosity is essentially thought of in Indo-Tibetan philosophy as reflexive. Otherwise it is difficult to understand exactly what is being referred to by the expression 'luminosity'. Geshe Kelsang comments that 'clarity' [luminosity] refers to the nature of the mind [consciousness], while 'cognizes' [awareness] refers to its function. Thus the mind is essentially luminous. Since for dGe lugs Madhyamaka only emptinesses are ultimate truths, the mind is of course a conventional truth. But as a conventional truth, in order for its nature to be luminosity it would seem that it should conventionally be reflexive, i.e. there should be *svasaṃvedana* conventionally in the sense in which Mi pham, following Śāntarakṣita, is going to explain it. On the other hand it would not be incoherent for a dGe lugs pa to reply that he grants the conventional existence of luminosity but denies that this is *svasaṃvedana*, since one cannot speak of self-*awareness* where there is no subject-object relationship, and, there-

Thus far Śāntarakṣita and his commentators have portrayed self-awareness as the very characteristic of consciousness, what distinguishes it from insentience, and this is said to correspond to the usage of the 'person-in-the-street'. But consciousness can take itself as an object without this being 'self-awareness' in the sense in which Śāntarakṣita is using the expression here. Such occurs for example in introspection, where we direct our attention at another (previous) consciousness-event. Clearly this could not itself be the defining characteristic of consciousness, for if all consciousnesses required themselves to be known by introspection we would have an infinite regress and, as Śāntarakṣita puts it in his *Tattvasaṃgraha* (following Dignāga and Dharmakīrti), in such a case there would be no awareness at all. Alternatively, if the series ends at some point, that terminating consciousness would have to be self-justifying, i.e. self-aware, and the same could therefore be said of other con-

fore, the expression 'self-awareness' has been given no meaning apart from saying it is what consciousness has that other things do not. 'Luminosity' is of course a metaphor. Incidentally, the need for consciousness to be defined in terms of luminosity *and* awareness (of something) is interesting. I have argued elsewhere (on Kantian grounds) that I have difficulty making sense of a state of consciousness which is literally nonconceptual and nonconceptualizable (see Williams, 1992a). Here, if we take a hypothetical case of a pure nonconceptual consciousness it would seem that in fact it would have to be luminous but not aware (of anything). In this hypothetical case, mere luminosity with no content could still not be distinguished from no experience at all. Thus the need to define consciousness in terms of luminosity (i.e., following Śāntarakṣita, reflexivity as its nature which distinguishes it from insentience) *and* awareness (i.e., intentionality, it takes an intentional object as content) would appear philosophically to be a sensible move.

sciousnesses. They are all the same in respect of being consciousnesses.[11] Śāntarakṣita sums up, therefore, his vision of *svasaṃvedana* in a manner which Matilal (1986, p. 156) refers to as a 're-definition from the Buddhist point of view'. What is meant by '*svasaṃvedana*' is (i) that consciousness does not depend on another thing in order to be known, and (ii) it is nevertheless known.[12] Therefore, it follows that it is self-known.

Thus the character of self-awareness here has nothing to do with taking itself as an *object* in a way which might lead to an infinite regress. Rather, self-awareness *means* reflexivity, where there is no sense of referring to an actual subject/object relationship and, therefore, no stage of validation beyond the consciousness itself. Kamalaśīla implies that it would not be correct to think of self-awareness on the model of 'x is aware of y' where $y = x$. In other words, the epistemological model based on act and agent where an agent acts on itself is inappropriate, and, therefore, the common criticism of self-awareness found in other Buddhist sources, grounded on the impossibility of an action directed towards itself, simply does not apply in

11 See *Tattvasaṃgraha* 2024-7. For Dignāga and Dharmakīrti see *Pramāṇasamuccaya* 1:12 in Hattori (1968), and Hattori's accompanying notes.

12 *Tattvasaṃgraha* 2011: svarūpavedanāyānyad vedakaṃ na vyapekṣate / na cāviditam astīdam ity artho'yaṃ svasaṃvidaḥ //. Note that although on balance it seems likely that this self-awareness (ii) strategy originated with Śāntarakṣita, it may have been a common interpretation in his time (8th century), or originated with someone else. It appears to be found very nicely stated in Vinītadeva's *Nyāyabinduṭīkā* (Vinītadeva 1971, p. 107). Consciousnesses reveal their own nature because that is their very nature. Like a lamp, they do not require another to render them known. Vinītadeva was perhaps an older contemporary of Śāntarakṣita.

this case.[13] *Svasaṃvedana* is essentially *not* a case of a subjective aspect (*grāhakākāra*) experiencing an objective aspect (*grāhyākāra*). Kamalaśīla comments that 'By self-cognition we do not mean the nature of a subject ("the perceiver"; *grāhaka*). Then what is it? It has as its nature illumination by itself, intrinsically; it is just like the glow in the sky.'[14] Likewise in his *Madhyamakālaṃkārapañjikā* Kamalaśīla observes that when we refer to *svasaṃvedana* we are not maintaining that it has the nature of object or subject (p. 188: *de bzhin du gzung ba dang 'dzin pa'i dngos por yang mi 'dod pa nyid do*). Both categories are inapplicable.[15] The crucial verse on this issue is *Madhyamakālaṃkāra* 17, in which Śāntarakṣita explains that in the case of self-awareness of consciousness it is not to be treated on the model of activity and agent, since as regards what is

---

[13] See, for example, *Bodhicaryāvatāra* 9:17 where we find a common reference to the Buddha's saying (in the *Laṅkāvatārasūtra* and elsewhere) that the mind cannot see the mind, any more than a sword can cut itself. Śāntarakṣita wants to say that the model here is wrong. Mi pham is able to refer to the *Ghanavyūhasūtra* where the Buddha says that the mind *is* seen by the mind (in good Cittamātra manner), although unrecognized (sna tshogs snang ba rang sems te // lus can rnams kyi bdag nyid gnyis // phyi dang nang dang thams cad du // gzung dang 'dzin pa lta bur gnas // sems kyis sems ni mthong yin yang // khong du mi chud dus pa rnams // kha gnyis sems de lus can gyi // yin yang shes par ma gyur pa //. See Mi pham (1975b), p. 211. That the act/agent model is inappropriate is made quite clear by Śāntarakṣita at *Madhyamakālaṃkāra* 17.

[14] Translated by Ichigo (1989), p. 173. This is Kamalaśīla's commentary to *Tattvasaṃgraha* 1999 (cited *ibid.*, p. 234 n. 63): na hi grāhakabhāvenātmasaṃvedanam abhipretam/ kiṃ tarhi / svayam prakṛtyā prakāśātmatayā nabhastalavarttyālokavat //.

[15] He refers to this as also being the view of the *Pramāṇavārttika* (*rnam par 'grel pa las kyang de bzhin nyid du ston to*). Cf. the *Pramāṇaviniścaya* 1:38cd cited above, note 8.

by nature a partless unity a threefold division (into action—'that which is done'— agent, and activity—the actual doing) is unacceptable.[16] Thus when we refer to self-awareness in this sense (self-awareness (ii)) it is not *self* awareness in the sense of an awareness that takes itself as an object. What referent a consciousness takes is another issue. But in its own nature as consciousness it is always reflexive.

Let me summarize now what it is I am saying about the relationships between self-awareness (i) and self-awareness (ii). They are clearly not the same, and things can be said about the one which cannot be said about the other. Self-awareness (i) is the result of a particular epistemological situation. It has an intentional structure ('intentional' in Brentano's sense of intending an object, i.e. taking a referent)—self-awareness (i) involves the subjective aspect experiencing the objective aspect. It is self-awareness in the sense that consciousness takes consciousness as an object. Because it is the result of a particular epistemological situation, in a hypothetical case of pure consciousness, i.e., consciousness which is not of anything, which has no epistemological content, there would also be no self-awareness (i), for there could be no case of a subjective aspect taking as an object the objective aspect, since there could be no objective aspect. In a case of literally pure consciousness there would be no perception *of* anything, and, therefore, no objective aspect, no consciousness taking-on the aspect of

---

16 gcig pa cha med rang bzhin la // gsum gyi rang bzhin mi 'thad phyir // de yi rang gi rig pa ni // bya dang byed pa'i dngos por min // = *Tattvasaṃgraha* v. 2000: kriyākarabhāvena na svasaṃvittir asya tu / ekasyānaṃśarūpasya trairūpyānupapattitaḥ //. For more on action, etc., see below ch. 3, n. 1 and references.

any object. Self-awareness (i) taken by itself, without the addition of self-awareness (ii), also suggests the problem of an infinite regress.[17] Self-awareness (ii) on the other hand is the essential characteristic of consciousness itself. For Śāntarakṣita this does not seem to be primarily a matter of argument. His tendency is to simply assert it. It is an articulated basic presupposition. There must be something which distinguishes *sui generis* consciousness from everything else, i.e. that which is insentient. This is reflexivity. Thus wherever there is consciousness there is that characteristic of reflexivity, and in the sense in which 'reflexivity' is being used here it can only characterize consciousness. It is what makes consciousness consciousness. It has nothing to do with a particular epistemological situation or theory as such, and the reflexivity of consciousness does not *in itself* involve any intentional situation. In other words 'self-

[17] See here Klein (1986), p. 113, writing from the dGe lugs Prāsaṅgika point of view: 'In any case, because the self-knower [*svasaṃvedana*] is a factor of experience that is one entity [*ngo bo gcig*—see ch. 1, n. 9 above] with the perceiving consciousness, the difficulty remains of explaining more fully how the two factors of a single directly perceiving consciousness relate to one another. For example, it is said that the self-knower observes the subjective apprehension aspect; yet, why should one consciousness or factor of consciousness need to appear to another one? Is the self-knower itself then generated in the image of the apprehension aspect? The Prāsaṅgika system rejects the existence of a self-knower because it considers that if a self-knower had to be posited in order to explain the self-awareness of an eye-consciousness, then that self-knower would also have to possess a self-knower, and so on infinitely.' Śāntarakṣita does not explain *svasaṃvedana,* either in the *Madhyamakālaṃkāra* or in the *Tattvasaṃgraha,* on the model of the subjective aspect experiencing the objective aspect (self-awareness (i)). His alternative model of reflexivity (self-awareness (ii)) is precisely intended to avoid these problems of infinite regress.

consciousness' here has nothing to do with a subject-object relationship, it essentially does *not* involve in itself consciousness *of* anything, and, therefore, is nothing to do with consciousness of (it)self. In a hypothetical case of pure consciousness there would by definition still be self-awareness (ii), since otherwise it would not be consciousness at all. Likewise, although self-awareness (ii) may have other problems associated with it, still, by definition again, it would avoid the difficulty of an infinite regress. Reflexive consciousness is self-validating in its occurrence, and does not require regress to a further validator. On the other hand to say that consciousness is reflexive is in itself to say nothing about particular perceptual situations. It is only to say that if there is a perceptual situation then inasmuch as *any* perceptual situation involves consciousness—including any ordinary everyday perception—that consciousness is reflexive, because such is what any consciousness must be in order to be other than insentience.

It should also be clear, however, that although I am arguing self-awareness (i) is different from self-awareness (ii), I do not wish to maintain that the one cannot be reduced to the other through a combination of (sometimes debatable) presuppositions and inference. Quite the reverse. It might be argued, for example, that in the case of self-awareness (i), since for Cittamātra there is no external reality causing the aspect of blue when the eye-consciousness takes on the aspect of blue, it follows that in reality the eye-consciousness cannot take on the aspect of blue.[18] Thus when the sub-

---

[18] Internal 'seeds' (*bija*) will not help here, since where (without an infinite regress) do the seeds come from? What distinguishes the seed for blue from that for, say, yellow? What causes one rather than another to occur at time *x*?

jective aspect experiences the objective aspect, pure awareness experiences pure awareness. If this is the case, there is no longer any differentiation into subjective and objective aspects. Therefore, if we have consciousness at all we must be left simply with self-reflective consciousness with absolutely no differentiation into subject and object—that is, it would seem, self-awareness (ii).

One could also argue for the reverse, and this was important for Śāntarakṣita himself. Śāntarakṣita wants to argue that since consciousness is by its very nature the exact opposite of insentience, it is not possible in reality for consciousness to contact insentient objects. Thus in knowing an object, consciousness must really be apprehending itself in the form of the object.[19] Therefore, from the reflexive nature of con-

---

[19] See *Madhyamakālaṃkāra* 18: de'i phyir 'di ni shes pa yi // rang bzhin yin pas bdag shes rung // don gyi rang bzhin gzhan dag la // de yis ji ltar shes par 'gyur // = *Tattvasaṃgraha* v. 2001: tad asya bodharūpatvād yuktaṃ tāvat svavedanam / parasya artharūpasya tena saṃvedanaṃ katham //. Cf. also Kamalaśīla (quoted Ichigo, p. 234 n. 60, trans. p. 173): tasmād ātmasaṃvedanam eva sadaiva jñānaṃ saty api bāhye santānāntara iti siddhyati vijñaptimātratā. As Ichigo puts it (p. 176), for Śāntarakṣita and his followers 'Knowledge, since it is immaterial, cannot grasp the insentient and material object which is distinct from knowledge.' Consciousness can only apprehend something of the same type, i.e. consciousness. Matilal (1986, p. 159) has observed that 'the usual mentalistic strategy is to introduce an insurmountable barrier between the mental and the non-mental (material) and then claim that the mental (a cognitive event, a mode of consciousness) cannot be connected with the material object unless it transforms the latter into a mental object. This would, therefore, create what has sometimes been called the 'veil of ideas'. An argument can usually be developed to show eventually that this veil of ideas becomes in fact our veil of ignorance about the external, material world: if this is so, then, in our explanation of knowledge

sciousness as its uniquely defining quality one moves to an epistemology where consciousness apprehends itself in the form of the object. That is, one moves from self-awareness (ii) to self-awareness (i). It is clear that Śāntarakṣita finally does want to argue from *svasaṃvedana* to a *cittamātra*-like position. However, Śāntarakṣita is a Mādhyamika, and as such he is not going to adopt the other Cittamātra (Yogācāra) premiss, that of the need for a *dravya* in order to explain the possibility of conceptual construction (see, for example, *Madhyamakālaṃkāra* 1). A complete universality of conceptual construction (= *prajñaptisat* = *niḥsvabhāvatā*) at least ultimately is the defining characteristic of all Madhyamaka. Therefore, Śāntarakṣita is left with a *cittamātra* position as an explanation of the *conventional* world, and his discussion of the reflexive nature of consciousness and its use in order to argue for mind-only is all occurring on the conventional level. Whether consciousness is reflexive or not, and whether it is coherent to speak of *cittamātra* conventionally, are thus on this level not issues of the Mādhyamika search for putative ultimates. They are in fact empirical issues (perhaps issues of science—the nature of consciousness, and whether it is reflexive or not, would be on this basis a matter of psychology). Mi pham is going to take from Śāntarakṣita the reflexive nature of consciousness and argue on such a foundation that whether consciousness is reflexive or not is nothing to do with the Prāsaṅgika critique of ultimate, inherent, existence. But Mi pham is certainly also going to want to deny (as himself a Prāsaṅgika Mādhyamika) that he is required to give a *cittamātra*-type explanation of the conventional world based on

and awareness, a reference to the external world would seem to be dispensable.'

the reflexivity of consciousness. Having pointed out that the Prāsaṅgika critiques do not entail a denial of the conventional status of *svasaṃvedana*, it is not necessary for Mi pham as a Prāsaṅgika to explain exactly how a reflexive consciousness knows material objects. Mi pham simply wants to argue for the obvious givenness of the fact that consciousness is reflexive. As Kamalaśīla said, it is obvious even to cowherders. Even conventional *cittamātra* does not have that same obvious givenness.

CHAPTER THREE

Madhyamakālaṃkāra 16-17 in Prajñākaramati's *Bodhicaryāvatārapañjikā* on *BCA* 9:21

Mi pham is going to argue that Śāntideva in his *Bodhicaryāvatāra* is not opposed to the conventional existence of *svasaṃvedana* as a characteristic of consciousness, and Mi pham's understanding of *svasaṃvedana* is clearly derived from Śāntarakṣita. But Prajñākaramati, possibly the earliest and principal Indian commentator to the *Bodhicaryāvatāra* actually cites *Madhyamakālaṃkāra* 16-17 as part of a defense by his *opponent*. Prajñākaramati has a good understanding of Śāntarakṣita's position, and the description he puts into the mouth of his opponent serves as an excellent summary commentary to *Madhyamakālaṃkāra* 16-17.

The opponent explains that consciousness is spoken of as self-awareness with reference to its self-luminosity. This is because the illumination of consciousness does not depend on another since it is produced from its own causes and conditions, with a nature which is indeed the exact opposite of that of insentience. Moreover, for us, the opponent points out, differentiation into a separate action *(karman/las)*, agent *(kartṛ/byed pa po)* and activity *(kriyā/bya ba)* is not acceptable with reference to the self-luminosity of consciousness. It is not reasonable to have these three natures (action, agent, and activity) applied to one (unitary) existent. There is not, therefore, for us the slightest defeat based on critical faults thought to stem from differentiation into a separate activity, etc. There is in fact no problem as regards a self-luminosity which was born from its own cause.[1]

---

1 Skt. text (Vaidya edition) on *BCA* 9:21: yasmāt jaḍasvabhāvavyāvṛttātmatayā svahetupratyayāt utpattir eva jñānasya prakāśāntaranirapekṣasya ātmaprakāśatā svasaṃvedanam ucyate /...na punar asmābhiḥ karma-kartṛkriyābhedena jñānasyātmaprakāśanam iśyate / ekasya sataḥ karmādisvabhāvatrayasyāyogāt / tan na kriyādibhedena dūṣaṇe'pi kiṃcid dūṣitam asmākaṃ syāt, svahetujanitasyātma-prakāśasyānupaghātāt / = Tib. (Derge) pp. 409-10: gang gi phyir rang gi rgyu dang rkyen las bems po'i rang bzhin las bzlog gi bdag nyid du bskyed pa'i shes pa nyid gsal ba gzhan la ma ltos par bdag nyid gsal ba la rang rig par brjod de / . . . yang kho bo cag rnams kyis las dang byed pa po dang bya ba tha dad pas shes pa'i bdag nyid gsal bar ni yod pa ma yin te / yod pa gcig la las la sogs pa'i rang bzhin gsum mi rigs pa'i phyir ro // de bya ba tha dad [410] pa'i sgo nas skyon brjod na yang kho bo ni cung zad kyang sun phyung ba ma yin te / rang gi rgyu las skyes pa'i bdag nyid kyi gsal ba ma nyams pa'i phyir ro //. The terms ***karman, kartṛ*** and ***kriyā*** as used here are derived from the Sanskrit grammatical tradition. I shall treat them in more detail subsequently. To avoid misunderstanding it is important to bear in mind that although ***karman*** is translated here by the

This is the context within which Prajñākaramati's opponent cites *Madhyamakālaṃkāra* 16-17. Prajñākaramati's reply is particularly interesting if we bear in mind that as far as Śāntideva and Prajñākaramati as Prāsaṅgika Mādhyamikas are concerned, the opponent wishes to establish *svasaṃvedana* as something found under ultimate analysis, that is, something which really, inherently exists, an ulti-

---

literal 'action', in the grammatical context it refers in the broadest possible sense to the direct *object* of the activity expressed by the verb ('that which is done'; a frequent equivalent is *āpya*, 'that to be obtained'). For handy definitions see Abhyankar and Shukla (1986). For the Tibetan context and considerations see Verhagen (1994). I now have some reservations incidentally as to whether Prajñākaramati's commentary is the earliest commentary to the *Bodhicaryāvatāra.* Thanks to the important textual work by Akira Saito on the Tun-huang versions of the Tibetan translation of the *Bodhicaryāvatāra* we know that there are two rather different versions of Śāntideva's text. What we might call the 'standard received' or 'canonical' text preserved in Sanskrit and the Tibetan Canon is much longer and different in certain important respects from that found in several versions at Tun-huang (and incidentally clearly called the *'Bodhisattvacaryāvatāra').* Bu ston and others speak of disputes in India—apparently from early times—concerning which was the correct version of Śāntideva's text. Saito considers (quite probably, but not certainly) that the shorter 'non-canonical' version is closer to the original than the canonical version. However, there is preserved in the bsTan 'gyur a commentary to the non-canonical version, the anonymous *Bodhisattvacaryāvatāravivṛttipañjikā* Apparently even the names of the translators of this commentary are unknown, so there is no accurate way of dating the translation, let alone the commentary. But the *Vivṛttipañjikā* is a commentary to what is very likely an earlier version of Śāntideva's text than the standard canonical version commented upon by Prajñākaramati. We could plausibly argue, therefore, a *prima facie* case that the *Vivṛttipañjikā* may also be an earlier commentary than that by Prajñākaramati. [I am grateful to Paul Harrison for introducing me to Saito's work and the gift of a copy of Saito (1993).]

mate existent, and Mi pham wants to claim that the Prāsaṅgika does not wish to deny also the conventional existence of *svasaṃvedana* (as the Prāsaṅgika would certainly wish to do, for example, with reference to a creator God or an inherently existent Self).

Prajñākaramati begins by denying that his opponent is going to be able to avoid the attribution of activity and agent in the case of self-awareness, since these distinctions are part of everyday transactional usage and a fault can be pointed out on the basis of common linguistic meaning. Behind this comment we can detect the linguistic model of Sanskrit semantics. In everyday language, activity and agent are thought necessary for verbal meaning, and the very expression '*svasaṃvedana*' is a verbal derivative. Thus from an everyday, non-analytic, point of view it must still involve activity and agent. Śāntarakṣita's point concerning the inapplicability of act, agent and so on to reflexive self-awareness contradicts the everyday perspective and therefore contradicts the conventional. Prajñākaramati adds that if his opponent wishes to avoid fault by abandoning commonly-agreed verbal usage, then it is the world which will censure him.[2] Of

---

2 kriyākārabhedena vyavahāraprasiddhaṃ śabdārtham adhigamya dūṣaṇam uktam, svasaṃvedanaśabdasya tadarthābhidhāyakatvāt / yadi punar doṣabhayāl lokaprasiddho'pi śabdārthaḥ parityajyate, tadā lokata eva bādhā bhavato bhaviṣyati / = bya ba dang byed pa po'i khyad par gyi tha snyad las grub pa'i sgra'i don rtogs pas nyes pa brjod pa yin te / rang rig pa'i sgras de'i don brjod pa'i phyir ro // gal te yang nyes pas 'jigs nas 'jig rten la grags pa'i sgra'i don yongs su spong na / de'i tshe khyed la 'jig rten pa nyid kyis gnod por 'gyur la /. One answer to this point is actually given by Mi pham, who argues that in terms of linguistic differences one can speak of agent, activity, etc. in the case of *svasaṃvedana,* i.e., one can legitimately make these distinctions (as in 'Consciousness knows itself'; they are different isolates), but this does not mean they

course, Śāntarakṣita could not deny that '*svasaṃvedana*' is a verbal derivative which, therefore, in accordance with Sanskrit grammar, implies act, agent and so on. His problem is that if he then goes on to deny that semantics reflects or indeed has anything much to do with ontology (as Mi pham will do quite happily) Śāntarakṣita might in context be taken as implicitly claiming that *svasaṃvedana* exists as an ultimate truth, and that would contradict his position as a Mādhyamika. For Prajñākaramati clearly, the conventional must be whatever does not contradict everyday usage, and to contradict the conventional is not a matter for criticism by the Prāsaṅgika as such but is rather a matter for censure from the world itself.

It could be argued, however, that Prajñākaramati is too restrictive here. 'The world' (i.e., the realm of concern of those who are not considering the ultimate way of things) has a number of layers. Since whatever are the latest scientific discoveries of psychologists, psychiatrists and neurosurgeons for example concerning the mind are not matters of ultimate truth, for the Mādhyamika they must come within the conventional. But they certainly do not correspond with the way things are understood by our person-in-the-street. There are specialists within the conventional realm, and indeed Prajñākaramati's comments rely on the considerably refined specialization of Sanskrit grammarians like Pāṇini and Patañjali. It is actually debatable whether the ordinary person-in-the-street always considers that verbs require agent,

are distinct realities (there are no ontological implications; they are one entity). These are perfectly respectable dGe lugs categories, and it is a perfectly respectable dGe lugs response. See the discussion in ch. 7 below.

action and so on. Our friend may well have not considered the matter. Prajñākaramati is in fact (not uncommonly in Indian philosophy, and for understandable cultural reasons) relying upon and privileging a very elite group, Sanskrit grammarians, for an idea of what is to constitute the conventional. For his opponent ('Śāntarakṣita'), I suggest, if issues concerning the nature of consciousness are no longer matters of ultimate truth, then in what could be represented as his proto-scientific attempt to uncover the nature of our empirical consciousness Śāntarakṣita may well find himself saying something which is not the everyday view of non-specialists, let alone specialists in another field, Sanskrit grammar. Prāsaṅgika Madhyamaka need not be thought to imply a contradiction with scientific investigation. In other words, what the empirical nature of consciousness is arguably should not be a matter of concern for Prajñākaramati *qua* Prāsaṅgika. Śāntarakṣita can perfectly consistently claim that Sanskrit grammar does not necessarily reflect *empirical* reality, and the conventional truth anyway means non-ultimate truth, not simply whatever is considered to be true by our poor benighted cowherder. Of course, the conventional should not *contradict* the truth of Gorakṣa the cowherder. In actual fact the discoveries of scientists, while sometimes different from the perspective of the person-in-the-street, do not contradict them, for they are derivable in an acceptable and commonly agreed way from the world of the cowherder.

I do not see that Prajñākaramati would find this an unwelcome conclusion. He rather implies in his phrasing that his concern is to warn (his opponent or) Śāntarakṣita that as it stands his disagreement is not with himself, Prajñākaramati, but rather with the world, and it is against that world that Śāntarakṣita will have to defend himself. It is not an issue for Prajñākaramati the Mādhyamika.[3] What Prajñākaramati does *not* say here, and this is the point I really want to stress, is that were he to argue for the conventional status of *svasaṃvedana*, Śāntarakṣita would also contradict Śāntideva. In other words, Prajñākaramati simply fails to state that for Śāntideva (according to Tibetan doxographers, a Prāsaṅgika Mādhyamika of the same tradition as Candrakīrti), *svasaṃvedana* is not the case even conventionally.[4]

---

[3] Looking back on it, I think I was groping towards a similar perspective on the issue of *svasaṃvedana* in Williams (1983) pp. 329-30 (Appendix 2 below), when I spoke of the possibility of seeing *svasaṃvedana* (by those who hold to it) as a *presupposition* of the everyday world, and therefore occupying a space between the everyday as the world of everyday people, and ultimate truth. As (arguably) a presupposition of a conventionality (that is how consciousness must be in order to *be* consciousness, a conventionality) *svasaṃvedana* must itself be a conventionality (only emptinesses are ultimate truths for Madhyamaka) and yet it is not an everyday conventionality of everyday folk. This is a category which the Prāsaṅgika has rather tended to ignore (at least, certain Prāsaṅgikas in particular, such as Mi bskyod rdo rje (see Williams 1983b, p. 328), who take the Prāsaṅgika as accepting conventionally only what is held by the completely naive pre-critical perspective of the cowherder), although, of course, the Prāsaṅgika can reply that it is not his or her concern *qua* Prāsaṅgika. Thus, given that it does not exist as an ultimate truth, whether there is *svasaṃvedana* conventionally becomes an empirical matter, and the Prāsaṅgika has not said that it does not. He or she has *as such* no interest in the matter. As we shall see, this is in fact the view of Mi pham.

[4] As we shall see, in spite of this being one of the fundamental points in the dGe lugs tradition for distinguishing Prāsaṅgika Madhyamaka from other forms of Buddhist philosophy, they are able to find only one short and controversial quotation from Candrakīrti in support (on *Madhyamakāvatāra* 6:73). The fact that no quotation is ever offered to the best of my knowledge from Śāntideva or his many commentators suggests a problem

Rather the reverse. Having told his opponent that he will have to defend himself against the everyday world for his view that activity and agent are not applicable to reflexive self-awareness, Prajñākaramati continues by *denying svasaṃvedana as an ultimate truth* (which is not the view of Śāntarakṣita).[5] In other

(even if one accepts the interpretation of Candrakīrti) in placing Śāntideva and Candrakīrti within the same subschool of Madhyamaka, at least if *svasaṃvedana* is part of the issue of definition.

[5] Of course, it could be pointed out against what I am arguing here, that Prajñākaramati considered himself to have first refuted the existence of *svasaṃvedana* conventionally, and now he is continuing to refute it ultimately. There is no doubt that he considers himself to have first *treated* self-awareness conventionally, and then ultimately. But whereas he as a Mādhyamika refutes *svasaṃvedana* ultimately, from the conventional perspective he simply points out a problem. It is the *world* which will attack the opponent on that level. My point is that Prajñākaramati does not seem to think that it is his job as a Mādhyamika to *refute* conventionally, at least, to refute *svasaṃvedana*. The issue of a creator God, for example, would be different. A God *could* only exist as an ultimate. Thus in refuting the ultimate existence of God one also refutes all possible forms of God's existence and therefore a God's merely conventional existence (which would be a contradiction). Therefore, while the Prāsaṅgika shows how for all *x*, *x* cannot be found under an analysis which investigates whether *x* has ultimate, inherent existence, the issue of conventional existence taken as a whole is still open for the Prāsaṅgika: (i) There are some things which if they exist, would have to exist ultimately (i.e., inherent existence, God, the True Self etc.). These things the Prāsaṅgika can consistently say do not exist either ultimately or conventionally as an implication of their not existing ultimately. (ii) There are other things which the Prāsaṅgika like anyone else can also say do not exist either ultimately or conventionally because they are straight contradictions (i.e., a square circle or, to use an Indian example, the son of a barren woman). These things do not exist in all possible worlds, ultimate and conventional. Their nonexistence is a necessary truth

(some in category (ii) may also come under category (i)). (iii) The nonexistence conventionally of other things (i.e., Meinong's golden mountain, unicorns or, perhaps, the reflexive nature of consciousness) is a contingent matter. There is a possible world (which may or may not be realized in our empirical world) in which they do exist. What I am suggesting then (as a background to appreciating Mi pham's defense of conventional *svasaṃvedana*) is that the Prāsaṅgika has no right and indeed no grounds, *qua Prāsaṅgika*, to say of one of these possible existents that it does not exist even conventionally, and equally no right to determine what would or would not be held to exist conventionally from one particular static perspective, least of all that of the-person-in-the-street (or, indeed, the Sanskrit grammarian). Of course, the Prāsaṅgika has every right to decide what is or is not the case conventionally as someone who is also a human being (even Prāsaṅgikas venture into the street sometimes), as a rational person, as someone who has looked, or as a scientist etc. And the Prāsaṅgika has every right to supplement the Prāsaṅgika perspective with any other perspective which concerns the conventional (the latest discoveries of science, Aristotelean, post-Aristotelean, Naiyāyika or Dharmakīrtian logic, medicine and so on) according to requirements. This is what occurs in Tibet, especially in the massive systematization found particularly in the use of Dharmakīrti by Tsong kha pa and his pupils. Assuming one accepts a supplement as *true*, it could then follow that certain things do not exist even conventionally (for example, if one supplemented the Prāsaṅgika perspective with a flat-earth cosmology as true it would follow by definition that a globular earth does not exist even conventionally), but this acceptance of the supplement is on conventional, and therefore contingent, rather than Prāsaṅgika grounds. Incidentally, understanding the concerns of conventional existence as not concerns of the Prāsaṅgika *qua* Prāsaṅgika, but as contingent matters,—and also recognizing different levels to the conventional (scientific, everyday, etc.)—should enable modern Prāsaṅgikas to be much more open to the perspective and discoveries of science, which after all are themselves contingent matters and not as such the concern of the Mādhyamika search for putative ultimate truths. Thus Mi pham too will want to urge that *svasaṃvedana* understood only as reflexivity stands or falls on whether it is as a mat-

words, as a Mādhyamika Prajñākaramati's concern (and by implication that of Śāntideva) is with claims of ultimate, inherent existence—not conventional status. Prajñākaramati observes that by his opponent's own reasoning there is no ultimately true establishment of *svasaṃvedana*. In the case of what is thus like a reflex, born from causes and conditions, we say it lacks inherent existence. Therefore, the reflexivity of consciousness very definitely does not exist, and this is because really *(tattvato)* an innate inherent existence does not exist. Moreover, being without inherent existence, a self-awareness of something which is of the nature of a sky-lotus is quite unreasonable.[6]

That Prajñākaramati's *own* argument is occurring entirely on the level of ultimate truth, which is the concern of the Mādhyamika, is even clearer from his further comments. For Mādhyamikas—patently *qua* Mādhyamikas, concerned with putative ultimate existence—there is not established the *in*sentient nature of anything (i.e., our chariot, walls and so on) *ul-*

---

ter of fact necessary to the nature of conventional consciousness or not. Not only is it not for Mi pham part of the Prāsaṅgika perspective but the Prāsaṅgika actually has *no right* to say that *svasaṃvedana* does not exist even conventionally. That is a matter of psychology and nothing to do with the Prāsaṅgika *as such*. I suggest that Prajñākaramati would not disagree.

6 ittham api na paramārthataḥ svasaṃvedanasiddhaḥ / tathā hi hetupratyayopajanitasya pratibimbasyeva niḥsvabhāvatvam uktam / tathā ca sutarāṃ na svasaṃvedanaṃ jñānasya, tattvato nijasvabhāvābhāvāt / na ca svabhāvābhāve gaganotpalasya ātmasaṃvedanam ucitam / = 'dis kyang rang rig don dam pa 'grub pa ma yin te / de bzhin du rgyu dang / rkyen las skyes pa'i gzugs brnyan rang bzhin med pa nyid du brjod la / de ltar rang rig pa'i shes pa ni shin tu yang med pa yin te / de kho na nyid du gnyug ma'i rang bzhin du med pa'i phyir ro // rang bzhin med par yang nam mkha'i ut pa la'i bdag nyid rang rig par yang rigs pa ma yin no //.

timately, by which one could derive the reflexivity of consciousness as the reverse of insentience, that is, not-insentience. Thus you, the opponent, Prajñākaramati says, should use this reasoning with the others, the 'Realists', those who hold to the inherent existence of something. Since there is absence of inherent existence, there is not established in any manner the reflexivity of consciousness.[7] Which is to say, the reflexivity of consciousness is not established, not found, under ultimate analysis, as an inherently-existing entity. Structurally it is clear that Prajñākaramati sees the Mādhyamika refutation of the reflexivity of consciousness as a corollary of the Mādhyamika denial of its opposite, those things which are insentient. Since there is no denial of insentient things conventionally contained in the Mādhyamika negations, it seems obvious that there is absolutely no implication here that Prajñākaramati sees the Mādhyamika denial of *svasaṃvedana* as a denial conventionally as well as ultimately. Whether *svasaṃvedana* exists conventionally or not appears to be no concern of Prajñākaramati *qua* (Prāsaṅgika) Mādhyamika. As we have seen, Prajñākaramati observes that his opponent should use his reasoning

---

7 na cāpi jaḍasvabhāvatā madhyamakavādinaṃ prati paramārthataḥ kasyacit siddhā, yena jaḍavyāvṛttam ajaḍaṃ svasaṃvedanaṃ syāt // tasmād anyān eva vastuvādinaḥ prati yuktam etad vaktuṃ / tato niḥsvabhāvatayā na kathaṃ cid api svasaṃvedanasiddhaḥ /. The Tibetan appears to be slightly but not really significantly different: dbu mar smra ba po rnams kyi dbang du byas te bems po'i rang bzhin yod pa ma yin zhing / gang gi bems po'i las bzlog pa bems po ma yin pa'i rang rig par 'gyur ba don dam par gang zhig kyang yod pa ma yin no / de lta bas dngos por smra ba gzhan nyid kyi dbang du byas te / 'di smra bar rigs pa yin no // de'i phyir na rang bzhin med pa nyid kyi nam yang rang rig pa grub pa ma yin no //.

with the Realists, not the Mādhyamika. This can only mean that Prajñākaramati is saying that the very reason why the Mādhyamika does not accept an argument for reflexivity as the reversal of insentience is because there are no insentient entities. The argument might work with the Realists, who accept insentient entities. Yet, even the Mādhyamika does not deny insentient entities *conventionally*. Therefore, Prajñākaramati is not denying the possibility (but it is as such no concern of his) that the argument may also work on the conventional level for showing the *conventional* fact of *svasaṃvedana*. It seems patently obvious to me that for Prajñākaramati there is no 'Prāsaṅgika' denial of the reflexive nature of consciousness even conventionally, and such a denial as a particular feature of an identifiable subschool of Madhyamaka never entered his mind.[8] We will find the same point

[8] We find the same with the commentary by Vibhūticandra, who as the only other Indian commentator who quotes Śāntarakṣita on this verse indicates here as so often in his commentary to the *Bodhicaryāvatāra* that he is essentially following Prajñākaramati: gang bshad pa / rnam shes bems po'i rang bzhin las // bzlog par rab tu skye ba ste // zhes bya ba la sogs pa des kyang rang rig tu mi 'grub ste / byas pa gzugs brnyan lta bu rang bzhin med pa'i phyir / rang gi rang bzhin med la bems po yang ma grub pas gang las log / (Derge p. 523). Among Tibetan commentators, as so often, it is Bu ston who is closest to Prajñākaramati and once more we find Śāntarakṣita referred to and no suggestion whatsoever that the refutation of *svasaṃvedana* is on the conventional as well as the ultimate level (p. 516): rang rgyu las bem po las ldog par skyes pa'i phyir ro // zhe na / rgyu rkyen las skyes na / de kho nar rang bzhin med pas khyab pas rang rig grub par 'gal zhing / nged la bem po ma grub pas de las ldog par grub pa 'gal lo //. Clearly the point in all of this is that an argument for establishing *svasaṃvedana*, that is, for finding *svasaṃvedana* under ultimate analysis, is contradictory because *svasaṃvedana*—being born from causes and conditions—truly lacks inherent existence.

suggested in turning to the crucial verse here from the *Bodhicaryāvatāra,* the verse on which Mi pham elaborated his own interpretation of the conventional existence of *svasaṃvedana.*

Insentient entities are not established for the Mādhyamika so their reversal could not establish reflexive sentience.

CHAPTER FOUR

The Verse

Prajñākaramati has his opponent introduce *Bodhicaryāvatāra* 9:26, with which Śāntideva ends his critique of *svasaṃvedana*, with the usual objection—that if there is no *svasaṃvedana* consciousness would lack its essential quality of sentience and therefore there could be no sensory awareness at all. Thus to deny the reflexive nature of awareness would also be to deny (conventional) transactional sensory experiences altogether.[1] Note that implicit here is a claim by the op-

[1] nanu yadi jñānam aviditasvarūpaṃ syāt, arthasyāpi pratītir na syāt / avyaktavyaktikatvād jñānasya, na hi arthasya vyaktiḥ / tadapratītau katham arthasya pratītiḥ?...sarvaś cāyaṃ dṛṣṭādi vyavahāro loke na syād ity āha yathā dṛṣṭam ity ādi / = Tib. p. 415: gal te shes pa rig pa'i ngo bor ma gyur na don yang rtogs par mi 'gyur ba ma yin nam shes pa ni mi gsal ba gsal bar byed pa'i phyir te don ni gsal ba ma yin la / de ma rtogs pa la don ci ltar rtogs par 'gyur te /...'jig rten na mthong ba'i tha snyad 'di thams cad med par 'gyur ro zhe na / ji ltar mthong thos shes pa la sogs pa gsungs te /. Cf. also Vibhūticandra: If there were no *svasaṃvedana*, then a pot could illuminate a cloth—'o na shes pa ma myong na don myong bar mi 'gyur / de ma myong na don gsal bar mi 'gyur ba'i phyir ro // de bshad pa shes pa ni rtogs pa'i don zhes so // de lta yin na bum pas ras kyang gsal bar byed do //.

ponent (a 'Śāntarakṣita') that reflexive-awareness is necessary to ordinary empirical experience. The issue is not one of whether the Mādhyamika negates as such conventionalities or not, but rather whether the Mādhyamika destroys empirical sensory awareness through negating *svasaṃvedana*.

Bodhicaryāvatāra 9:26 (9:25 in the Tibetan)

yathā dṛṣṭaṃ śrutaṃ jñātaṃ
  naiveha pratiṣidhyate /
satyataḥ kalpanā tvatra
  duḥkhahetur nivāryate //

ji ltar mthong thos shes pa dag /
'dir ni dgag pa bya min te /
'dir ni sdug bsngal rgyur gyur pa /
bden par rtog pa bzlog bya yin //

There is not [Tib.: ' to be'] negated here
  [something] as seen, heard, or cognised /
Rather, here, there is [Tib.: 'to be'] reversed
  the construction of truth, which is the cause of
  suffering //[2]

Śāntideva is quite clear about what is being negated in the Mādhyamika analysis. It is the construction of truth *(satyataḥ kalpanā)* in things which do not have

---

[2] The Tun-huang copies of this verse deciphered by Saito (1993) have a slightly different version of the first part, which gives perhaps a better reading: 'di ltar mthong dang thos pa kun // 'di la dgag par bya myed kyi //. Saito restores a Sanskrit version: yathā (should this be tathā?) dṛṣṭaṃ śrutaṃ sarvaṃ naiveha pratiṣidhyate / = 'Thus there is not [to be] negated here all the seen and heard, but...'.

truth. By 'construction of truth', Prajñākaramati explains, we mean the superimposition of an ultimate status, in other words, of course, the imposition of an inherent existence *(satyataḥ paramārthataḥ / kalpanā āropaḥ)*. However, it is not immediately clear whether Śāntideva wants to say that it is specifically something seen, heard and cognised which is not negated by the Mādhyamika, or whether he is using this expression to stand for sensory experience in general, whatever that sensory experience may involve and therefore including the possibility of *svasaṃvedana* as also not being negated by the Mādhyamika.

It seems that the expression '[something] as seen, heard or cognised' must be intended to stand for *something* in addition to its own contents, since Śāntideva surely could not be taken as wanting to exclude in this context, say, something as touched or smelt. So the expression should be taken as including at least the experiences of the six senses. Moreover, in context Śāntideva could not be concerned with something as seen etc. *qua* things—objects or sensations—as such. Rather his concern is with them as *visual* and so on, that is, Śāntideva's concern here is with all sensory cognitive experience. The crucial question, however, is whether Śāntideva would also want to say that *svasaṃvedana*, as (according to some) necessary to cognitive experience *qua* experience, is not being negated here either.[3]

---

[3] It should be clear from what has been said already concerning Prajñākaramati that this option would not commit Śāntideva to holding that there actually is *svasaṃvedana* conventionally. All it would commit him to holding is that the conventional existence of *svasaṃvedana* is not negated by the Mādhyamika *qua* Mādhyamika. Whether it exists or not conventionally is a matter for 'the world' and not the Mādhya-

Mi pham and those who hold to the conventional existence of reflexive-awareness would want to maintain that since the opponent's (say, a Śāntarakṣita's) argument is that the reflexive nature of consciousness is necessary for any conscious experience to take place at all, what Śāntideva is claiming not to negate conventionally here is conscious experience as such and thus also *svasaṃvedana* as the essential constitutive feature of conscious experience, consciousness as *consciousness.* The expression '[something] as seen, heard or cognised' must on the premisses of the opponent's argument include *svasaṃvedana.* Otherwise Śāntideva would have to make explicit and explain against the opponent's objections not only that he considers the negation of *svasaṃvedana* to apply also to the conventional as well as the ultimate level—although this conventional as well as ultimate negation does not apply to sensory experience as such—but also how this could be. He does neither. The dGe lugs tradition, on the other hand, would want to argue that Śāntideva's half-verse should be taken as at the most referring to the six forms of sensory experience, which, as Tsong kha pa holds, do not require *svasaṃvedana* to

---

mika. It is perhaps worth noting at this point that when I refer here and elsewhere to what *Śāntideva* intended in a particular verse, I mean 'Śāntideva' as an expression for the author of the received canonical version of verse *x* as we now have it, *whoever that person or persons may have been.* This is the person (quite possibly a composite figure) Prajñākaramati and our Tibetan commentators considered to be Śāntideva. The textual archaeology of which verses or parts were really by Śāntideva, while fascinating although probably insoluble if the search is for even reasonable certainty, is not relevant to my purposes or concerns here. Mi pham and his critics certainly thought Śāntideva wrote (or uttered) the received canonical version.

take place.[4] Thus Śāntideva is explicitly stating that ordinary sensory experience is not denied as such (conventionally) by the Mādhyamika, but this does not carry with it a claim not to deny (conventionally) *svasaṃvedana,* for the reflexive nature of awareness is completely unnecessary to experience even conventionally.

Initially it is not entirely clear which of these interpretations Śāntideva would favor. But it is clear, I think, what Śāntideva's main concern is. His concern is with overcoming suffering, which he attributes to a false construction of truth, and he sees the Mādhyamika negations as those negations necessary to achieve this goal. Thus I suggest that *Bodhicaryāvatāra* 9:26 is best read as a whole, where what is said *not* to be negated *as such* by the Mādhyamika in the first part of the verse should be understood as the exact contradictory of what is said to be negated in the second half-verse (i.e., what is not negated is {not inherent existence}). Thus, structurally, Śāntideva is stating that inherent existence is negated by the Mādhyamika analysis—which is an ultimate analysis investigating whether a putative ultimate existent really has that ultimate existence or not—while that which is not a putative ultimate existent is not the subject of the Mādhyamika analysis and therefore a Mādhyamika negation. Śāntideva's concern is to negate the cause of suffering. What is not the cause of suffering is not the concern of his negations. Thus whether *x* exists or not as a non-inherently existing entity (assuming it is *possible* for *x* to exist in this way) is not a matter concerning the cause of suffering (because it is not being posited, constructed, as true), and therefore it is not a

[4] For Tsong kha pa's arguments here, and sources, see Williams (1983), pp. 324-6 (Appendix 2 below).

matter for the Mādhyamika *qua* Mādhyamika. It may be a matter for the world, on its own grounds, and it is, therefore, up to the world whether or not there exists a non-inherently existent (i.e., conventional) *svasaṃvedana.*

It is worth noting that, among those I have examined, not a single commentary to the *Bodhicaryāvatāra* prior to the dGe lugs commentary of rGyal tshab rje, Indian or Tibetan, explicitly states that the purport of Śāntideva's critique of *svasaṃvedana* is to negate *svasaṃvedana* as existing even conventionally.[5] Most commentaries simply omit to discuss the issue, taking it for granted, I suggest, that the Mādhyamika is concerned with ultimate analysis and therefore putative inherent existents, and is not thus concerned with what does or does not exist conventionally. As we shall see, however, some commentaries on *Bodhicaryāvatāra* 9:26 nevertheless do state in passing that the negation is of an ultimate *svasaṃvedana,* thereby in context showing that Śāntideva's acceptance of sensory experience in the first half-verse does not in itself include a denial of a conventional *svasaṃvedana.*

Prajñākaramati asks his opponent whether he considers that all these transactional experiences would be denied as a result of the Mādhyamika arguments against *svasaṃvedana* (i) from an ultimate or (ii) from a conventional point of view?

---

[5] Note that this includes even Tsong kha pa's own commentary, although we know from elsewhere that he certainly does hold that the negation of *svasaṃvedana* is even from a conventional point of view. Perhaps Tsong kha pa's short commentary to the ninth chapter of the *Bodhicaryāvatāra* was delivered prior to his formulating his final view on the matter.

(I) DENIAL FROM AN ULTIMATE POINT OF VIEW

In the first case—the denial of *svasaṃvedana* from an ultimate point of view—the opponent's position is that all empirical transactional experiences are denied from an ultimate point of view by the Mādhyamika arguments. Unfortunately, Prajñākaramati's response is obscured by a textual problem. According to the Sanskrit version Prajñākaramati's reply is *tadāpriyam idam asmākam,* which could mean either (a) that this is what we (the Mādhyamika) accept—in other words, we agree with this—or (b) the exact opposite. P.L. Vaidya, in editing the Sanskrit text, has shown his preference for the first interpretation *(tadā priyam).* In support of this reading is first, that it is what one might expect a Mādhyamika to say. The Mādhyamika does indeed deny transactional experiences from an ultimate point of view. Moreover, both the commentaries which follow Prajñākaramati most closely—those by Vibhūticandra and Bu ston—clearly read his intention this way. Vibhūticandra states quite simply that if one asserts here that transactions such as something as seen and so on do not exist ultimately, then we accept it.[6] Against this reading is the fact that this is not the way the text was read by Sumatikīrti and his collaborators a century earlier than Vibhūticandra, when translating the *Bodhi-*

[6] Vibhūticandra Derge p. 525: mthong ba la sogs pa'i tha ṡnyad kyi don dam par med par 'gyur ba'am / yang na kun rdzob tu med par 'gyur ro // de la don dam par med par 'gyur zer na 'dod pa nyid /. See also Bu ston p. 518: shes pa rang ma rig na / shes pa chos can / gzugs sgra mthong thos kyi tha snyad mi 'thad par thal / rang ma rig pa'i phyir zhe na / don dam par med par thal ba la bsal ba med /. Note also that Bu ston explicitly refers in this context to transactional conventions of form, sound, seeing and hearing.

caryāvatārapañjikā into Tibetan. They just as clearly saw Prajñākaramati as denying that the Mādhyamika accepts that all empirical transactional experiences are negated from an ultimate point of view (*tadā apriyam*).[7] Prajñākaramati continues with: 'For there is no engaging in ultimate examination on the conventional level' (*na hi sāṃvṛtasya paramārthacintāyām avatāro'sti / kun rdzob tu don dam pa la dpyad pa 'jug pa yod pa ma yin no*). If we take reading (a), then what Prajñākaramati is stating is that the Mādhyamika accepts the negation of transactional experiences on an ultimate level, since Mādhyamika negations cannot occur on the conventional level as the Mādhyamika does not engage in his or her sort of investigations with reference to the conventional. The conventional still remains. In other words, granted that there *are* Mādhyamika *qua* Mādhyamika negations, all these negations must be taken with reference to the ultimate level. Vibhūticandra comments that the negation of transactional experiences on an ultimate level is accepted 'because there does not exist there [on the ultimate level] all the conventional' (*kun rdzob pa kun de la med pa'i phyir ro*). Since it is certain that Prajñākaramati would not want to hold that there *do* exist transactional experiences on the ultimate level, reading (a) must embody in some sense *a* correct reading.

If we follow Sumatikīrti and take reading (b), with Prajñākaramati denying that the explanation in this context is that the Mādhyamika accepts that all empir-

---

[7] yad ucyate dṛṣṭādivyavahāro na syād iti, sa kiṃ paramārtho na syāt, saṃvṛtyā vā? tatra yadi paramārtho na syad ity ucyate, tadāpriyam idam asmākam / = Tib.: gang mthong ba la sogs pa'i tha snyad med par 'gyur ro zhes pa de don dam pa'am / kun rdzob tu med par 'gyur / de la don dam par med par 'gyur ro zhes brjod na de'i tshe 'di ni bdag 'dod pa ma yin te /.

ical transactional experiences are negated from an ultimate point of view, then, of course, the reason must be contained in Prajñākaramati's comment 'for there is no engaging in ultimate examination on the conventional level'. One possible way of taking this is that Prajñākaramati wishes to stress that since we are talking of *transactional conventional* experiences it makes no sense to refer to them as negated on an ultimate level. 'Negation on an ultimate level' means 'lacking ultimate status, inherent existence'. The negation is precisely in showing that a putative ultimate existent is not ultimately existent and therefore, if existent at all, is existent only conventionally. Transactional, conventional experiences by definition lack inherent existence. Once it is granted that they are only transactional conventional experiences without an inherent ultimate nature, as unenlightened beings think, then as merely conventional it is inappropriate to continue to apply ultimate examination. The ultimate examination has done its work precisely in showing that these *are* merely conventional.[8]

I confess to finding reading (b) and this interpretation, while possible, forced. Vibhūticandra is surely right in stating that, for the Mādhyamika, none of the

---

[8] Of course, another possible interpretation is that Prajñākaramati holds that the Mādhyamika has no position at all, and therefore the Mādhyamika does not have the position that transactional experiences are negated on an ultimate level.. There are obvious paradoxes here, but paradoxes would not be enough to show that this is not Prajñākaramati's purpose. If this had been his intention, however, I am sure Prajñākaramati would have made it clearer. It would concern issues of ultimate analysis (that is, it would not be the case that the Mādhyamika holds the view that transactional experiences lack ultimate existence, for example), and would not fit obviously with the reason he gives.

conventional exists on the ultimate level, and therefore it is correct for the Mādhyamika to accept in a straightforward way the assertion that conventional transactional experiences are denied on the ultimate level. Moreover, it would, I think, be stylistically unusual for Prajñākaramati to set up a dilemma for his opponent and follow the first lemma not with a *reductio* but out of the blue with the statement 'This is not what we, the Mādhyamika, accept'. The opponent had not based any argument on the fact that this is held by the Mādhyamika. In constructing his dilemma, on the other hand, Prajñākaramati can indeed construct one lemma against his opponent by saying that such is indeed our Mādhyamika position. Notwithstanding Sumatikīrti's Tibetan translation, therefore, even though it is earlier than Vibhūticandra and Bu ston, I suspect that the latter have the correct reading, which is more straightforward and makes better sense.[9]

If we apply (i) with the reading (a) to the issue of *svasaṃvedana,* we find that the argument that the negation of *svasaṃvedana* denies the ultimate status of transactional experiences is precisely acceptable to the Mādhyamika. Nothing has any ultimate status. Thus the negation of *svasaṃvedana* which latter is a condition for experience provides an additional acceptable argument for why experiences cannot be found under ultimate analysis and therefore lack ultimate status. One way of reading Prajñākaramati

---

[9] Note, incidentally, that Bu ston has no discussion of this textual problem, in spite of the obvious difference between the Tibetan translation of Prajñākaramati, and Vibhūticandra. Bu ston is usually quite good at picking up such difficulties. I doubt Bu ston had a different 'correct' Tibetan translation of Prajñākaramati. It seems he was working directly from a Sanskrit text (see Saito (1993), p. 26), and chose to read the text in what appears to be a more obvious manner.

here—in harmony with his treatment of Śāntarakṣita on *Bodhicaryāvatāra* 9:21—is as accepting (at least for the sake of argument) the necessity of *svasaṃvedana* in order for experiences to occur. If there is from an ultimate point of view no *svasaṃvedana,* then ultimately there can be no experiences either. Prajñākaramati *qua* Mādhyamika is once again concerned only with putative ultimate existence. Prajñākaramati's addition of 'for there is no engaging in ultimate examination on the conventional level' is of central importance here, for we can see quite explicitly what we have already seen implicitly—for Prajñākaramati the Mādhyamika analyses are not concerned with what does or does not exist conventionally.

(II) DENIAL FROM A CONVENTIONAL POINT OF VIEW

In the second case (see above, p. 56), the Mādhyamika denial of empirical transactional experiences as a result of its denial of *svasaṃvedana* is from a conventional point of view. It is in this context, Prajñākaramati tells us, that Śāntideva has stated *Bodhicaryāvatāra* 9:26 ab. The Mādhyamika does not negate worldly transaction. Whatever is well renowned in the world, as it is so, is thus acceptable providing it is of an unexamined nature. Thereby it is worldly-renowned, but it is not ultimately the case. Therefore, Prajñākaramati adds, the faults that there would be no cognition of referents and so on because there is no (reflexive) awareness of consciousness, do not get started in the case of one who holds (solely) to the side of the ultimate.[10] Prajñākaramati is placing the em-

[10] yad yathā lokataḥ pratīyate / tat tahaiva avicāritasvarūpam abhyupagamyate lokaprasiddhitaḥ, na tu punah paramārthataḥ / tena jñānasaṃvedanābhāvād arthānadhigamādayo'pi

phasis here on the ultimate::conventional distinction, not on whether or not certain things exist within the conventional. The opponent alleges that a conventional *svasaṃvedana* is necessary to empirical transactional experiences. For Prajñākaramati, if this is acceptable from the world's own perspective, still it is not an ultimate fact (as the Cittamātrin wishes it to be). Thus were the world to require that *svasaṃvedana* exists in order for empirical experiences to take place this, and worldly experiences themselves, would not be undermined by the complete rejection of *svasaṃvedana* ultimately, when subjected to ultimate analysis to see whether it has truth, inherent existence. For the Mādhyamika, concerned *qua* Mādhyamika solely with the ultimate, the opponent's faults do not apply for clearly there are no transactional experiences on the ultimate level. The Mādhyamika arguments are against *svasaṃvedana* existing ultimately. Problems concerning the conventional level are to be dealt with on the conventional level by those whose concern is the conventional level. The Mādhyamika ultimate does not undermine the conventional, and problems for the conventional do not touch the Mādhyamika ultimate.

This way of reading Prajñākaramati is not only the most obvious, but is also supported by his following comments. In that case, the opponent asks, what actu-

---

doṣāḥ paramārthapakṣavādina iha nāvataranti /. Cf. Tib.: gang ji ltar 'jig rten na rab tu grags pa de de bzhin nyid du ma dpyad pa'i ngo bo khas blangs nas 'jig rten grags pa yin te don dam pa ni ma yin no // des na shes pa'i rig pa med pas don rtogs pa la sogs pa med ces pa'i nyes pa don dam pa'i phyogs smra ba la 'dir glags mi rnyed do //. Cf. also Vibhūticandra: de thams cad dgag pa ni ma yin gyi ma dpyad par legs par shog / don dam par ma yin no //...de shes pa ma rig na don mi rtogs pa la sogs pa'i skyon don dam par med do //.

ally *is* negated by the Mādhyamika *(yadi tat tathaivabhyupagamyate, kiṃ nāma tarhi pratiṣidhyate ity āha)*? If Prajñākaramati holds to a complete denial of *svasaṃvedana* even conventionally, one would expect him to say so here. He does not. Rather, he introduces *Bodhicaryāvatāra* 9:26 cd. What the Mādhyamika negates—and, the implication is, *only* what the Mādhyamika negates—is the superimposition of inherent existence. Thus an inherently existent, ultimate, reflexive nature of awareness is negated. It is not here Prajñākaramati's concern to negate conventionally. Therefore, Prajñākaramati concludes, the Mādhyamika maintains here the simple negation of the craving which constructs the superimposition of what is not existent (Tib.: 'not true'). The Mādhyamika does not go round negating even the slightest thing. But, he adds, the slightest consciousness which is reflexively aware is not reasonable. The point here is not that it is negated on both ultimate and conventional levels, but that it is not reasonable, i.e. not found under the Mādhyamika analysis. Prajñākaramati ends by returning to his critique of the inherently-existent reflexively-aware consciousness maintained by Cittamātra, a critique which takes place, of course, with reference to the ultimate level.[11]

---

[11] tasmād asatsamāropakalpanābhiniveśapratiṣedhamātram atrābhipretam, na tu vāstvaṃ kiṃcit pratiṣidhyate iti / tad evaṃ svasaṃvedanaṃ jñānasya na kathaṃcid acid api yujyate / = de lta bas na 'dir ni bden pa ma yin pa'i 'dogs pa rtogs pa'i mngon par zhen pa dgag pa tsam bzhed pa yin la / dngos po cung zad gcig ni 'dir dgag pa ma yin no // de'i phyir de ltar na rang rig pa'i shes pa cung zad kyang rigs pa ma yin te /. That Prajñakaramati returns to the ultimate level is reinforced by his concluding quote, from the *Bodhicittavivaraṇa* (v. 45): na bodhyabodhakākāraṃ cittaṃ dṛṣṭaṃ tathāgataiḥ / yatra boddhā ca bodhyaṃ ca tatra bodhir na vidyate // = rtogs bya rtogs

I have argued that Prajñākaramati does not consider that the Mādhyamika negation of *svasaṃvedana* includes the conventional as well as the ultimate levels. As a Mādhyamika he has no view on whether consciousness is reflexive conventionally or not. This way of reading Prajñākaramati is clearly the way it was taken by Vibhūticandra at the beginning of the thirteenth century, for Vibhūticandra—who frequently follows Prajñākaramati—ends his commentary to *Bodhicaryāvatāra* 9:26 (just prior to repeating Prajñākaramati's quote from the *Bodhicittavivaraṇa*) with the observation that 'therefore there does not exist *ultimately* the reflexive nature of awareness' *(de bas rig pa rang rig don dam par med do)*. In other words, Vibhūticandra is quite explicit that Śāntideva's point in *Bodhicaryāvatāra* 9:26 is to show that the ultimate negation of *svasaṃvedana* does not in itself entail its nega-

---

byed rnam pa'i sems / de bzhin gshegs pas gzigs pa med / gang du rtogs dang rtogs byed pa / de la byang chub sems yod min //. This same quote is given with some variations by Vibhūticandra (Derge p. 525): rtogs bya rtogs byed rnam pa can / sems ni rgyal bas ma gzigs so // gang la rtogs bya rtogs byed yod / deng ni byang chub med pa nyid //. Prajñākaramati ends by referring to *svasaṃvedana* as unreasonable and speaks of the Buddha's nonperception of mind. This is a return to ultimate analytic unfindability. Ultimately there is no *svasaṃvedana,* and no mind as the Cittamātrin thinks. The declaration of *cittamātra* by the Buddha is with intentional purport, like the skandhas and so on (yat tu kvacid bhagavatā cittamātratāstitvam uktam, tat skandhāyatanādivan neyārthatayeti kathayiṣyate / = gang der cung zad bcom ldan 'das kyis sems tsam nyid du yod par gsungs pa de phung po dang skye mched la sogs pa bzhin du drang ba'i don nyid yin par bshad par 'gyur ro). Yet again, Prajñākaramati precisely takes the 'transcendental turn' when he negates *svasaṃvedana.* Yet again he precisely fails to say that it is also negated from a conventional point of view.

tion conventionally. The Mādhyamika has shown only that *svasaṃvedana* does not exist ultimately, inherently.[12]

Only one Indian commentary, the anonymous commentary *Bodhisattvacaryāvatāravivṛttipañjikā*, specifically considers the issue of whether *svasaṃvedana* is negated conventionally as well as ultimately—to dismiss immediately the idea that it is also negated conventionally as a nihilistic misunderstanding. An opponent objects that there could be no memory because there is no ultimately real self-awareness. The reply is that memory can occur since even though there does not exist an ultimate *svasaṃvedana*, nevertheless self-awareness does exist conventionally. But, the opponent objects, *svasaṃvedana* is not asserted to exist even conventionally, for there is lack of inherent existence. It is in response to this comment, our anonymous author tells us, that Śāntideva taught *Bodhicaryāvatāra* 9:26. One negates inherent existence, craving for Reality—such craving being the cause for suffering—but one does not negate conventional existence.[13] Thus the negation of *svasaṃvedana* even

---

[12] The fact that Vibhūticandra clearly uses and follows Prajñākaramati, incidentally, should not be taken to mean that his commentary is merely a summary of the latter. He does sometimes differ from Prajñākaramati (although not here), and Vibhūticandra's commentary also includes *Bodhicaryāvatāra* ch. 10.

[13] 'o na te rang rig pa don dam pa de yod pa de nyid du ma grub pa ni phyis dran pa'i shes pa skye ba mi 'thad do zhe na / don dam pa med kyang rang rig pa kun rdzob tu yod pa'i dbang gis dran pa'i shes pa skye ba'i phyir de dran zhes gsungs so // 'o na te kun rdzob tu yod pa nyid yang mi 'thad do // rang bzhin med par khas len pa'i phyir ro zhe na / 'di ltar zhes bya ba la sogs pa smos te / mthong ba dang thos pa la sogs pa kun rdzob pa ni 'dir mi 'gog pa'i phyir dang / 'o na dir ci zhig 'gog snyam pa la 'dir ni zhes bya ba la sogs pa smos te / 'dir ni sdug bsngal

conventionally is the result of mistakenly thinking that the Mādhyamika negates the conventional when in fact he or she only negates inherent existence. Implicit here is the idea that if the Mādhyamika *were* to negate conventionally as well as ultimately, it would be the result of illegitimately extending the Mādhyamika negation of inherent existence. If the Mādhyamika only negates inherent existence, then it precisely does not negate conventional existence. It does not follow that because *svasaṃvedana* lacks ultimate (inherent) existence, it lacks conventional existence. On the contrary, in this commentary it is specifically affirmed that *svasaṃvedana* does exist conventionally.[14]

Other commentators to the *Bodhicaryāvatāra* are not so explicit in treating our theme as in this anonymous commentary. But equally, it seems that commentators on Śāntideva prior to the early dGe lugs pa do not state that the negation of reflexivity *is* on the

---

thams cad 'byung ba'i rgyu dngos por zhen pa dgag pa'i phyir rang bzhin 'gog go snyam du bsam pa'o // (Derge p. 685). Note that the version of this same discussion in the *Bodhisattvacaryāvatāravivṛtti*, the anonymous commentary to just the last two chapters, is identical except for adding *yang dag pa'i* to *rang bzhin 'gog go* (Derge p. 364).

[14] Of course, if the issue of whether something exists conventionally or not is not a matter for the Mādhyamika *qua* (Prāsaṅgika) Mādhyamika, then in seeking to avoid the nihilism of the opponent it could be argued that our anonymous commentator has overstretched himself. Perhaps this commentator was a follower of Śāntarakṣita's Yogācāra-Svātantrika Madhyamaka. Whether he was or not, in reading Śāntideva (according to Tibetans a Prāsaṅgika) in this way it shows the problem of trying to compartmentalize texts and teachers on the later Tibetan doxographic model. Note incidentally that as I pointed out above (ch. 3, n. 1), the *Vivṛttipañjikā* may be the earliest commentary to the *Bodhicaryāvatāra*.

conventional as well as the ultimate level. The twelfth century Sa skya lama bSod nams rtse mo portrays his opponent as arguing on the basis of the refutation of *svasaṃvedana* that if consciousness does not truly exist, it would be necessary to deny also the direct perceptual establishment of something as seen and so on. Not so, bSod nams rtse mo replies, for such is conventional and we do not refute that. Thus bSod nams rtse mo appears to accept the opponent's presupposition that *svasaṃvedana* is essential to consciousness, in that a refutation of reflexivity is a refutation of consciousness. At least, bSod nams rtse mo is not concerned to reply by distinguishing between *svasaṃvedana*, which is refuted conventionally as well as ultimately, and consciousness which is refuted only ultimately. bSod nams rtse mo's response is almost dismissive. His opponent's argument is void because these things are merely conventional, and the Mādhyamika is not concerned with the merely conventional. The Mādhyamika is concerned only with the opposition between ultimate refutation and conventional acceptability. This is clear from bSod nams rtse mo's response to the opponent's inevitable question as to what exactly is refuted by the Mādhyamika. Even more clearly than Prajñākaramati, bSod nams rtse mo tells us that 'if it exists ultimately, it is refuted'.[15] Thus if *svasaṃvedana* is posited as existing ultimately, it too is

---

[15] bSod nams rtse mo p. 497.4: gal te shes pa de kho nar med na mthong ba dang thos pa la sogs pa mngon sum du grub pa'ang bsal dgos zhe na / de ni kun rdzob pa yin la de ma bkag go // zhes ston pa ni // [9:26 ab (Tib. 25)] // zhes pa'o // 'o na gang 'gog ce na don dam par yod na 'gog go zhes bya bar ston pa ni / [9:26 cd] // ces bya ba'o //. bSod nams rtse mo's quotation of the verse has some minor variants (i.e., *grags* for *dgag*) which are probably due to scribal error.

refuted. This is the sole concern of the Mādhyamika *qua* (Prāsaṅgika) Mādhyamika.

bSod nams rtse mo was writing perhaps a generation earlier than Vibhūticandra. Maybe nearly two hundred years later, Bu ston and a number of his eminent contemporaries also indicate that they would not consider the Mādhyamika refutation of the reflexive nature of consciousness in Śāntideva's *Bodhicaryāvatāra* to extend to the conventional as well as the ultimate level. As does Vibhūticandra, Bu ston ends his refutation of *svasaṃvedana*—after pointing out that the conventional is not refuted, but only the ascription of true ultimate reality *(dngos po bden pa ma yin pa la don dam pa'i bden par rtog pa de / bzlog par bya ba yin te)*—with the comment that 'therefore there does not exist even the slightest *svasaṃvedana* ultimately' (p. 518: *des na don dam par rang rig cung zad kyang med)*. Given the context of distinguishing between what is refuted ultimately and what remains conventionally, it seems clear here that Bu ston did not consider the refutation of *svasaṃvedana* to be also a refutation conventionally. Earlier, Bu ston had observed that something having *svasaṃvedana* does not exist because all *dharmas* are ultimately emptiness (p. 515: *don dam par chos thams cad stong nyid yin pas rang rig pa med de)*. In other words, the very reason for reflexive-awareness not existing is a result of the way things are from an ultimate, not a conventional, point of view.[16]

---

[16] It may be worth noting here that according to some later sources Bu ston was a follower of Yogācāra-Svātantrika Madhyamaka (see Ruegg 1966, p. 12). If true, then on the model supplied by dGe lugs doxographers not only would Bu ston hold that *svasaṃvedana* is not refuted by the Mādhyamika conventionally, but following Śāntarakṣita he would hold that *svasaṃvedana* actually exists conventionally. Bu ston's treatment of *svasaṃvedana* in his commentary to the *Bodhicaryāvatāra*

could provide the first stage of an argument in support of Bu ston's allegiance to Yogācāra-Svātantrika Madhyamaka. Certainly, from a dGe lugs point of view, if Bu ston does not hold to the nonexistence even conventionally of *svasaṃvedana,* then he is not a pure Prāsaṅgika. However, I doubt that applying the model of philosophical school distinctions derived by later dGe lugs scholars to earlier teachers is very accurate or helpful. I am arguing that on such a basis neither Prajñākaramati nor for that matter Śāntideva himself were pure Prāsaṅgika. Perhaps on those grounds there were no pure Prāsaṅgikas before Tsong kha pa, although it would be necessary to examine also earlier Tibetan commentaries to the *Madhyamakāvatāra* before drawing such a conclusion. Tsong kha pa's own teacher Red mda' ba discusses the issue in his *dBu ma la 'jug pa'i rnam bshad De kho na nyid gsal ba'i sgron ma* (pp. 173 ff.). It is possible that Red mda' ba in commenting on *Madhyamakāvatāra* 6:73 (p. 174) is wanting to say that *svasaṃvedana* is not the case even conventionally, in which case Tsong kha pa may have been influenced in this respect by his teacher (tha snyad du shes pa rang rig pa grub pa ma yin te / shes pa'i don rtogs par 'jig rten na tha snyad byed pa'i phyir ro //). On the other hand, as we shall see, Mi pham certainly does not hold that this is what *Candrakīrti* is saying at 6:73, and Mi pham might be able to offer a corresponding interpretation of Red mda' ba. Red mda' ba seems to hold the view that conventionally things just happen (for example, memory just occurs), and the conventional as conventional is not to be examined critically at all (pp. 175-6). (Cf. also my passing comments on whether Red mda' ba holds the 'no-view' interpretation of Madhyamaka in Williams 1985, p. 212.) Thus it makes no sense to talk of needing *svasaṃvedana* to explain the conventional. On the other hand Mi pham would say that not to assert or need *svasaṃvedana* conventionally is not the same as asserting that it positively does not exist conventionally. Mi pham could accept the first for the Prāsaṅgika, but it simply does not follow that we can therefore conclude *svasaṃvedana* does not exist even conventionally. If Red mda' ba is indeed saying that *svasaṃvedana* is not the case even conventionally, then he certainly does not seem to make the same capital out of it as does the later dGe lugs tradition. Gareth Sparham (1993) has recently argued that Tsong kha pa's *Yid dang kun gzhi'i dka' ba'i gnas rgya cher 'grel pa Legs bshad pa'i rgya mtsho,* in which he

Bu ston's friend and contemporary, the Sa skya pa bLa ma dam pa bSod nams rgyal mtshan (1312-75), in his own commentary to the *Bodhicaryāvatāra,* has the opponent introduce his objection with the comment that 'if *svasaṃvedana* does not exist, then it follows that consciousness would not cognize itself. If that is agreed, it also would not cognize the referent' (p. 332: *gal te rang rig med na shes pa rang nyid mi rtogs par thal la / 'dod na don yang mi rtogs par 'gyur la).* bLa ma dam pa's response to this is that 'it is agreed from an ultimate point of view' *(don dam par ni 'dod pa yin).* The ex-

---

treats *inter alia* the Cittamātra substratum consciousness *(ālayavijñāna)* is probably Tsong kha pa's first major work, and in it Tsong kha pa seems to be prepared to consider that the *ālayavijñāna* may be acceptable to the Prāsaṅgika conventionally, even if not ultimately. As we shall see, the issue of the *ālayavijñāna* is intimately related to that of self-awareness. For the later Tsong kha pa and dGe lugs doxographers both are completely unacceptable even conventionally to the Prāsaṅgika. Thus it seems quite possible that the early Tsong kha pa would have been prepared to accept the conventional existence of self-awareness. It is not surprising, therefore, that earlier Tibetan scholars also held this view. The real question, however, is whether Tsong kha pa changed his mind due to teaching from Red mda' ba, or the evolution of his own thought. I strongly suspect the latter, and I see no clear evidence otherwise. Certainly the story of Tsong kha pa receiving elucidation of difficult points concerning the Madhyamaka directly from Mañjuśrī (initially through lama dBu ma pa, who could be significant here although as far as I know there are no works by dBu ma pa to examine) suggests that many aspects of Tsong kha pa's understanding of Madhyamaka which differed from his contemporaries and predecessors were the result of his inner development. Anyway, whatever is concluded as regards Red mda' ba's own views, one still feels that with Tsong kha pa and his disciples *everything changes.* It is here that we find the nonexistence even conventionally of *svasaṃvedana* consciously understood and articulated, and made into a doxographical strategy.

pression '[it] is agreed' *('dod)* in the objection is mirrored in the response. *What* is agreed? The only answer must be that what is agreed is contained in the argument that 'if *svasaṃvedana* does not exist, then it follows that consciousness would not cognize itself'. But what is agreed here is not the hypothetical inference, for bLa ma dam pa could not be saying that it is the hypothetical inference which is agreed ultimately but not conventionally. In other words, he could not be saying that it is ultimately the case but not the case conventionally that 'If the reflexive nature of awareness does not exist consciousness would not cognize itself'. There could not be a case (at least in this context) of consciousness cognizing itself conventionally without the conventional existence of *svasaṃvedana*. That would make no sense. bLa ma dam pa must be saying that he accepts the inference, that without *svasaṃvedana* consciousness would not cognize itself, and therefore there would be no cognition of referents.[17] But this entire situation applies only on the ultimate level, and does not interfere with the conventional. Thus bLa ma dam pa seems to indicate pretty clearly that conventionally if there is cognition of referents, there must conventionally be *svasaṃvedana*. The Mādhyamika critique is directed only at putative ultimates.

Another contemporary and acquaintance of Bu ston, rGyal sras Thogs med, introduces his discussion of *svasaṃvedana* with the observation that it involves pointing out the faults in ultimate *svasaṃvedana* (p. 319: *rang rig don dam la gnod pa brjod pa)*, and uses the ex-

[17] Of course, there could hypothetically be the case of subsequent introspection taking an earlier consciousness as its referent, without necessarily positing *svasaṃvedana*. But that could not be what is meant in this particular context.

pression 'ultimately' with reference to the refutation of self-awareness at a number of points in his analysis (e.g., p. 321: *gal te don dam du rang rig gzhan rig gang yang ma grub pas*...). bLa ma dam pa's pupil, Sa bzang mati paṇchen 'Jam dbyangs blo gros, interprets Śāntideva here in much the same way as his teacher, placing the emphasis on the Mādhyamika critical enterprise as the means of discovering what is ultimately the case. The opponent objects that if self-awareness *(svasaṃvedana)* does not exist, awareness of others (i.e., referents) also would not be acceptable. Thus there would not exist cognitive transactional experiences. Sa bzang mati paṇchen replies (expanding the verse) that even though it does not exist (or 'they do not exist') when critically examined, according to mere appearance, conventional transactions of something as seen through direct perception and so on are not to be negated in this world. This is because it is (they are) affirmed for the noncritical understanding according to conventional worldly renown.[18] Once more,

[18] Sa bzang mati p. 338: gal te rang rig med na gzhan rig kyang mi 'thad pa'i phyir / 'jig rten na mthong thos shes pa la sogs pa'i tha snyad thams cad med par 'gyur ro zhe na / dpyad na med kyang snang tsam du ji ltar mngon sum gyis mthong ba dang lung las thos pa dang rjes dpag gis shes pa la sogs pa'i tha snyad dag 'jig rten 'dir ni dgag par bya ba min te kun rdzob ji ltar grags pa bzhin du ma dpyad pa'i blo ngor khas len pa'i phyir ro //. An alternative interpretation is that bLa ma dam pa wants to say that it is true that with no *svasaṃvedana* there would be no empirical experiences. But this is a form of critical examination. Thus even though empirical experiences do not exist when critically examined, they (those experiences) are not denied as experienced empirically. This interpretation would enable a reading of bLa ma dam pa as denying *svasaṃvedana* even conventionally. But it would certainly be less adequate philosophically and, I suspect, syntactically *(rang rig med na...dpyad na med kyang)*.

we find that Sa bzang mati paṇchen accepts the initial argument of the opponent, while replying that its conclusions apply only on the ultimate level. The opponent begins with 'if self-awareness does not exist' *(gal te rang rig med na)*. Sa bzang mati paṇchen appears to echo this with 'even though it does not exist (they do not exist?) when critically examined' *(dpyad na med kyang)*. At least one way of reading what Sa bzang mati paṇchen is saying here is that *svasaṃvedana* does not exist *when examined,* and the implication is that the Mādhyamika as a Prāsaṅgika Mādhyamika does not wish to object to *svasaṃvedana* as such when it is not subject to critical ultimate analysis, that is, the analysis which seeks to find whether it really inherently exists.

By way of contrast, let us look now at some dGe lugs discussions of Śāntideva's treatment of *svasaṃvedana* in *Bodhicaryāvatāra* 9:26. This contrast is marked immediately in Tsong kha pa's treatment. In *Bodhicaryāvatāra* 9:24 Śāntideva had introduced and refuted the memory argument for *svasaṃvedana.* In the following verse Śāntideva moves from the memory argument to another quite different argument, before clarifying in verse 26 what is and what is not being refuted in the Mādhyamika negations. In commenting on verse 26, Tsong kha pa (initially inexplicably) returns to *Bodhicaryāvatāra* 9:24. It is clear that as far as Tsong kha pa is concerned the memory argument, as an argument concerning the operation of conventional consciousness, can also be read as an argument for the *conventional* existence of reflexivity. Thus through this strategy Tsong kha pa is able to introduce into his commentary the suggestion that Śāntideva is refuting not only the ultimate but also the conventional existence of *svasaṃvedana*.[19] Śāntideva had already refuted the memory argument for *svasaṃvedana* in verse 24. In contrast to all the other commentaries we have examined, Tsong kha pa's opponent in *Bodhicaryāvatāra* 9:26 wishes to argue for reflexivity not on the basis that were there no reflexivity there could be no consciousness of referents, but rather were there no reflexivity there could be no *memory*, and therefore no consciousness of referents. In other words, for Tsong kha pa the opponent is appealing not to an argument concerning the nature of consciousness as such (the 'Śāntarakṣita' argument), but is merely producing a slightly modified version of an argument Śāntideva had already refuted (perhaps a 'Dignāga' argument).[20] Thus when Śānti-

---

[19] This notwithstanding the fact that it is clear in context that the opponent is using the memory argument as an *argument* for *svasaṃvedana*. In other words the opponent intends the memory argument to show that *svasaṃvedana* can withstand analysis and thus exist inherently, i.e. not merely conventionally.

[20] Tsong kha pa (1956) folio 8b: des na rang rig la khyad par ma sbyar bar tha snyad du rang rig grub pa'ang slob dpon 'di mi bzhed par gsal te / rang rig [mi] bzhed na rnam shes dran par ji ltar 'gyur / zhes pa'i lan du gzhan myong ba dang 'brel pa las zhes sogs smas mi dgos kyi / rang rig pa'i rgyu mtshan gyis yin no zhes smos pas chog pas so // ci ste rang rig med na dran pa med pas yul myong ba dang mthong thos sogs med par 'gyur ro zhe na / ji ltar sogs rkang pa bzhi ste /. I have amended the text on the basis that here Tsong kha pa must be alluding to *Bodhicaryāvatāra* 9:24 which reads: gal te rang rig yod min na / rnam shes dran par ji ltar 'gyur /. The alternative in this context makes no sense. Cf. here also rGyal tshab rje, who certainly mentions the opponent who might want to maintain that *svasaṃvedana* exists conventionally even if not ultimately, but specifically mentions him or her only in the context of the memory argument on *Bodhicaryāvatāra* 9:24, concluding in this context (1973 p. 222): spyod 'jug gi dgongs pa ni tha snyad du rang rig 'gog pa min zhes pa ni rgyal sras chen

deva responds that something as seen and so on is not refuted, the contrast is with something as seen plus *svasaṃvedana* as necessary to memory. Śāntideva had already refuted *svasaṃvedana* as necessary to memory. In such a context and interpretation, all we are left with is something as seen, minus *svasaṃvedana* which is, therefore, not included within the scope of what remains after the Mādhyamika negations and is, therefore, refuted even conventionally. In his summary commentary, his notes, to *Bodhicaryāvatāra* chapter nine, Tsong kha pa clearly introduced what appears to be an innovative and strikingly clever way of reading verse 26, given his overall concern to show

---

po'i bzhed pa gtan min zhes gsung ngo //. By the time of rGyal tshab rje the whole claim that *svasaṃvedana* might exist conventionally—or at least that its conventional existence is not refuted by the Prāsaṅgika—had become blended with the refutation of the memory argument. Thub bstan chos kyi grags pa on the other hand seems to want to integrate Tsong kha pa's introduction of the memory argument more neatly into the impossibility of sensation without *svasaṃvedana*, with which he would be perfectly familiar from the Indian commentaries. Thus Thub bstan comments (1990a p. 608) that 'if reflexivity does not exist then there would not exist experiencing the object through seeing, hearing and so on. If that did not exist then there would not exist memory and because of that it would follow that even the transactional conventions of [something] seen and heard and so on expressed in terms like "I saw" or "I heard" would cease to exist (rang rig med na mthong thos sogs kyis yul myong ba med la de med na dran pa med pas ngas mthong ngas thos zhes pa'i mthong thos sogs kyi tha snyad kyang med par thal lo zhe na). It is in this context that Śāntideva taught *Bodhicaryāvatāra* 9:26. Thus while Tsong kha pa seems to say that without reflexivity there is no memory and therefore no sensation, Thub bstan appears to reverse it. Without reflexivity there is no sensation and therefore no memory. Still, again the memory argument is integrated into the commentary in a way which seems to be characteristically dGe lugs and will serve to negate *svasaṃvedana* even conventionally.

that Prāsaṅgika Mādhyamikas like Śāntideva do not accept *svasaṃvedana* even conventionally. Yet this way of reading the verse is paradoxical, for there is no indication anywhere in Śāntideva's text, or in the previous commentarial tradition, that verse 26 should be linked to Śāntideva's treatment of the memory argument. Quite the reverse. The introduction of an altogether different argument for *svasaṃvedana* by the opponent after the memory argument in verse 24 and before the treatment of what remains in the light of the Mādhyamika negations in verse 26 indicates fairly conclusively that Śāntideva did *not* see *Bodhicaryāvatāra* 9:26 as having anything to do with a memory argument for reflexivity.

In the light of subsequent dGe lugs discussions of Śāntideva's critique of *svasaṃvedana*, there may well have been another important reason why Tsong kha pa linked his interpretation of *Bodhicaryāvatāra* 9:26 to the memory argument. It is indeed striking that in spite of the dGe lugs claim that a Prāsaṅgika Mādhyamika does not hold to *svasaṃvedana* even conventionally, dGe lugs sources repeatedly give the same single quotation in support of their position. It comes from Candrakīrti's *Madhyamakāvatāra* (on 6:73), and occurs specifically within the context of the memory argument. Candrakīrti observes that 'if one appeals to worldly transaction, still, even on such a basis there is not possible memory which has reflexivity as a cause'.[21] I do not want to discuss Candrakīrti's

[21] de la Vallee Poussin edition, p. 169: 'on te 'jig rten gyi tha snyad kyi dbang du yin te de lta na yang rang rig pa'i rgyu can gyi dran pa mi srid pa nyid do //. This reference is quoted for example by Tsong kha pa in the *Drang nges legs bshad snying po* (see Thurman 1984, p. 318; text 1973b, p. 175), mKhas grub rje in his *sTong thun chen mo* (text p. 422; Cabezón p. 349), by Thub bstan chos kyi grags pa (1990b) p. 756 and by Mi pham's oppo-

own refutation of *svasaṃvedana* here. I have made some comments elsewhere (Williams, 1983; Appendix 2 below), and I shall treat subsequently Mi pham's response to this particular quotation from Candrakīrti. The verse occurs very much within the context of the memory argument and it is evident that if this is the clearest Indian textual support for the claim that Prāsaṅgikas refute *svasaṃvedana* even conventionally then this is an additional strong reason for linking Candrakīrti's refutation with the other principal Indian refutation held to be Prāsaṅgika, Śāntideva's discussion in the *Bodhicaryāvatāra*. This link is effected through inserting the memory argument into Śāntideva's treatment of what is not negated by the Prāsaṅgika. It is important to dGe lugs exegesis that on these issues there is no difference between Candrakīrti (whose view is held to have been recommended to Tsong kha pa as the final correct view by Mañjuśrī himself) and Śāntideva, for both are identified as members of the same philosophical subschool, Prāsaṅgika Madhyamaka. Thus, for example, Thub bstan chos kyi grags pa introduces his use of the quotation from Candrakīrti with the comment that 'in both this text [the *Bodhicaryāvatāra*], and also the *Madhyamakāvatāra*, reflexivity is negated not only ultimately but even transactionally' (1990b p. 756: *gzhung 'di dang dbu ma 'jug pa gnyis kar don dam du ma zad tha snyad du'ang rang rig bkag pa yin te)*.

For Tsong kha pa, what Śāntideva is claiming not to negate are the objects of the six consciousnesses, what is seen, heard and so on, and presumably also the consciousnesses themselves. He observes that it is not necessary to negate those, and anyway taken as

---

nent Tre bo brag dkar sprul sku (Mi pham 1975b, p. 198).

merely themselves they do not generate suffering.[22] Also those transactional conventions exist even for Arhats. One is not able to negate them, for if one were to refute them it would have to be through textual support and reasoning. In such a case, the textual support and reasoning would also be refuted (as involved in the six consciousnesses). Thus one would become a complete nihilist. Therefore, it is only the construction of truth applied to those referents, which acts as a cause of suffering, which is opposed here.[23] One could observe that Mi pham would want to make precisely the same points as regards the reflexivity of consciousness, for if consciousness is not reflexive in the sense in which he is using the term, then it is not consciousness. And without consciousness at all the same faults would follow.

Thus far we have followed mainly Tsong kha pa in dGe lugs exegesis. rGyal tshab rje quotes all of

---

22 Mi pham is going to want to suggest that, as Śāntideva says, it is the conception of inherent existence which generates suffering. Thus there is no reason why we should assume that *svasaṃvedana* as merely itself *(de tsam)*, i.e. conventionally, not inherently, existing, should generate suffering. The dGe lugs pa will have to argue that like the Tīrthaka's Self or God, if there is *svasaṃvedana* it could *only* exist inherently. But, Mi pham is going to want to say, following Śāntarakṣita, that is patently not true in the sense in which he is using the term *svasaṃvedana.*

23 Tsong kha pa folio (1956) 9a: rnam shes drug gi yul mthong thos sogs 'dir dgag pa min te / de dgag mi dgos te / de tsam gyis sdug bsngal bskyed pa min te / dgra bcom pa rnams la yang tha snyad de dag yod pa'i phyir ro // dgag mi nus te / 'gog na lung rigs kyis 'gog dgos na de 'gog na lung rigs la yang mtshungs pa'i phyir ro // bkag na skyon yod de / chad lhag [= cha lta: rGyal tshab rje 1973, p. 223] can du 'gyur ba'i phyir ro // des na 'dir sdug bsngal gyi rgyur gyur ba'i yul de dag bden par rtog pa bzlog bya yin no //.

Tsong kha pa's discussion on *Bodhicaryāvatāra* 9:26, but adds some observations of his own related to other important features of the dGe lugs understanding of Prāsaṅgika Madhyamaka, particularly the claim that Arhats and Pratyekabuddhas genuinely and directly cognize the emptiness of *dharmas* as well as emptiness of persons. These other features involve much more defensible claims than the position that the Prāsaṅgika negates *svasaṃvedana* even conventionally. Tsong kha pa had argued at length for the assertion that Arhats and Pratyekabuddhas discern complete emptiness in his *dBu ma dgongs pa rab gsal* commentary to the *Madhyamakāvatāra* (Tsong kha pa 1973a, pp. 46 ff.; Hopkins trans. 1980, pp. 150 ff.). Here in the *Bodhicaryāvatāra,* rGyal tshab rje tells us, it is clearly maintained that Arhats and Pratyekabuddhas cognize the absence of self of *dharmas,* since it is said that the root of *saṃsāra* is the apprehension of truth (i.e., inherent existence) with reference to forms, sounds and so on. Thus Arhats and Pratyekabuddhas must have overcome the apprehension of truth in anything, including *dharmas,* in order to have overcome *saṃsāra* and genuinely be Arhats and Pratyekabuddhas.[24] Moreover, rGyal tshab rje adds,

---

[24] rGyal tshab rje (1973) pp. 223-4, taking-up the end of Tsong kha pa's comments: des na 'dir sdug bsngal rgyur gyur pa yul de dag bden par rtog pa ldog bya yin te de nyid 'khor ba'i rtsa ba yin pa'i phyir / 'khor ba'i rtsa ba ma log na 'khor ba mi ldog cing gzugs sgra sogs bden 'dzin 'khor ba'i rtsa bar bstan pas nyan rang la chos kyi bdag med rtogs pa *'od* [omit on basis of parallel passage in Thub bstan chos kyi grags pa (1990a) p. 608?] gsal [224] bar bzhed pa yin no /. Thub bstan chos kyi grags pa explains that when we affirm that the very construction of truth—because it acts as the root or cause of the suffering which is *saṃsāra*—is to be reversed by correct awareness, we are referring to the apprehension of truth which is the apprehension of

we should note that not only should there not be negated mere appearance to our sensory consciousnesses, but also the claim that here (the Prāsaṅgika) is to negate even the apprehended object as anything, such as permanent or impermanent, existent or non-existent, is tantamount to a revival of the position of the Chinese scholar (Hoshang Mahāyāna). In other words, it is crucial in Madhyamaka to realize not only that one should not over negate by negating even sensory experiences, but also one should not negate so much that all discernment—even philosophically correct and relevant to the path—is lost in striving to remain in a state of 'non-conceptual' and non-affirmative blank-mindedness. It is not the case that the Mādhyamika has no views and no positively-determining arguments, even correct ones, and what is to be negated by the Mādhyamika is only but completely inherent existence, the cause of *saṃsāra* and thereby suffering.[25]

Even though we affirm that there exists experience in the sense of mere verbal attribution (i.e., with-

---

things as established from their own side, in the light of the innate mundane mind, not as dependent on examinations by tenet-systems. The cause of *saṃsāra* is not just erroneous philosophical systems! (grub mthas dpyad pa la ma ltos par 'jig rten pa'i blo lhan skyes kyi ngor rang ngos nas grub par 'dzin pa'i bden 'dzin nyid 'khor ba'i sdug bsngal gyi rtsa ba'am rgyur gyur pa yin pas bden par rtog pa de nyid rig pa yang dag gis bzlog bya yin par 'dod pa'i phyir ro).

25 kha rag pa la sogs pa dbang shes la snang tsam dgag bya min la de la rtag mi rtag dang yod med sogs gang du gzung yang dgag bya yin no zhes zer ba ni rgya nag gi mkhan po slar 'ongs pa yin no //. On some philosophical problems with the concept of non-conceptuality, and the position of Hoshang Mahāyāna, see my 1992a paper. On the dGe lugs treatment of whether or not the Prāsaṅgika has no views see Ruegg 1981a and mKhas grub rje (text pp. 294 ff.; Cabezón trans. pp. 257 ff.).

out any metaphysical implications of inherent existence), Thub bstan chos kyi grags pa points out, still we do not affirm that there exists any self-experience or other-experience. It is like the case when even though we affirm that there exists production, still we do not affirm that there exists any self-production or other-production, or when in transactional usage—even though we affirm that a lamp has the nature of illumination—still we do not maintain at all that a lamp is self-illuminated or other-illuminated. Thus even the dGe lugs pa has no objection as such to the simple usage of everyday expressions like 'I myself know myself.' This is not properly speaking what is meant when we refer in this technical context to the issue of self-experience.[26] Thub bstan chos kyi grags pa's introduction of the case of causality is interesting, for although Candrakīrti states that production from another is unacceptable even conventionally, Tsong kha pa makes it clear that the Mādhyamika *can* accept causation between things which are at least nominally different from each other. Such is simply not what we mean in this critical context by 'production from another'. The denial of production from another

---

26 Thub bstan chos kyi grags pa 1990b p. 755: 'dir ming gis btags tsam gyis myong ba yod par 'dod kyang rang myong dang gzhan myong gang yang yod par mi 'dod de / dper na ming gis btags tsam gyi skye ba yod kyang bdag skye dang gzhan skye gang yang mi 'dod pa dang / tha snyad du mar me gsal ba'i rang bzhin du 'dod kyang rang gis gsal ba dang gzhan gyis gsal ba gang du'ang khas mi len pa bzhin no // 'dir rang myong mi 'dod de / tha snyad tsam du nga rang gis nga rang rig zhes pa tsam 'dod kyang de la rang myong gi don mi tshang zhing /. See also Tsong kha pa's *Drang nges legs bshad snying po* (1973b text pp. 177-8; Thurman trans. pp. 320-1) and mKhas grub rje's *sTong thun chen mo* (text p. 421; Cabezón trans. p. 347).

is held by Tsong kha pa to be the case only as found under analysis. Since to be found under analysis is to exist inherently, Tsong kha pa effectively neutralizes Candrakīrti's claim that production from another is not the case even conventionally.[27] From this perspec-

[27] See Newland (1992) pp. 298-9. Newland is treating here the problem of whether the Buddha sees his own mind or not. If he does then at, least in the case of the Buddha, consciousness can see (nondualistically) consciousness (i.e., there is at least some sort of *svasaṃvedana*). If not, then the Buddha would appear not to be omniscient. Newland treats alternative views found in writers such as rGyal tshab rje, mKhas grub rje, Paṇchen bSod nams grags pa, Sera rje btsun Chos kyi rgyal mtshan, and 'Jam dbyangs bzhad pa. It is while treating the view of 'Jam dbyangs bzhad pa that Newland suggests that perhaps 'Jam dbyangs bzhad pa would want to apply to the issue of self-awareness (at least in the case of the Buddha's cognition) the same approach which Tsong kha pa takes to production from another, i.e. that it is inherently-existent production from another which is being negated: 'It is difficult to see where this argument will leave the Prāsaṅgika refutation of self-consciousness. Jam-yang-shay-ba's approach may suggest that, unlike Gyel-tsap and Kay-drup, he tends to regard the refutation of self-consciousness as a refutation of inherently existent self-cognition....Thus, like the assertion of "production from other" *(gzhan skye),* the assertion of self-consciousness is, for non-Prāsaṅgikas, inextricably bound up with the conception of inherent existence. However, perhaps a Prāsaṅgika can hold that, in merely conventional terms, a consciousness can know itself.' (p. 208). 'However, if this is correct, it would mean that a statement such as "self-consciousness is refuted even conventionally" could be read as an utter denial of a self-consciousness that is findable under analysis. For someone who refutes inherent existence, it might still be possible to hold that a consciousness can know itself' (p. 299). Of course, for the Buddha's omniscient but, nevertheless, conventional consciousness to know itself in a direct and non-dualistic way is not the same as maintaining that consciousness *as such* must be reflexive, albeit, of course, as a purely conventionally-existent consciousness and in a purely conventional way. But it is interesting that a

tive the Mādhyamika çritique of causation is based on searching for an inherently-existing causal relationship between inherently-existing causes and effects. Under those circumstances there is no possibility of self-causation, other-causation, both or neither. Thus it should follow that the Mādhyamika has no comment to make concerning whether something is or is not the case conventionally, and the Mādhyamika should not be averse to analysis on the conventional level (scientific or proto-scientific research, for example). It is only self-experience (i.e., self-awareness, *svasaṃvedana)* when searched for under analysis, that is, as inherently-existing, which is denied by the Mādhyamika. The issue of the conventional status of *svasaṃvedana,* a Śāntarakṣita or a Mi pham might argue, is an issue concerning the conventional conditions of conventional experience. It is at a level deeper than the ordinary perception of the cowherder, but it is (arguably) necessary to the ordinary perception of the cowherder, it is implicit in his behavior, and is thus no less and no more a *conventional* issue than the ordinary perception of the cowherder itself.[28]

---

case could be made-out for a dGe lugs pa like 'Jam dbyangs bzhad pa possibly being willing to countenance (or being forced into the position of) the conventional existence of self-awareness under certain circumstances. What would that do to the distinctions between philosophical tenet-systems?

[28] Cf. Candrakīrti on *Madhyamakāvatāra* 6:75: 'di yang 'jig rten tshul lugs ying gyi shin tu dpyad par bya ba mi ma yin te / rdzun pa'i don can nyid kyiṣ 'jig rten gyi tha snyad yin pa'i phyir ro /. The idea that when things are analyzed they are found to be false, and therefore the position of the world is to be accepted without analysis, is open to misunderstanding. It seems that the Prāsaṅgika position is that whatever the world considers to be the case *in its worldly terms* (and not ultimate terms) can be taken to be the case without further analysis as to its *real* existence. If we were to carry out the analysis into reality

Now perhaps we have reached an appropriate point to begin looking more closely at Mi pham's own contribution to this debate.

the world would not be found. But within the world it does not follow that the Prāsaṅgika (as a scientist, for example) cannot analyze or investigate in worldly terms to discover more accurate worldly 'truth'. What the 'world' considers to be the case changes, and the change does (often) embody greater accuracy (as Popper has pointed out somewhere, the notion of greater accuracy, incidentally, need not imply any notion of perfect accuracy, or 'Truth').

CHAPTER 5

Mi Pham on *Bodhicaryāvatāra* 9:26 (Tibetan 9:25)

Mi pham's clear advocacy of the conventional existence of *svasaṃvedana* in his commentary to the ninth chapter of the *Bodhicaryāvatāra* evoked a fierce response from his dGe lugs pa critics. We shall be concerned in particular with the attack by Tre bo brag dkar sprul sku bLo bzang dpal ldan bstan 'dzin, for it is in reply to bLo bzang dpal ldan bstan 'dzin's criticisms that Mi pham developed probably his most extensive discussion of *svasaṃvedana*. Perhaps one of the reasons why Mi pham's treatment so infuriated dGe lugs scholars was not simply that he advocated wrong views—they were quite familiar with followers of other traditions who did *that*—but rather that Mi pham had spent at least some time in a dGe lugs monastery, clearly knew perfectly well the dGe lugs approach and tenet, and not only chose to write commentaries on texts long considered by dGe lugs scholars to be their own particular areas of expertise, but also used or alluded to dGe lugs commentaries in an approving as well as a critical way where appropriate. I have shown elsewhere that Mi pham had in front of him when writing his commentary to the *Bodhicaryāvatāra* the standard dGe lugs commentary by rGyal tshab rje, which quotes extensively (although usually without direct acknowledgment) the commentary to the ninth chapter by Tsong kha pa.[1]

On *Bodhicaryāvatāra* 9:26 too, Mi pham shows his use of Tsong kha pa, probably through rGyal tshab rje. The opponent (the 'Vijñaptivādin') introduces a reference to the standard definition of consciousness as accepted also by the dGe lugs tradition. Consciousness is defined in terms of luminosity and awareness.[2] If consciousness is not luminous and aware, then, because it does not illuminate itself, it would not be able to illuminate others. This would be to annihilate all empirical transactional conventions, since they are all founded in dependence upon consciousness which (we all agree) is luminosity and awareness. Otherwise they simply do not occur at all. Mi pham's response is in accordance with what we have seen in (most) other commentaries. If the opponent is speaking of empirical experience ([something] as seen etc.) as it occurs on the basis of mere unexamined convenience, then we do not negate that. For, Mi pham adds, undoubtedly echoing here Tsong kha pa, one is not able to negate that, and also it is not necessary to negate it. As to what *is* refuted by the Prāsaṅgika, it is the construction of true reality in the

[1] See Williams (1992b), p. 545.

[2] See also above, ch. 2, n. 10. Mi pham discusses the importance of consciousness as luminosity and awareness in this context in his commentary to Śāntarakṣita's *Madhyamakālaṃkāra* (Mi pham 1976a, pp. 143-5).

case of all entities, which serves as the cause of suffering.[3]

[3] Mi pham 1975a, p. 21: de la rnam rig smra ba na re / shes pa nyid gsal zhing rig pa min na rang mi gsal bas gzhan yang gsal mi nus la / de ltar na mig gis mthong ba dang / rna bas thos pa dang / yid kyis shes pa'i tha snyad thams cad rgyun chad par 'gyur te / 'di kun gsal rig gi shes pa la brten nas rnam gzhag bya dgos kyi gzhan du mi srid pa'i phyir zhe na / ji ltar mthong thos dang shes pa 'di dag ma brtags nyams dga' ba tsam gyi dbang du byas te brjod na ni / 'dir dgag pa min te de dgag mi nus la dgag kyang mi dgos pa'i phyir / 'o na ci zhig 'gog ce na / 'dir sdug bsngal gyi rgyur gyur pa dngos po kun la de bzhin gyi bden par rtog pa bzlog bya yin no //. Cf. here also Mi pham's commentary to the *Madhyamakāvatāra* (1979 p. 500): As for the Prāsaṅgika system—since the mind is that which brings about cognition, it indirectly understands that it is a cognizer (as in the case when a lamp illuminates, a sword cuts and so on). Because the mind cognizes a referent this is enough for proving that it cognizes itself as well. The six sensory groupings (sense organs, referents and resultant consciousnesses) are indeed enough for cognizing all possible referents. But even though a transactional convention of *svasaṃvedana* is not made (in the Prāsaṅgika system), still it is appropriate. What Mi pham is saying here is that it is not necessary to the Prāsaṅgika as such to explain how it is that consciousness cognizes, and therefore the Prāsaṅgika makes no statement about the conventional existence of reflexivity. It is enough for the Prāsaṅgika that consciousness cognizes. Nevertheless, in that it *does* cognize, it is necessary to the nature of consciousness that it is reflexively aware. Therefore, the conventional status of *svasaṃvedana* is still appropriate to the Prāsaṅgika in that the Prāsaṅgika accepts conventionally cognition and thereby cannot contradict it. Thus, Mi pham continues, *truly*...in the case of *svasaṃvedana* it is like the example of a sword cutting itself (and so on, i.e. it is impossible). But that is all in accordance with ultimate analysis searching for inherent existence. The establishment through conceptual-imputation of a transactional convention of *svasaṃvedana* is not refuted. One is not able to negate that, and it is not necessary even to refute a correct conceptually imputed transactional convention (thal 'gyur lugs la /

Thus Mi pham's opponent appeals to the empirical definition of consciousness, something on which there would have been a broad agreement. The image of luminosity is, of course, based on that of the lamp, which in illuminating objects does not require another lamp to illuminate itself but rather illuminates itself in the very act of illuminating others. Śāntideva had already refuted at *Bodhicaryāvatāra* 9:18 (Tib. 18 cd/19 ab) the model of the lamp as an example to demonstrate the real (inherent) existence of *svasaṃvedana,* the reflexive nature of consciousness as found under ultimate analysis. Mi pham's opponent is not going to be able to use an appeal to the nature of consciousness as luminosity and awareness in order to demonstrate the inherent existence of reflexivity. But in introducing into his commentary an agreed definition of consciousness acceptable to the Prāsaṅgika (including the dGe lugs pa), Mi pham gives rise to a genuine question as to what exactly it means to call consciousness (conventional consciousness) 'luminosity and awareness'. To call consciousness 'luminous' must mean, if it is to mean anything at all, that consciousness is of such a nature that it makes itself known in the very act of rendering objects known. It does not require another illuminator for its cognition (see also

---

blo shes byed yin pa nyid kyis shes pa yin pa shugs rtogs dang / mar me gsal byed / ral gri gcod byed sogs kun la 'dra / blo yul shes pas rang nyid de shes par grub pa nyid kyis chog go / tshogs drug gis yul dus shes pas chog gi rang rig gi tha snyad ma byas kyang rung / yang dag par na mar me la gsal byed gzhan mi dgos par grub pa yin mod / rang gsal ba min te / mun gyis sgrib pa min pas so // rang rig na mun pas rang sgrib ral gris rang gcod ltar 'gyur te 'di ni don dam par dpyod pa'o // rang rig gi tha snyad btags pas grub pa ni mi 'gog ste khegs mi nus la / btags pa'i tha snyad don mthun 'gog kyang mi dgos so //.

note 7 below). The model is that of the lamp, but this time not as an example to prove the real inherent existence of *svasaṃvedana*.[4] All this discussion is occur-

---

[4] Mi pham observes in his commentary on the *Madhyamakālaṃkāra* (pp. 143-4) that referents like a pot and so on are insentient. Thus it is not possible that they are luminous and aware. Therefore, in order to bring about an awareness of their nature one must necessarily depend upon a mind which illuminates and is aware of that which is other than itself. But in the case of this consciousness, since its own nature is not like an insentient thing, it is not necessary for it to depend on another condition for its nature to be known. Thus the conventional formulation of 'self-awareness' is indeed acceptable. Since it is something that has the nature of luminosity and awareness from merely itself, if there does not exist another aware agent for it, even though it is aware of others, then we cannot say that it is not self-aware. It is as we say that a lamp illuminates itself by itself. We call a lamp self-luminous in conventional parlance since when the lamp has illuminated a pot and so on in a dark house *it is not necessary that there is another cause to illuminate the lamp itself. We do not mean that the lamp illuminates itself having made itself a referent* (yul bum pa sogs bem po yin pas de dag la gsal zhing rig pa mi srid la / des na de dag gi ngo bor rig par byed pa rang las gzhan pa gsal zhing rig pa'i blo la ltos dgos kyang / shes pa 'di ni rang gi ngo bo bem po lta bu ma yin pas rang gi ngo bo rig par bya ba rkyen gzhan la ltos mi dgos pa de phyir rang rig ces bzhag pa tha snyad ches 'thad de / kho rang tsam nas gsal rig gi rang bzhin can yin pas / khos gzhan rig kyang kho la rig mkhan gzhan med na rang mi rig pa ma yin pas /...mar me rang gis rang gsal zer ba dang 'dra ste / de'ang mun khang nang gi bum pa sogs mar mes snang bar byas kyang / mar me rang snang bar byed pa la rgyu gzhan mi dgos pas rang gsal zhes tha snyad btags pa las mar mes rang gis rang yul du byas nas gsal ba min pa lta bu'o). In other words, Mi pham is saying, the 'self' in 'self-awareness' must be understood here structurally as the equivalent of 'not-other'. 'Self-awareness', as used conventionally, is strictly equivalent to 'not made known through another'. And this is something we all recognize conventionally, as in the case of the lamp which is self-luminous, i.e. not illuminated through another. As an

ring simply at the level of the conventional—Mi pham's 'unexamined convenience', but here 'unexamined' in the sense of no examination into its real inherent existence, not no examination into how it is conventionally. If to call conventional consciousness 'luminous' means that conventional consciousness is of such a nature that it makes itself known in rendering objects known, Mi pham wants to say, this is what we *mean* by saying that conventionally consciousness is reflexive, that there is *svasaṃvedana* conventionally. Following Śāntarakṣita, the issue is what distinguishes sentience from insentience. It is not enough to say, as might Tsong kha pa, that to be conscious of blue is all that is needed, we do not need the additional factor of reflexivity. We have defined consciousness as luminosity and awareness, in opposition to insentience. The issue is not one of whether or not consciousness is conscious of, say, blue, but rather what this *means* and how it is possible. For Mi pham (as for the dGe lugs pa) in order for consciousness to be consciousness it has to be luminous and aware. Insen-

---

everyday conventional fact, how could this be denied? Thus if one understands in this manner the way of proving a merely transactional thing called 'self-awareness', Mi pham comments, there is no harm in maintaining transactionally, conventionally, *svasaṃvedana* (des na rang rig ces pa'i tha snyad tsam zhig sgrub tshul de ltar shes na kun rdzob tu rang rig 'thad pa la gnod pa gang yang mi 'bab ste). The well-known Mādhyamika counter-arguments, such as that if a lamp could illuminate itself darkness should darken itself, all apply if one asserts *svasaṃvedana* to be a true reality (mar mes rang gsal na mun pas rang bsgribs par thal ba sogs kyi rigs pa thams cad / rang rig bden par khas blangs na 'jug ste). That is, they all apply if we are searching to find an inherently existent *svasaṃvedana*, a *svasaṃvedana* which could be found under ultimate analysis. Mi pham makes the same point in his commentary to the *Madhyamakāvatāra*.

tient things are not like that. What it means to be luminous and aware is that, *inter alia*, consciousness makes itself known in rendering objects known. What else could luminosity and awareness be here? With Śāntarakṣita, consciousness as consciousness must be reflexive.[5]

Thus Mi pham continues his commentary to *Bodhicaryāvatāra* 9:26 with the observation that 'in short, as for the refutation of *svasaṃvedana*, even though it is a refutation ultimately, as the mere reverse of insentience *(bem po las log tsam)* there is no refutation of that manner of conceiving *svasaṃvedana* transactionally (or "as transactional")'.[6] The mention of 'the mere reverse of insentience' is, of course, a direct reference to Śāntarakṣita, a direct reference to an argument for the conventional existence of a reflexivity which is quite different from the inherently-existent *svasaṃvedana* which is advocated by their opponent, the Vijñaptivādin (Cittamātrin), a type of *svasaṃvedana* which cannot be found under the ulti-

---

[5] Note also that the bridge enabling Mi pham to move from what he sees as the Prāsaṅgikas not denying the conventional existence of *svasaṃvedana,* to his wish to positively affirm it, is the definition of consciousness as luminous and aware. It is arguable that the definition of consciousness as such is nothing to do with the Prāsaṅgika *qua* Prāsaṅgika. It is a conventional matter (a matter for certain philosophers, psychologists or scientists to argue over). Thus while the Prāsaṅgika as such simply does not negate the conventional existence of reflexivity, a wider context allows us to affirm it. But this wider context here, Mi pham wants to say, is accepted by the dGe lugs pa who, for Mi pham, has not thought through its implications and has not properly appreciated the minimal sense of '*svasaṃvedana*' indicated by Śāntarakṣita.

[6] mdor na rang rig pa 'gog pa ni don dam par 'gog pa yin gyi bem po las log tsam la [22] tha snyad du rang rig par 'dogs pa'i tshul de 'gog pa ma yin te /.

mate analysis carried out by the Mādhyamika. If one were to negate this conventional *svasaṃvedana,* various absurd results would follow which would parallel and eventually lead to the absurd results mentioned by Tsong kha pa and his tradition themselves as following from the negation of conventional empirical transactions, since one would in fact be negating consciousness *qua* consciousness, sentience as distinguished from insentience.

THE FIRST ABSURD RESULT

(i) To negate *svasaṃvedana* understood in this sense would necessarily be to hold that one's own mind is a hidden object for oneself *(de bkag na rang blo rang la lkog tu gyur par khas len dgos pas).* The reference here is to a distinction derived from Dignāga and Dharmakīrti, well-known in dGe lugs circles, between evident things which can be known through direct empirical experience without dependence upon inference, those which are hidden and thus have to be known normally through inference, and very hidden objects like the exact details of the workings of *karma* and rebirth, which short of becoming a Buddha oneself have to be known from some authoritative source such as the Buddha (see Gyatso 1993, p. 53). Of course, an omniscient mind knows all things through direct experience. Thus what Mi pham is saying here is that if one's own consciousness at time *t* is not itself also known by oneself directly in experiencing objects at time *t* (i.e., reflexivity), then it would have to be known through some subsequent means such as inference, which is absurd. It would mean that experience lacks validation, that we never know we are experiencing when we are experiencing.[7]

---

[7] Of course, one's own consciousness is a knowable *(shes bya)* and always a knowable, so it must be known by *some* means. The epistemology of all this is dealt with by Mi pham in his *Don dam par nges pa shes rab ral gri mchan bcas* (Mi pham 1976c, pp. 795-6; this text has also been used by Matthew Kapstein (1988), who briefly summarizes material relevant to *svasaṃvedana* on p. 158). If it is necessary to know a consciousness by a further consciousness, then there would be an infinite regress. Even if it were simultaneous or not simultaneous with the original experience, there would still be an infinite regress. Thus consciousness is the reverse of a chariot, a wall and so on. It has the nature of luminosity and awareness. The expression 'self-awareness' here is self-luminosity to itself of also its own nature without needing to depend on another, at the same time as cognizing an external referent. It enables the activity which is the very perceptual nature, where there is experience by the other three direct perceptual types (direct sensory perception, mental direct perception, and yogic perception). If *svasaṃvedana* did not exist, there could be no other manner of establishing direct perception. If blue for example is established by visual consciousness, by what perception or inference is visual consciousness established? If it is suggested that it could be established through (another) direct perception, such could not be either simultaneous or not simultaneous with the initial sensory perception. If we say it could be established by inference, inference does not exist since direct perception does not exist. (It has not yet been shown to exist since no means has yet been established for its experiential validation. Unless we not only have a perception but also know in a reflexive sense that we have a perception, Mi pham wants to say, we cannot be said to have a perception and therefore derive any inferences from it.) Inference is generated in dependence upon a perceptually-experienced sign (the perception of smoke as an indication of fire on the mountain). Therefore, the very root of inference is direct perception, and that perception is (itself) ascertained by self-awareness (*rang sems la yang* nyams su myong ba'i sgo nas gzhan la mi ltos par sgro 'dogs gcod pa *de yod na* // de rang rig gis ma shes par *de* la *shes* mkhan *gzhan yod* na de

THE SECOND ABSURD RESULT

(ii) Because of (i) it would follow that there would be no distinction in the manner of determination by

---

la'ang shes mkhan gzhan yod dgos pa sogs *thug med 'gyur //* te dus mnyam pa dang mi mnyam pa'i shes pa'ang gzhan gang yod kyang thug med du 'gyur ro // *de phyir* shes pa ni shing rta dang rtsigs pa sogs las bzlog ste / *gsal rig ngo bo* nyid du gyur pa yis // phyi rol gyi *yul shes* pa *bzhin tu rang nyid kyang //* rang gzhan la *ltos pa med par* rang la *rang gsal ba // 'di la rang rig ces su brjod // mngon sum gzhan* gsum *gyis nyams myong gang //* la *mngon sum* yin pa *nyid du // des byed pa // rang rig las yin* pas *de med na // tshul gzhan gang gis* mngon sum de *'grub mi 'gyur //* te sngon po mig shes kyis grub na mig shes mngon rjes gang gis grub / mngon sum gyis grub na mngon sum dbang don dus mnyam mi mnyam gnyis ka mi 'thad rjes dpag gis grub na de med de mngon sum med pas so // *rjes dpag* ni *mngon sum* myong ba'i rtags la brten [796] nas skye bas mngon sum gyi *rtsa ba can //* yin la / *mngon sum* de ni *rang rig nyid kyis nges //*). This text incorporates a word commentary to a previous work by Mi pham himself. The root text is given in italics. See also Mi pham's commentary to the *Madhyamakālaṃkāra* (1976a p. 145) on how *svasaṃvedana* offers that luminous experiential quality which completes the perception of a referent. Thus if one affirms the perceptual system one cannot say that *svasaṃvedana* does not exist (mngon sum don rig kyang mthar gsal bar nyams su myong ba'i rang rig gis tshar phyin pa yin pas tshur mthong tshad ma'i rnam gzhag zhig 'dod na rang rig med du mi rung ba yin pas). In the specific case of an omniscient mind, as we saw above (ch. 4, n. 27), there would occur further difficulties for the Buddha's own awareness, since the Buddha sees all things non-dualistically and simultaneously through direct experience. Thus if there were no *svasaṃvedana* in the case of the Buddha's own consciousness, the Buddha would be unable to know his own consciousness at all. Also, Mi pham might add, it could not be that the Buddha's consciousness *qua* consciousness is fundamentally different from the consciousnesses of unenlightened beings. Thus we could not escape this problem by saying that the Buddha's consciousness alone has reflexivity. If there is reflexivity it is a quality of consciousness as such.

consciousness of the minds of oneself and another *(rang gzhan gyi blo shes pas gcod tshul la khyad med du thal ba)*. It seems at least *prima facie* obvious *(pace* Gilbert Ryle) that one should have privileged access to one's own mind, yet if consciousness lacks reflexivity and becomes a hidden object for oneself it is difficult to see how privileged access can be sustained, and, likewise, any difference between modes of presentation to oneself of one's own mind and that of another. In fact, Mi pham may be thinking, just as one has to infer the existence of other minds, so one would have to infer the existence of one's own mind. Absurdly, one would know one's own mind in just the same way as one knows of the minds of other sentient beings.

The Third Absurd Result

(iii) Moreover, proving that there exists a mind in one's own continuum would be unreasonable *(dang rang rgyud la blo yod pa'i sgrub byed mi rigs pa)*. If one's own mind is a hidden object for oneself and therefore known on the same basis as one knows of the minds of others, then how would it be possible ever to prove to oneself that one has a mind? In fact the problem of knowing one's own mind would be the same as the problem of knowing other minds. It seems, for example, that there could be no inferential derivation of other minds on the analogical basis of one's own mind. Since one could not prove other minds, and one's own mind is held by the opponent to be known on the same basis as other minds, how, therefore, could one prove to oneself that one has a mind of one's own? Moreover, there could be no inference based on data provided from experience, since one has yet to prove one's own mind and therefore the possibility of experience.

THE FOURTH ABSURD RESULT

(iv) Eventually, the transactional conventions of awareness of referents would also be annihilated.[8] Obviously if one could not know one's own mind then there could be no conscious awareness of cognitive referents. These and other arguments, Mi pham notes, can be derived from the Lord of Reasoning.[9]

Thus what Mi pham has shown to his own satisfaction is that the correctness of the opponent's objection in *Bodhicaryāvatāra* 9:26 does indeed follow if the conventional (but not the ultimate) existence of the reflexive nature of consciousness is denied. Therefore, Śāntideva's claim in this verse that conventional transactional experiences are not denied by the Mādhyamika' must be taken to include reflexivity in the sense in which Śāntarakṣita (basing himself on Dignāga and Dharmakīrti, but with a Mādhyamika denial of inherent existence) and Mi pham understand it. All the variety of reasonings which refute *svasaṃvedana,* Mi pham notes, refute it on the ultimate level, like the reasonings which refute the aggregates

---

8 mthar don rig gi tha snyad kyang rgyun chad par 'gyur ba sogs. Cf. Tsong kha pa's comments in the previous chapter on annihilation from negating the conventional. Mi pham has skillfully thrown the dGe lugs analysis of *Bodhicaryāvatāra* 9:26, and the dGe lugs horror of negating the conventional, back at them. He has done this also through using Dharmakīrti, a writer integrated into the overall (Madhyamaka) project on the conventional level particularly by the dGe lugs tradition.

9 The Lord of Reasoning *(Rig[s] pa'i dbang phyug)* must be Dharmakīrti. He is referred to under this description again by Mi pham in his *Madhyamakālaṃkāra* commentary (p. 145), as the one whose texts are to be consulted for the overcoming of the non-acceptance of *svasaṃvedana* and the correct way of proving it.

(skandhas) and so on *(rang rig 'gog pa'i rigs pa ji snyed pa thams cad phung sogs 'gog pa'i rigs pa bzhin don dam par 'gog gi)*. Mi pham wants to say, therefore, that the ontological status of *svasaṃvedana* is no more and no less than that of the aggregates, and also the *dhātus* and *āyatanas*. All these were taught by the Buddha, are part of the conventional way of things, but were negated in the *Prajñāpāramitā* literature and by the Mādhyamika from an ultimate point of view. They cannot resist ultimate analysis. Mi pham's granting of the same ontological status to *svasaṃvedana* as to the *skandhas, dhātus* and *āyatanas* is not surprising. These categories include consciousnesses. The ontological status of reflexivity as the nature of consciousness *qua* consciousness could not be different from the ontological status of consciousness itself.

Mi pham is perfectly aware that someone might wish to argue that it is not at all inappropriate to negate here *svasaṃvedana* transactionally, and, what is more, in this school (Prāsaṅgika Madhyamaka) even conventionally *svasaṃvedana* and a substratum *(kun gzhi [rnam shes])* are simply not accepted. We can reply, Mi pham says, that here in Prāsaṅgika Madhyamaka there is neither negation nor proof transactionally. There is simply negating from an ultimate point of view.[10] For Mi pham what is or is not

[10] tha snyad du bkag pa'i gtan med ma yin par shes dgos shing / lugs 'dir tha snyad du'ang rig kun gzhi khas mi len zer yang 'dir tha snyad du ni dgag pa'ang med la sgrub pa'ang med kyi don dam par bkag pa kho na yin no // [p. 22]. That the expression *rig kun gzhi* = *rang rig dang kun gzhi* is clear from Mi pham's critic bLo bzang dpa ldan bstan 'dzin who glosses it this way in Mi pham 1975b p. 199. Cf. Mi pham's commentary to the *Madhyamakāvatāra* (1979 pp. 499-500): Supposing someone asks whether the Prāsaṅgika holds that *svasaṃvedana* and the substratum exist or do not exist transactionally? If one thinks in

the case conventionally is not the immediate concern of the Prāsaṅgika as such. His or her concern is simply the search for putative ultimate existents. Therefore, it is not the Prāsaṅgika *qua* Prāsaṅgika who positively affirms as part of his or her system the conventional existence of *svasaṃvedana*. The job of Madhyamaka is the negative one of negating ultimate existence. It is quite possible for someone to add to the Mādhyamika perspective various conventionalities as and where they are found to be true and/or helpful from a conventional point of view.[11] One of these is the

---

terms of a systematic formulaic acceptance by the Prāsaṅgika of those transactionally, then such is certainly not the case. Under those circumstances they are certainly accepted as nonexistent. But it is not the case that the Prāsaṅgika holds that they do not exist transactionally in general (thal 'gyur [500] pa'i lugs la rang rig dang kun gzhi tha snyad du yod med gang khas len zer na / tha snyad du de'i rnam bzhag med pa'i cha nas med par khas len mod / des de spyir tha snyad du med par mi 'gyur te). In other words, Mi pham is saying that the Prāsaṅgika *qua* Prāsaṅgika does not positively advocate the conventional existence of *svasaṃvedana* and the substratum as part of the Prāsaṅgika system. But equally the Prāsaṅgika does not argue for their nonexistence conventionally as a general fact. This seems to support my contention that for Mi pham the Prāsaṅgika *qua* Prāsaṅgika has nothing to say about what exists or does not exist *conventionally*. In case this should lead to any misunderstanding, however, one should be clear that Mi pham is not one of those for whom the Prāsaṅgika has no views at all. The Prāsaṅgika certainly has a view and a position on the ultimate. All *dharmas* lack inherent existence. Mi pham is simply saying that the Prāsaṅgika *qua* Prāsaṅgika does not have any position on whether or not *x* exists conventionally (where *x* is a possible conventional, i.e. not a logical contradiction, or something which could only exist ultimately if it existed at all).

11 Of course, such an approach also makes it possible in another context to argue that one might be able to add to the purely negative Prāsaṅgika perspective an Ultimate Reality, providing it

conventional existence of the reflexive nature of consciousness. Another, Mi pham is going to want to arguc, is the substratum *(kun gzhi)*—when understood correctly.

We know from much earlier Tibetan writings that as well as maintaining that the Prāsaṅgika does not negate conventionally *svasaṃvedana,* there were previous Tibetan scholars who also argued that the Prāsaṅgika does not negate conventionally the substratum-consciousness *(ālayavijñāna/kun gzhi rnam shes),* a form of consciousness which is normally associated with the Cittamātra (see Williams 1983, p. 32; Appendix 2 below). It should be clear from his treatment of *svasaṃvedana,* however, that whatever substratum *(kun gzhi/ālaya)* Mi pham might want to suggest exists conventionally could not be identified with the *ālayavijñāna* maintained to exist by Cittamātra (Yogācāra) and thought by Cittamātra to be resistant to

---

is construed in such a way as to make it not accessible to the Mādhyamika negations. We should not forget that elsewhere in his commentary to the *Bodhicaryāvatāra* and in many other texts Mi pham—who was after all a rNying ma pa and follower of rDzogs chen—argues for the Great Madhyamaka, one interpretation of which is that of a *tathāgatagarbha* Reality. See my 1992b paper pp. 545-8, and also my 'Identifying the object of negation'. See also in particular Mi pham (1976b). Note incidentally that unless I state otherwise, I am using the term 'Madhyamaka' throughout this monograph to refer to what is normally meant by the term in Western writings, spoken of in rNying ma pa circles as the 'Outer Madhyamaka of the Prāsaṅgika and Svātantrika' (Dudjom Rinpoche 1991, p. 206). This is to be distinguished in certain respects from 'Madhyamaka' as it is used to refer in rNying ma sources to the 'Inner Madhyamaka', which is this Great Madhyamaka *(dBu ma chen po)* and appears often to be associated in this context with a form of *gzhan stong* absolutism. See Dudjom Rinpoche 1991, pp. 164-77. Again, I shall say a few more words about this topic later.

the Mādhyamika ultimate analysis. Moreover, if Mi pham is right that the Prāsaṅgika neither negates nor affirms anything conventionally, then it would follow, of course, that the Prāsaṅgika as such could neither negate nor affirm the substratum-consciousness conventionally. Whether or not a substratum-consciousness or indeed any other sort of substratum exists conventionally would depend upon other factors outside the concerns of the Prāsaṅgika *qua* Prāsaṅgika.

I do not want to consider here Mi pham's treatment of the conventional substratum as such. But in speaking of the substratum at this point in his commentary to the *Bodhicaryāvatāra,* Mi pham shows that he thinks the same broad principles apply in Prāsaṅgika Madhyamaka to the ontology of the substratum as to reflexivity. Thus Mi pham's opponent suggests that someone might say that if a person is a Mādhyamika he or she should not accept a substratum, for such is a tenet of the Vijñaptivādin (Yogācāra Cittamātrin). As far as Mi pham is concerned, this matter has not been well understood. If the substratum is not accepted as something truly-established (i.e., really, inherently existent), what harm is done to the Mādhyamika tradition by accepting it conventionally?[12] Mi pham goes right to the point. The conventional existence of something should be of no concern to the Mādhyamika as such. The Mādhyamika is concerned with negating putative ultimate existents, for they are what generate suffering. His textual basis for this approach to Madhyamaka is precisely *Bodhi-*

[12] de la kha cig gis dbu ma pa yin na kun gzhi khas len par mi bya ste / kun gzhi ni rnam rig pa'i lugs yin zer yang legs par ma brtags pa ste / kun gzhi bden grub tu khas ma blangs na tha snyad du khas blangs pas dbu ma'i tshul ci zhig nyams /.

caryāvatāra 9:26. Why should the Mādhyamika care whether something is accepted conventionally? Why is the Mādhyamika worrying himself with such matters? Of course, Mi pham wants to say, the Mādhyamika in another context, perhaps as a Buddhist, should certainly care if *svasaṃvedana* is *not* accepted conventionally, for the denial of *svasaṃvedana* conventionally will lead to the denial of all worldly transactions. Mi pham here seeks to liberate the Mādhyamika from all concern with those matters which should be outside his or her range of involvement *qua* Mādhyamika. The Mādhyamika's concern—limited but important—is simply with liberation from *saṃsāra* through cutting adherence to inherent existence.

Mi pham also has an additional argument against those who would suggest that the substratum (or the reflexive nature of consciousness) is not suitable to be accepted even conventionally. Whoever says this is, in fact, saying that these things are like the permanent generality or universal *(spyi rtag pa)* and so on which are actually harmed by a valid cognizer which critically examines the transactional. We can know through inference on the conventional level that there can be no such entity as a permanent universal, of course, therefore, even conventionally. We cannot argue that the same applies to the substratum or to the reflexive nature of consciousness. It is simply not legitimate to argue that the nature of consciousness as consciousness (luminosity and awareness, which implies reflexivity) is no more acceptable than the permanent universal accepted by, say, the Hindu Naiyāyikas. Reflexivity was after all, Mi pham might be thinking, taught by great scholars like Dharmakīrti. To say that the reflexive nature of consciousness is not the case even conventionally would in fact be to say that it is as unreal as the Hindu's universal. In order to prove this to be the case it would have to be refuted by a conventional valid cognizer, on the conventional level, not by the Mādhyamika's ultimate analysis searching for inherent existence. In other words, it would have to be negated by whatever means of critical investigation is appropriate for an empirical conventional phenomenon.[13] On the other hand if it is maintained that the reasoning employed in the Madhyamaka is not accepted as that of a valid cognizer which negates with ultimate reasoning (searching for inherent existence), then one would necessarily have to maintain as unacceptable also the *skandhas, dhātus* and *āyatanas*. This would appear to be because, since the Mādhyamika does indeed negate the aggregates and so on, if it is denied that there is any distinction between negating from an ultimate and negating from a conventional point of view, and all Mādhyamika negations are from both points of view, it would follow that conventionally too there would be no *skandhas, dhātus* and *āyatanas*.[14]

In spite of this, Mi pham tells us, even though in Prāsaṅgika treatises the substratum (and *svasaṃvedana*) are negated ultimately and there is no refutation conventionally, still there is no actual proving of their conventional existence by the Prāsaṅgika in the light of a systematic formulaic acceptance of

---

[13] Mi pham makes the same point in his commentary to the *Madhyamakāvatāra* (1979 p. 500), this time using the common case (used in elementary dGe lugs manuals, for example) of a permanent sound ('gyur na tha snyad dpyod byed kyis khegs dgos te sgra rtag pa bzhin no).

[14] tha snyad du khas len mi rung ba ni tha snyad dpyod byed kyi tshad mas gnod pa spyi rtag pa la sogs pa lta bu yin gyi / don dam pa'i rigs pas bkag tshad khas mi len na phung khams skye mched kyang gten med du khas blang dgos so //.

it.[15] On the other hand the opponent might want to suggest that the acceptance of *svasaṃvedana* conventionally is thus merely based on an habitual addiction to logic and is quite irrelevant. Mi pham agrees that there certainly is no necessity for reflexive awareness and the substratum in the light of the ultimate. Nevertheless, it is simply not appropriate to say that *svasaṃvedana* does not exist when one critically examines on its own level the conventional transactional framework.[16] If *svasaṃvedana* (or anything else) is established by a valid cognizer which critically examines the conventional then, Mi pham argues, of course, there cannot exist any reasoning which refutes *svasaṃvedana* as not existent conventionally.[17] In other words if the reflexive nature of consciousness is found to be the case by ordinary empirical critical investigation of a type quite different from the ultimate analysis employed by the Prāsaṅgika, the Prāsaṅgika can have no right and no rational grounds to say that

---

15 de phyir thal 'gyur ba'i gzhung du kun gzhi don dam par bkag gi tha snyad du mi 'gog kyang de'i rnam gzhag mdzad de sgrub pa'ang min no //. See also Mi pham on the *Madhyamakāvatāra* in note 10 above.

16 Notice Mi pham's repeated stress on conventional transactional analysis *(tha snyad kyi [rnam bzhag] dpyod pa)*. Mi pham does not consider that the conventional is only what is left unanalyzed—say, for example, the view of the uncritical person-in-the-street. The conventional includes whatever is found to be necessary to the conventional through critical analysis on the conventional level. But critical conventional analysis and ultimate analysis are mutually exclusive.

17 de bzhin du rang rig tha snyad du khas len pa ni rtog ge'i bag chags goms pa'i dbang gis yin gyi khas blang bar mi bya zer ba'ang gyin ste / don dam pa gtan la 'bebs pa la rang rig dang kun gzhi mi dgos mod / tha snyad kyi rnam bzhag dpyod pa la med du mi rung zhing tha snyad dpyod pa'i tshad mas grub na de tha snyad du med ces 'gog pa'i rigs pa ni med do //.

the reflexive nature of consciousness does not exist *conventionally*. Of course, it would also follow for Mi pham that if the Prāsaṅgika *were* to negate *svasaṃvedana* conventionally it would have to be on grounds of its incoherence in the light of empirical conventional investigation. At that point the Prāsaṅgika would no longer be analyzing *qua* Prāsaṅgika. Perhaps the Prāsaṅgika would have to become an empirical scientist.

Mi pham was a master of authorial style, and with fine dramatic touch one can almost begin to feel his opponent losing patience here. How can one say that there is no reasoning which negates *svasaṃvedana* conventionally? Do we not see manifold reasonings in the treatises of Candrakīrti, Śāntideva and others? Mi pham's response is that the refutation of self-awareness in those texts is exactly the same as the refutation of referential-awareness *(don rig)*. In other words those texts do not distinguish in terms of level of negation between the refutation of *svasaṃvedana* and the refutation of the normal sensory awareness of objects. The opponent's response is to argue that these refutations are not the same, since referential-awareness, unlike self-awareness, is not negated transactionally. The opponent is, of course, begging the question. Mi pham's point is that there are good empirical conventional grounds for *svasaṃvedana,* and there appears to be neither refutation nor proof of *svasaṃvedana* conventionally in Mādhyamika texts. Self-awareness is indeed refuted, but the scope of its refutation is not distinguished from that of the refutation of referential-awareness. The opponent is thus simply reasserting the point Mi pham had just disproved. Therefore, Mi pham's response here is the appropriate one—he re-expresses in clearer terms the normal empirical awareness we all must have of consciousness knowing itself. How can there be a refutation transactionally of even one's own sensations of happiness and so on? Of course, there is not, and thus (returning to the context of the *Bodhicaryāvatāra*) even though reflexivity is not acceptable in the case of one who affirms a mind *(sems)* to be truly established—in other words, a mind as understood by Cittamātra *(sems tsam)*—still, one should know that the transactional convention of reflexivity in the case of one who affirms it as not true (and, therefore, not a cause of suffering) is perfectly acceptable.[18]

The use of sensations of happiness and so on as an empirical means for establishing conventional reflexivity can be traced to Dharmakīrti. The argument is that when we see for example an attractive object we not only see the object but also feel happy. This happiness is a dimension of subjective response. When I have happiness at seeing *x*, that happiness is a reflex of *seeing x*, not *x* as such. Our visual sense sees the object, but the accompanying happiness must be connected with the awareness, and it must be involved in an awareness *that* we are seeing the object, in other words reflexivity.[19] This response to seeing *x*, which

---

18 Mi pham 1975a p. 23: gal te rigs pa ci ste med / zla grags zhi lha la sogs pa'i gzhung na ji snyed cig bshad pa 'di ma mthong ngam zhe na / de don rig la'ang mtshungs so // mi mtshungs te don rig ni tha snyad du mi 'gog go zhen na / bde sogs rang gis nyams su myong ba yang tha snyad du ji ltar 'gog ste mi 'gog go // des na sems bden grub tu 'dod pa la rang rig pa mi thad kyang bden med du 'dod pa la rang rig pa'i tha snyad shin tu 'thad par yang shes par bya ste …

19 Happiness involves not merely experiencing an object but also being aware that one is experiencing the object, and the particular mode of this awareness-that is happiness (awareness-that it is a strawberry, awareness-that in happiness mode). There could be no happiness without awareness-that,

is simultaneous with and part of seeing *x*, is possible only because in seeing *x* there is also a seeing that one sees *x*. The response of happiness which is part of seeing the attractive object is not in this example the result of seeing the object and *then* thinking 'It is *x*; I should be happy.' Rather the happiness is *part of* seeing *x*, and this shows that in seeing *x* one not only saw *x* but a dimension of that very seeing was self-awareness, an awareness that one is seeing *x*, or reflexivity. We do not require an additional mental act on seeing *x* also to feel happy at seeing *x*. Were there no reflexivity conventionally we would have subsequently to reflect on our earlier experiences in order to feel happy. Quite clearly we do not and, Mi pham wants to say, this is something we all know from our own immediate experience.[20]

i.e. reflexivity.

[20] See Dharmakīrti's *Pramāṇavārttika* 2:249 ff., *Pramāṇaviniścaya* 1:19d ff. (Vetter ed. pp. 62 ff.) and Dharmottara's *Nyāyabinduṭīkā* on 1:10: tasmād asātān nīlādy arthād anyad evasātam anubhūyate nīlānubhavakāle / tac ca jñānam eva / tato'sti jñānānubhavaḥ / = Tib.: de bas na sngon po myong ba'i tshe bde ba ma yin pa'i sngon po'i don las gzhan kho na'i bde ba myong ba yin no // de yang shes pa nyid pa de bas na shes pa nyams su myong ba ni yod do //. Matilal (1986 p. 155) refers to a rather weak reply by Udayana to Dharmakīrti's argument here. Pleasure, pain etc. are cognised the moment they arise due to their characteristic intensity. This is to confuse types of explanation. The issue is what it is to experience pleasure, pain etc. A pleasure has no intensity at all if it is not experienced, so experience is prior to its intensity. But the experience of pleasure is only possible, Dharmakīrti wants to say, because pleasure is of the nature of cognition and therefore cognition experiences itself. To experience the object is also to experience the subjective response of pleasure. See also Shah (1967) pp. 213-7.

CHAPTER 6

The Response of Tre bo brag dkar sprul sku bLo bzang dpal ldan bstan 'dzin

Mi pham's approach to Prāsaṅgika Madhyamaka is philosophically sophisticated in a way which reflects someone familiar with the training of dGe lugs monasteries, and yet it is so different from the dGe lugs approach in certain essentials that it was bound to evoke a spirited response. It is nice to see that in his *Sher 'grel brgal lan nyin byed snang ba,* written as a response to criticisms by bLo bzang dpal ldan bstan 'dzin and containing extensive quotations from the latter as *pūrvapakṣa,* Mi pham refers to his critic throughout with the greatest respect, a respect all the more pointed given that bLo bzang dpal ldan bstan 'dzin is not over-respectful in return.[1] Mi pham commonly refers to

[1] We should note also the considerable respect that Mi pham (1975b) shows for Tsong kha pa, and also his knowledge of

bLo bzang dpal ldan bstan 'dzin by his title of *sprul sku,* his critic is described as coming from the great monastery of 'Bras spungs *(dpal ldan 'bras spungs kyi chos sde chen po),* and Mi pham speaks of bLo bzang dpal ldan bstan 'dzin as one of clearly renowned understanding *(blo gros gsal bar grags pa).* He has written a good treatise called the *Zab mo dbu ma'i gnad brjod pa bLo gsal dga' ba'i gtam,* Mi pham observes, which clearly explains the position of his own tradition. He has disagreed with me and has, therefore, taken this up, and not only am I not unhappy about it but—like the peacock who hears the thunder—my happiness, Mi pham tells us, has been enhanced![2]

Tsong kha pa's works: des na bod gangs can nas sangs rgyas kyi bstan pa la phrin las 'gran zla dang bral ba rje btsun chen po tsong kha pa'i gzhung gsal zhing legs par bshad pa rnams la gus shing bka' [101] drin che bar shes mod /. This respect for his dGe lugs opponents and humility is also reflected in a note Mi pham wrote quoted by Dudjom Rinpoche in his history of the rNying ma tradition (Dudjom Rinpoche 1991, pp. 872-3): 'I never felt, even in dreams, such motivations as hostility towards other traditions, or self-congratulatory pride...if those who possess the eye of the doctrine refute me in accord with correct scriptural authority and logic, I should rely upon them like doctors. Such persons must never be refuted out of hostility. For these reasons, it is with a fair mind that I have sometimes entered into debate.'

[2] Mi pham 1975b p. 101: rang lugs kyi rjes brjod gsal por mdzad pa'i gzhung legs pa zhig bris te bdag la brgal ba'i phyir 'dir 'byor ba la mi dga' ba med par ma zad rma byas dbyar rnga thos pa ltar dga' ba'i gsos su gyur te...The reference to *blo gsal* in the title of bLo bzang dpal ldan bstan 'dzin's text suggests that our critic was from 'Bras spungs bLo gsal gling monastery. It may also be an allusion to Tsong kha pa's own commentary to the *Bodhicaryāvatāra,* the *sPyod 'jug shes rab le'u'i ṭikkā bLo gsal ba.* One feels that in referring to bLo bzang dpal ldan bstan 'dzin as having composed his attack according to the position of his own tradition, Mi pham is both expressing admiration at the

In truth though, given the late and ostensibly sophisticated dGe lugs' philosophical culture from which it comes, and given that Mi pham's work differs in several fundamental respects from the dGe lugs Madhyamaka vision, bLo bzang dpal ldan bstan 'dzin's attack on Mi pham's treatment of reflexivity and the substratum-consciousness when all is said and done seems rather disappointing. He does not refer to Mi pham by name, but speaks of 'a certain contemporary author of a commentary to the *Bodhicaryāvatāra*' *(deng sang gi spyod 'jug ṭī ka byed pa kha cig)*. bLo bzang dpal ldan bstan 'dzin quotes verbatim extensively from Mi pham's commentary in order to give the main points of Mi pham's perspective (Mi pham 1975b, pp. 198-9).

> (a) *Svasaṃvedana* is negated ultimately, but it is not negated conventionally as the mere reversal of insentience.
>
> (b) If it were, one's own mind would become a hidden object for oneself, and also all the other faults mentioned above would follow.

From these two points it follows that Mi pham is arguing for the conventional existence of reflexivity as a quality of consciousness, in a sense probably derived ultimately from Śāntarakṣita. bLo bzang dpal ldan bstan 'dzin then moves to the end of Mi pham's account.

> (c) In Prāsaṅgika Madhyamaka there is neither refutation nor proof transactionally. There

---

way in which the partisans of a tradition respond to defend their tradition, but also perhaps an exasperation at their inability to take a fresh critical look at the material and arguments.

is simply refuting from an ultimate point of view .

From this point one can see that Mi pham is not arguing for the conventional existence of reflexivity as a tenet of Prāsaṅgika Madhyamaka. Equally he is not arguing for the nonexistence conventionally of reflexivity as a tenet of Prāsaṅgika. Prāsaṅgika Madhyamaka is simply concerned with the search for putative ultimates. As a skeleton-summary of Mi pham's perspective this appears to be excellent. Yet one senses bLo bzang dpal ldan's exasperation. He terminates his quotation from Mi pham before reaching the formal end of the sentence with the comment that even though all this is said, actually it is merely Mi pham's own opinion.[3] He cites various reasons for this:

(i) In Prāsaṅgika Madhyamaka not only is *svasaṃvedana* negated ultimately but it is also negated conventionally *(lugs 'dir don dam du ma zad tha snyad du'ang rang rig bkag pa yin)*.

(ii) Such is clearly explained in the (ubiquitous) quote from Candrakīrti's *Madhyamakāvatārabhāṣya* on 6:73.

(iii) Moreover, bLo bzang dpal ldan bstan 'dzin tells us, if *svasaṃvedana* were not negated conventionally there could not exist the *prasaṅga*-reversal *(thal bzlog)* which entails activity, agent and action to be established from their own side conventionally.

---

[3] This may be a rather charitable way of reading bLo bzang dpal ldan bstan 'dzin's comment here. *Rang gi nang cha bstan pa tsam du zad de* could mean that this is merely the teaching of Mi pham's own bowels!

The third reason is an obscure point which bLo bzang dpal ldan fails to clarify, and as we shall see it is not clear that Mi pham fully understood what bLo bzang dpal ldan was getting at.[4] The reversal of the *prasaṅga* occurs when in the case of a *prasaṅga*-statement '*x* is *y*, because of *z*', a new *prasaṅga* is formed through replacing the predicate with the negative of the reason, and the reason with the negative of the predicate. Thus '*x* is not-*z*, because of not-*y*'. For example, the reversal of the *prasaṅga* 'It follows that the subject, all *dharmas*, lack inherent existence because they are dependently originated' is 'It follows that the subject, all *dharmas*, are not dependently-originated because they have inherent existence.'

---

4 gzhan yang tha snyad du rang rig bkag pa ma yin na tha snyad du bya byed las gsum po de rang ngos nas grub par thal ba'i thal ba bzlog tu med pa'i phyir /. When he replies to this argument (p. 202) Mi pham glosses it as: tha snyad du rang rig yod na bya byed las gsum rang ngos grub par thal ba bzlog tu med do. The issue of *prasaṅga*-reversal has been discussed at length by David Seyfort Ruegg (1991, pp. 292-6). The following attempt to reconstruct bLo bzang dpal ldan's argument is an imaginative and extremely tentative suggestion. It may have some plausibility. I would welcome alternatives. As we shall see, Mi pham simply side-steps the whole discussion as an ultimate analysis which misses his point here. One might object that on this basis Mi pham could accept anything (the notorious unicorn) conventionally, since counter-arguments by other Mādhyamikas will always be said to refer only to ultimate analysis. This would be to misunderstand the situation. Mādhyamika *qua* Prāsaṅgika Mādhyamika arguments do indeed refer only to a particular sort of solid coherence expected of putative existents on the ultimate level. Debate concerning the conventional operates with different sorts of methods of analysis and criteria for coherence and should not be confused with the Prāsaṅgika sort of analysis. Mi pham considers that he has very good reasons for accepting *svasaṃvedana* (but not the unicorn) conventionally.

One *possible* interpretation of bLo bzang dpal ldan bstan 'dzin's obscure point here is that he is relying on an assumption that there is no middle, in the case of *svasaṃvedana,* between inherent existence and complete nonexistence. This would be to see *svasaṃvedana* as the same sort of phenomenon as the True Self of the Hindus, God, or the permanent universal (cf. ch. 3 n. 5 above). If these things exist at all they would have to inherently exist. Thus if *svasaṃvedana* is the nature of consciousness, *svasaṃvedana* would have to exist inherently and, therefore, at least in this case action, agent and activity would not only be the same—a common accusation against reflexivity in Prāsaṅgika writings (see, for example, *Bodhicaryāvatāra* 9:17 (Tib. 17 cd-18 ab))—but also exist from their own side. Mi pham would, of course, consider all this quite absurd, since he holds that there are overwhelming arguments on the conventional level for consciousness as reflexive, and very good arguments against its inherent ultimate existence. Moreover, with Śāntarakṣita, Mi pham simply does not accept the applicability of the action-agent-activity model as such to *svasaṃvedana* (but see below, next chapter).

Nevertheless, there are apparently some important indications in dGe lugs sources as to why they might wish to maintain that *svasaṃvedana* could only exist inherently, and why, therefore, they would consider that with *svasaṃvedana* action, agent and activity would also have to exist from their own side, inherently. According to Guy Newland, expounding the dGe lugs position, 'if a consciousness could set itself up as a knower without depending on something else as the known, then this would point to its being an autonomous, i.e. inherently existent, knower. Refuting inherent existence, Prāsaṅgikas accordingly argue that self-consciousness is impossible' (1992 p.

204).[5] Thus it is argued that *svasaṃvedana* would involve a consciousness which does not as such rely on a referent. It, therefore, does not arise in dependence upon a referent and must thereby be, it is argued, independent and consequently inherently existent.

I confess I find this argument as such rather unclear and anyway on both possible alternatives unconvincing. It is not clear to me whether the opponent is suggesting that (a) a consciousness would inherently exist were there *svasaṃvedana;* or (b) *svasaṃvedana* must itself inherently exist, with no specific reference to the consciousness itself characterized by *svasaṃvedana.* In the first case the argument is that if consciousness is incontrovertibly and directly aware of itself then it is self-validating. If it is self-validating then it does not exist in dependence upon its object, and, therefore, it is independent and thus inherently existent. I shall say a little more about this argument in the final chapter below. For the moment it seems clear to me that it simply does not follow that because consciousness is self-validating it does not arise in dependence upon its causes, and one of those causes is indeed the object. If we take argument (b), then Mi pham at least is certainly not maintaining that *svasaṃvedana* is some strange sort of consciousness, in the way that a consciousness of blue is a consciousness (i.e., self-awareness (i)), which takes as a referent itself and, therefore, does not have any ac-

---

[5] Therefore, if there is *svasaṃvedana* it must be inherently existent. Since the construction of truth—inherent existence—is the cause of suffering in *saṃsāra,* this implication is perhaps behind the easy slide in dGe lugs writings from the negation of the construction of truth in *Bodhicaryāvatāra* 9:26 to the negation of *svasaṃvedana,* which as we have seen otherwise, and certainly for certain other commentators, does not seem to follow at all.

tual referent which is external to it. *Svasaṃvedana* is what makes consciousness consciousness (self-awareness (ii)). Thus the fact that (to use an old Buddhist formula) a consciousness comes into existence in dependence upon *inter alia* a referent does not imply that *svasaṃvedana* as *svasaṃvedana* requires a referent, although the consciousness itself characterized by *svasaṃvedana* can be taken here to do so (ignoring Śāntarakṣita's 'idealistic turn'). None of this entails, however, that *svasaṃvedana* is independent of causes and conditions, and, therefore, inherently existent. Inasmuch as *svasaṃvedana* is the characteristic of a consciousness-moment as such, it is as dependent as the consciousness-moment itself is. The *svasaṃvedana* of consciousness-moment *y* arises among other things in dependence upon the *svasaṃvedana* of the immediately preceding consciousness-moment *x*, and also consciousness-moment *x* itself. Indeed inasmuch as consciousness moment *x* arises in dependence upon its referent so, indirectly, we can also claim that the *svasaṃvedana* of consciousness moment *x* arises in dependence upon the referent. Thus just as any consciousness-moment is dependently-originated and, therefore, lacking in inherent existence, so the same applies to any reflexivity as characterizing that consciousness-moment.

Supposing that bLo bzang dpal ldan bstan 'dzin considered that if *svasaṃvedana* exists at all, its very implications would entail that it would have to exist inherently, then we can see one *prasaṅga* as:

> It follows that the subjects—conventional activity, agent and action in the case of consciousness—depend on an object, because they do not exist from their own side.

Conventional activity, agent and action in the case of a consciousness (which for bLo bzang dpal ldan includes putative *svasaṃvedana*) do not exist from their own side, but arise in dependence upon causes and conditions. In the case of consciousnesses, normally the principal conditions are the object and the preceding moment of consciousness of the same type. Therefore, conventional activity, agent and action in the case of consciousnesses arise in dependence upon an object. It also follows that all consciousnesses lack inherent existence and therefore there can be no *svasaṃvedana*. The *prasaṅga*-reversal is that in the case of any putative *svasaṃvedana:*

> It follows that the subjects—conventional activity, agent and action in the case of consciousness—exist from their own side, because they do not depend on an object.

In other words if there is *svasaṃvedana,* because it is reflexive it refers to itself. Activity, agent and action are the same and exist independently of an object and therefore (it is argued) they exist independently of a cause. Thus if there is *svasaṃvedana* it exists inherently, and not conventionally. I suggest, therefore, that one possible reading of bLo bzang dpal ldan bstan 'dzin's objection to Mi pham's claim that *svasaṃvedana* exists conventionally is that if *svasaṃvedana* existed conventionally it would also have to exist ultimately. If *svasaṃvedana* existed at all, then even conventionally activity, agent and action in the case of consciousness would exist from their own side. If this were the case, then Mi pham could not at the time of searching through ultimate analysis draw a *prasaṅga*-reversal against the opponent who holds to an inherent *svasaṃvedana*—that it would absurdly entail activity, agent and action existing from their own side. He himself must hold this too.

> (iv) In denying that there is *svasaṃvedana* even conventionally, bLo bzang dpal ldan bstan 'dzin tells us, we are not forced into the position that one's own mind becomes a hidden object for oneself, or there is an annihilation of the transactional conventions of ordinary referential-awareness and so on. It is necessary to explain the occurrence of memory even though there does not exist *svasaṃvedana,* and it is necessary to explain things in such a way that one does not mix up lower and higher tenet-systems.[6]

We note here the dGe lugs linking of the negation of *svasaṃvedana* with the issue of memory, and also a prescriptive insistence on the framework provided by clearly delineated tenet-systems.

This is reflected in bLo bzang dpal ldan's next point. He moves to a consideration of any affirmation of a conventional substratum-consciousness. Concerning this, our critic appears to begin to loose his patience. 'How can it be reasonable for someone to assert the existence conventionally of even the *ālayavijñāna*?' If that were the case, the Prāsaṅgika would necessarily refute also the external object. But there are authoritative sources which tell us that it is not reasonable to refute the external object, and it is all quite unacceptable.[7] In other words, any affirmation conven-

---

[6] rang blo rang la lkog tu gyur pa dang / don rig gi tha snyad rgyun chad par 'gyur ba sogs dgos med kyi dgag pa rnams kyang 'dod du rigs te / gong *[gang?]* du rang rig med kyang dran pa skye ba 'chad pa la dgos pa yod cing / grub mtha' gong 'og gi lugs [200] rnams so so nas ma 'dres par 'chad dgos pa'i phyir ro //.

[7] de bzhin du kun gzhi'i rnam shes pa'ang tha snyad du yod ces

tionally of a substratum-consciousness could only be a substratum-consciousness under the terms of its acceptance in those tenet-systems which are recognized as accepting the substratum-consciousness. Those tenet-systems which accept a substratum-consciousness do so as part of a rejection of a referential object external to the consciousness continuum. All discussion has to occur within the framework provided by the four tenet-systems of Vaibhāṣika, Sautrāntika, Cittamātra and Madhyamaka, with their clearly distinguished subschools. It is part of the characterization of the Prāsaṅgika subschool of Madhyamaka that it accepts neither the *ālayavijñāna* nor *svasaṃvedana*

---

smra ba ga la rigs te de ltar na lugs 'dis phyi rol gyi doṇ yang 'gog dgos par 'gyur la / des na mdo sde sa bcu pa dang de'i dgongs 'grel sogs las phyi don 'gog tu mi rigs par gsungs pa sogs don med pa nyid du thal bas 'dod du ga la nus te mi nus so //. Note that Mi pham himself, when speaking from his own side, perhaps to make an intentional distinction, prefers to use the expression ***kun gzhi*** (substratum) rather than ***kun gzhi rnam shes*** (substratum-consciousness), which is associated with Cittamātra. bLo bzang dpal ldan, on the other hand, takes it as obvious that Mi pham is speaking of the ***kun gzhi rnam shes*** associated with Cittamātra. Of course, one response to Mi pham's defence of the conventional existence of ***kun gzhi*** and ***svasaṃvedana*** might be simply to say that Mi pham is not a Prāsaṅgika but a Yogācāra-Svātantrika Mādhyamika (like Śāntarakṣita). Whether one could maintain this systematically, using the dGe lugs distinctions between tenet-systems, I do not know. But it would be to beg the question, for Mi pham claims to be a Prāsaṅgika and does not see an incompatibility between the conventional existence of what he refers to as the ***kun gzhi*** and ***svasaṃvedana*** on the one hand, and the Prāsaṅgika position on the other. Thus for Mi pham nothing ***in this*** shows that he is not a perfectly good Prāsaṅgika. On the uses of the terms ***kun gzhi*** and ***kun gzhi rnam shes*** in rDzogs chen see Karmay (1988), pp. 178-84. On the distinction of the rDzogs chen ***gzhan stong*** (q.v.) view from Cittamātra see Dudjom Rinpoche (1991), ch. 4.

even conventionally. If it did, then it would be accepting the tenets of other systems, with all that entails, and it would not be Prāsaṅgika Madhyamaka.

With that, bLo bzang dpal ldan bstan 'dzin has finished his constructive critical comments on Mi pham's position regarding the substratum and reflexivity. In this commentary of yours, he tells Mi pham, even though there are many supporting arguments for this verbal garland of feeble explanation, I have no intention of negating them individually. I have but taught the mere beginnings of the authoritative testimony and reasoning which would undermine this commentary. But if one were to critically examine these arguments of Mi pham precisely in detail then there would be a complete refutation. Therefore, let that sort of precise intellect undertake a superior proper examination.[8]

[8] gzhan yang khyod kyi 'grel pa 'dir 'khogs bshad kyi tshig phreng 'di dang rigs mthun pa mang du mchis kyang re re nas dgag tu ma langs mod / 'on kyang 'dir gnod pa'i lung rigs kyi sgo tsam bstan la 'di rnams la zhib tu dpyad na phal cher 'gog par yod pas zhib mo'i blos go bsdur mi dman re mdzod /. The expression *'khogs pa* (feeble) means weak due to age (= senile?). Could this be a reference to Mi pham's own age?

CHAPTER 7

Mi Pham's Reply

Perhaps the precise intellect required to make a proper examination was that of Mi pham! bLo bzang dpal ldan bstan 'dzin's attack could scarcely be called detailed or devastating, but it did provide Mi pham with the opportunity to repeat at much greater length his vision of Prāsaṅgika Madhyamaka and his defense of the conventional existence of reflexivity, clarifying and refining as he did so, while also developing new arguments against anyone who would wish to deny his thesis. Mi pham begins by stating that he will restrict his examination to just the sūtra perspective, omitting that of tantra *(lan mdo tsam brjod na)*. In the context of the *Bodhicaryāvatāra* this is appropriate, but it also draws the attention of an opponent to the use of expressions in tantric discourse connoting the reflexivity of consciousness (e.g., *so so rang rig pa'i ye shes tsam*), and the additional problem Mi pham's opponent would have were Mi pham also to extend the discussion to the tantras.

Generally, Mi pham observes, it is clearly the case from their own treatises that in the Prāsaṅgika system there is an acceptance of the six consciousness-groups—each of the six sense-bases, the six types of referential object, and the six resultant consciousnesses—and the Prāsaṅgika does not make a systematic formulaic acceptance of *svasaṃvedana* and so on. Thus, of course, as far as consciousness is concerned the Prāsaṅgika simply accepts that there are six types of consciousness associated with seeing, hearing, smelling, tasting, touching and (in a broad sense) mental activity. This Mi pham is prepared to grant. The issue, however, is not which consciousnesses are accepted, but what it is to be a consciousness. Mi pham does not believe that we find this issue treated as such in Prāsaṅgika texts. He does not wish to argue, therefore, that we find in Prāsaṅgika texts an explicit avowal and integration into the Prāsaṅgika perspective of the conventional existence of *svasaṃvedana*. His point at this stage is primarily one of logic, but also one of the broader context of Prāsaṅgika Madhyamaka within a whole integrated Buddhist system. How, Mi pham asks, is someone able to ascertain with such certitude that *svasaṃvedana* does not exist transactionally just through the mere absence in Prāsaṅgika texts of its affirmation transactionally? As a matter of general principle, it is impossible to infer *x* is not the case from the fact that no one has said that *x* is the case. Both Mi pham and his dGe lugs critics agree that there are many things accepted within the broader contexts of their respective systems which are not mentioned in Prāsaṅgika texts, but one cannot conclude from this that they do not exist or would be unacceptable to the Prāsaṅgika as a Buddhist practitioner or indeed as a human being. For example, Mi pham continues, take the case of such conventions as the innate mind *(gnyug sems)* or great bliss *(bde ba chen po)* and so on. We do not fail to affirm those transactionally even though they do not occur in the Prāsaṅgika system.[1]

Mi pham's choice of these examples (where the Prāsaṅgika perspective is supplemented incidentally by important concepts developed, if not originating, within the context of Tantric practice) is interesting. It is one thing to argue as I have done that, in terms of the Indian commentarial tradition on the *Bodhicaryāvatāra, svasaṃvedana* was not negated conventionally because it never crossed any commentator's mind that this was an issue for the Prāsaṅgika. Whether something exists conventionally or not was not at stake. From this perspective, as Mi pham is aware, the Prāsaṅgika neither affirms nor denies a conventional *svasaṃvedana.* It is not considered. It appears to be a matter of supreme indifference. It is, however, another thing to argue that a conventional *svasaṃvedana* is important, and in order for the Prāsaṅgika perspective to be integrated into a whole Buddhist theoretical and practical system it has to be supplemented with this concept from elsewhere. Mi pham wishes to *add* to Prāsaṅgika Madhyamaka, and what he is doing here is drawing attention not only to the logic of the situation but also to the fact that all Tibetan traditions, including the dGe lugs, involve an integration of the Prāsaṅgika perspective into a wider spiritual context of a path and vision of the goal where concepts which are not mentioned in Prāsaṅgika texts

[1] de la lan mdo tsam brjod na / spyir dbu ma thal 'gyur ba'i lugs la rnam shes tshogs drug tu bzhed pa dang / rang rig gi rnam bzhag sogs ma mdzad pa ni rang gzhung na gsal mod / der tha snyad du zhal bzhes med pa tsam zhig gis tha snyad du med nges su go dgos [201] pa'i nges pa ga la yod de / dper na thal 'gyur ba'i lugs la gnyug sems dang bde ba chen po sogs kyi tha snyad sbyor don med kyang de dag tha snyad du mi 'thad pa ma yin pa bzhin no //.

have their place and significance.[2] Of course, Mi pham is prepared to grant that whatever these concepts involve they refer to things which are ontologically only conventions and do not inherently exist. Nevertheless, they do exist in the way that conventions exist, and as parts of the wider Buddhist context they are crucially important. Understood this way there are ontological issues—the conventional existence of many things—which are not covered by Prāsaṅgika Madhyamaka. Mi pham feels he has good rational reasons for wishing to add to the Prāsaṅgika refutation of the inherent existence of *svasaṃvedana* its remaining conventional existence. He cannot see any Prāsaṅgika grounds not to do this and, he is saying, all agree that the Prāsaṅgika system is not complete in itself.

In order to be able to respond to Mi pham the opponent has to be able to show that the conventional existence of *svasaṃvedana* is not the same as other conventional concepts which are acceptable alongside Prāsaṅgika Madhyamaka, such as the great bliss. 'How are the cases similar?', the opponent asks. It is quite clear, he stresses, that the negation of *svasaṃvedana* by the Prāsaṅgika is made very strongly—it occupies a major role in Prāsaṅgika treatises—and because of this the refutation of *svasaṃvedana* as not existent conventionally is one of the distinctive features of the Prāsaṅgika perspective. Mi pham's response to this is that while it is certainly

---

2 Even if one accepts with the dGe lugs tradition that Prāsaṅgika Madhyamaka is the highest view *(lta ba)*, still it by no means follows that how things are *conventionally* is completed contained within Prāsaṅgika. Rather the reverse, Mi pham wants to say. How things are conventionally is in general not contained within Prāsaṅgika at all.

the case that the reflexive nature of awareness is negated with serious urgency in Mādhyamika texts, those texts negate it from an ultimate point of view and they do not refute it transactionally. Serious urgency, strength of refutation, Mi pham wants to say, do not change the level of refutation, just as shouting does not make something true, and the fact that for Tsong kha pa the nonexistence even conventionally of *svasaṃvedana* is a distinctive feature of Prāsaṅgika Madhyamaka does not make that true either. According to Mi pham the Prāsaṅgika refutation of self-awareness is on the same level as the refutation of the awareness of others. Both are negated in Mādhyamika texts and he can find no distinction in terms of level of negation made between them. If we maintain that self-awareness is not the case even conventionally, then we should also maintain that awareness of others is not the case conventionally either.

Supposing we wonder why we should maintain that *svasaṃvedana* is not refuted conventionally? Well, Mi pham says, if the reflexive nature of awareness were to be refuted even transactionally then it would follow that it would be just like a permanent sound, or the creator Lord (God) of the theists, which would also be harmed by a valid cognizer which examines the transactional. But that is not possible here.[3] Mi pham is making a crucial methodological point. There is a

[3] de dang ga la 'dra ste rang rig la dgag pa nan tan mdzad par dngos su gsal bas tha snyad du med par 'gog pa de thal 'gyur ba'i khyad chos su 'jog go zhe na / dbu ma'i gzhung na rang rig nan gyis bkag pa yod mod kyi / de dag gis don dam par bkag par 'gyur gyi tha snyad du mi khegs te dper na gzhan rig bzhin no //ci'i phyir mi khegs snyan [*snyam?]* na tha snyad du yang med ces 'gog na rtag pa'i sgra dang dbang phyug byed pa po la sogs pa bzhin du tha snyad dpyod byed kyi tshad mas gnod pa dngos su yod pa dgos na 'di la de mi srid pa'i phyir ro //.

fundamental distinction between (i) reasoning which examines something to see whether it has inherent existence, that is, whether it is resistant to this sort of reasoning and therefore exists inherently, i.e. ultimately, and (ii) reasoning which examines something to see whether or not it exists conventionally, empirically, i.e. transactionally. Prāsaṅgika texts usually involve (i). When they involve (ii) they say so. Certain things, like the permanent sound and the creator God, are refuted in Prāsaṅgika texts as existing both ultimately and conventionally, and therefore, according to Mi pham, they must also be harmed by a valid cognizer which examines the conventional. Of course, as things which do not exist conventionally this must be the case. I suggest, however, that Mi pham would hold permanent sounds and creator Gods to be of such a nature that if they are refuted ultimately they must be refuted conventionally as well. In other words, in their being harmed by a valid cognizer which examines the ultimate, they are implicitly and indirectly also harmed by a valid cognizer which examines the conventional. This is because they are either of such a nature that they imply simple logical contradictions and therefore could not be existents in any possible world, or if they exist they are necessary existents and thus could only exist as inherently-existent ultimates. A creator God, like inherent existence itself, could not be merely an empirical possibility. I have indicated earlier that it is possible Mi pham's dGe lugs critic considered *svasaṃvedana* to fall into this second category. Mi pham, on the other hand, considers it patently obvious that reflexivity is an empirical possible which not only is not refuted by a valid cognizer which examines the conventional, but also has compelling supporting arguments. Mi pham would simply deny as absurd the suggestion that if awareness is reflexive the reflexivity could exist only inherently.

What the opponent has to do is to be able to show where in Mādhyamika texts it is explicitly stated that *svasaṃvedana* is negated conventionally as well as ultimately. There remains only one direct supporting quotation, Candrakīrti on *Madhyamakāvatāra* 6:73:

> If one appeals to worldly transaction, still, even on such a basis memory which has reflexivity as a cause is not possible.[4]

We might argue that the most this quotation will show in isolation is that Candrakīrti (not necessarily Śāntideva) considered that even from a transactional point of view memory could not serve as an argument to prove reflexivity. Mi pham, however, adopts another approach. He had argued that *svasaṃvedana* is negated in Madhyamaka treatises by ultimate analysis and not by conventional analysis. Mi pham's strategy for verse 73 is to return it to its context in the *Madhyamakāvatāra*. He quotes most of the following verse (74 a-c):

> Even if it is accepted that reflexivity is indeed proved, still it is not reasonable that there is recollection by memory. This is because they are other, as occurs in a mental continuum where there was no previous experience.[5]

What Candrakīrti means, Mi pham explains, is that in the case of separately existing former and later

---

[4] 'on te 'jig rten tha snyad kyi dbang du yin na ni / de lta na'ang rang rig pa'i rgyu can gyi dran pa mi srid pa nyid du /.

[5] rang rig pa ni grub la rag mod kyi / de lta'ang dran pa'i dran pa rigs min te / gzhan phyir ma shes rgyud la skyes pa bzhin /. Mi pham reads for line b: de lta'ang dran pas dran par rigs min te /.

consciousnesses, established with their own characteristics *(svalakṣaṇa)* as postulated by the Cittamātrin opponent, even though one might have formerly experienced oneself, still there is reasoning showing that there can be no memory now. This, Mi pham implies, is because, as Candrakīrti says, these are (inherently) other, i.e. quite separate events within the mental continuum. In the case of what is experienced by one person, it is not recollected by another person. Here, what arises subsequently bears no connection to what was experienced previously, and is therefore no different from a case of no memory, experiencing now something not previously experienced at all (see *Madhyamakāvatārabhāṣya* on 6:74). Nevertheless, Mi pham says, there does not exist here any reasoning which harms the existence of *svasaṃvedana* in worldly transaction. In other words, all Candrakīrti has shown is that even in worldly transaction there is no memory with reflexivity as a cause where memory is posited as occurring between inherently existent former and later moments of consciousness. Even if there is reflexivity, where consciousness moments are inherently separate there could be no memory. Therefore, by merely quoting *Madhyamakāvatāra* 6:73 there is proved nothing.[6]

In Mi pham's critical version of his argument, bLo bzang dpal ldan bstan 'dzin, unable to appeal any more to his quotation, resorts to the argument that if *svasaṃvedana* exists conventionally there could not exist the *prasaṅga*-reversal *(thal bzlog)* which entails that

---

[6] Mi pham p. 201: snga phyi'i shes pa rang mtshan gyis grub pa'i so so ba la sngar rang gis rang myong du chug kyang da lta dran mi srid par ston pa'i rigs par 'dug gi / 'jig rten tha [202] snyad du rang rig yod pa la gnod nges kyi rigs pa gang yang mi 'dug na de tsam zhig brjod pas ci yang mi 'grub bo //.

activity, agent and action would be established from their own side. But this does not follow (*rgyu mtshan ma nges pa'i tshig tsam*—there is an uncertain reason). In the Madhyamaka, Mi pham explains, the expression 'established from its own side' means withstanding analysis by a reasoning which examines the ultimate. Under those circumstances it is accepted that *svasaṃvedana* is not established. On the other hand if one knows by oneself one's own mind conventionally *(svasaṃvedana)* there is no reason at all for any necessity that activity, agent and action are established from their own side. Mi pham clearly fails to see what the connection is between activity, agent and action withstanding analysis by reasoning which examines the ultimate, and conventionally being reflexively aware of one's own consciousness. Once again Mi pham tells us that the situation with self-awareness is just the same as awareness of external referents. It does not follow that just because there is an awareness of external referents conventionally, activity, agent and action must be established from their own side.[7]

Mi pham entertains the possibility that someone might reason as follows: the activity, agent and action referred to here when we speak of self-awareness are in fact the activity of being aware, the agent who is aware, and that of which one is aware. But these do not exist separately in the case of *self*-awareness, and un-

---

[7] rigs pa yod de gong du brjod pa ltar tha snyad du rang rig yod na bya byed las gsum rang ngos grub par thal ba bzlog tu med do zer na 'di rgyu mtshan ma nges pa'i tshig tsam ste / rang ngos nas grub pa zhes pa dbu ma'i skabs 'dir don dam dpyod pa'i rigs pas dpyad bzod la brjod pa yin la / des rang rig ma grub par ni 'dod cing tha snyad du rang blo rang gis rig na bya byed las gsum rang ngos nas grub dgos pa'i rgyu mtshan rdul tsam med de don rig bzhin no //.

der such circumstances one can scarcely speak of 'self-awareness' since we do not have here even in conventional terms an *awareness* (an action directed towards an object) in any meaningful sense. On the one hand if one examines the case of engaging in an action *(byed pa)* directed towards oneself, if object and subject really are separate then this would not be a case of self-awareness. It would in fact be a case of other-awareness, that is, awareness of another thing. If they are not separate, on the other hand, there would be no engaging in an action, since activity, agent and action would be the same. This is as in the case (mentioned in the *Laṅkāvatāra Sūtra*, for example) where it is said that a sword cannot cut itself.[8] In the case of *svasaṃvedana* the possibility that subject and object are different is excluded by the premisses of those who would argue for self-awareness. If subject and object are different there is not self-awareness but other-awareness, and the need to validate awareness itself is going to lead to an infinite regress. But if subject and object are the same then, it is argued, there is no action since to be aware is a transitive action. Self-awareness is thus simply a contradiction in terms.[9]

---

8 gal te 'di'i skabs kyi bya byed las gsum zhes pa rig bya rig byed rig pa'i bya ba gsum tha dad du med pa la / rig pa'i tha snyad kyang mi thob cing / rang gis rang la byed pa 'jug pa la dpyad na yul yul can tha dad du yod na'ang rang rig tu mi 'gyur te gzhan rig tu 'gyur ro // tha dad du med na'ang byed pa mi 'jug ste bya byed las gsum gcig tu 'gyur bas ral gris rang gis rang mi gcod pa bzhin no snyam na //. *'Byed pa'* here must refer to the action (= *kriyā;* see Verhagen 1994, p. 339), rather than the actor *(byed pa (po))* in the specific context of activity, agent and action. On *rig bya* used here with reference to the *kriyā* and *rig bya'i bya* for the *karman* cf. notes 29, 41 and 58 below.

9 The suggestion that self-awareness is a contradiction in terms could be serious for Mi pham, since if something is simply and

To an extent Mi pham agrees *(de ltar yin mod de)*. Take the example of a consciousness apprehending blue, and blue. If we critically examine whether they are two or not and so on, using common Mādhyamika critical strategies, then certainly we will conclude that there is in fact not possible any apprehension of blue by that consciousness. But for Mi pham the point which the opponent fails to realize is that these have become ultimate investigations. They do not entail a rejection of the consciousness which ex-

---

straightforwardly a contradiction then it cannot exist ultimately or conventionally. But as we have seen already, and will see again, Mi pham argues following Śāntarakṣita that self-awareness cannot be analyzed in terms of the activity-agent-action model, at least if the activity-agent-action model is taken literally and with its normal implications. Self-awareness as reflexivity, the unique characteristic of consciousness, is a special case. Put another way, the term 'awareness' in 'self-awareness' is not being used in the same way as it is used in 'awareness of strawberries'. Mi pham is required, therefore, to explain how he is using the expression, and he devotes much space to doing so ('self-awareness' in the sense that there is awareness (i.e., there is not lack of awareness) and yet that awareness does not require another to make itself known etc.). Even granted that activity-agent-action must be transitive, self-awareness is not transitive although other-awareness is. There can, of course, be verbs that contain acts referring to themselves, and anyway language does not dictate reality, even conventional reality. Because the word 'awareness' is used, and because awareness is normally of something (other-awareness), it does not follow that 'awareness' cannot be used in the case of self-awareness. All that follows is that it should be explained how and why the term is being used here. Śāntarakṣita and Mi pham have included as part of that explanation a denial of the implications of the normal transitive activity-agent-action model. That is as such something they are perfectly entitled to do provided they explain themselves. Which is what Mi pham intends to do.

periences blue in everyday life.[10] What we have here is a distinction between something which is well-acknowledged in the world as occurring, and the failure to discover its basic coherence when a particular sort of investigation is carried out. However the Prāsaṅgika carries out his or her analytic investigations, we have seen already from Śāntideva that it is crucial the investigation should not be taken to deny what are accepted as the facts of everyday conventions. Thus when Mi pham defends himself against an attack by his opponent on the basis that all the analyses by the opponent are ultimate analyses and do not touch the conventional existence of *svasaṃvedana,* Mi pham's criterion for applying this strategy is that the reflexive nature of awareness is clearly evident and therefore well-known at least at some level in worldly transaction. A critical analysis which shows something clearly evident and accepted in worldly transaction not to be the case must be an ultimate analysis.[11] Thus the opponent's critical investigation of

---

[10] de ltar yin mod de dper na sngo 'dzin shes pa dang sngon po gnyis bar bcas pa dang ma bcas pa'am snga phyi ji ltar yin dpyad na gang ltar kyang des de 'dzin pa mi srid mod kyi dpyad pa de dag don dam dpyod [203] par song gi 'jig rten tha snyad du sngon po nyams su myong ba'i shes pa gtan med par mi 'gro ba bzhin du /.

[11] Of course, it does not follow that everything which is well-known in worldly transaction is accepted by the Prāsaṅgika conventionally. Inherently existent entities are well-known in worldly transaction, but if they existed they would have to exist ultimately. Thus ultimate analysis also shows that inherently existent entities do not exist even conventionally. But if *x* could exist conventionally, and those who are best qualified in terms of criteria applied by the world to know hold that it does exist, then the type of critical analysis (found in Madhyamaka) which shows it does not exist is an ultimate analysis and should not contradict the conventional acceptance of *x*.

svasaṃvedana in terms of the incoherence of self-awareness must also be an ultimate analysis.

No Mādhyamika doubts, least of all Mi pham, that self-awareness is incoherent in such terms. Nevertheless, Mi pham adds, what we mean by 'self-awareness' is that even though activity, agent and action do not exist separately in the case of self-awareness, still, not being a hidden object from its mere occurrence as having its own-mental-event-quality *(rang blo nyid),* experience takes place with the nature of luminosity and awareness. That self-awareness exists in terms of worldly transaction. If we have to decide between whether there is actually awareness or lack of awareness, by one's own mind, of its own continuum conventionally, if we opt for the decision that there is lack of awareness then we would have to accept that one's own mind is an object hidden from itself—and that is scarcely credible.[12] Mi pham's approach is purely structural. He is not committed to any complex conclusions, ramifications and implications which his opponent might wish to insist follow from his acceptance of reflexivity conventionally. His point is simply that consciousness is consciousness, and it is the nature of consciousness that it is not {non-reflexive}. Consciousness either actually is or is not aware of itself. If it is not then the absurd result follows that the nature of consciousness is to know others but not to know whether itself exists or not. It would, therefore, be insentient. Thus consciousness is not {non-aware of

---

12 rang rig la'ang bya byed las gsum tha dad du med kyang rang blo nyid skyes tsam nas lkog tu ma gyur par myong ba gsal rig gi ngo bor skyes pa la rang rig ces brjod la de 'jig rten tha snyad du yód de tha snyad du rang rgyud kyi blo rang gis dngos su rig pa'am mi rig pa gnyis su kha tshon chod pa las mi rig par 'dod na rang blo rang la lkog gyur du khas len pa las 'os med do //.

itself}. It is a reflexive sort of thing. Nothing else follows as such for Mi pham. Simply, an absurdity which would be an absurdity for worldly convention is avoided. It is in this context that Mi pham chooses to quote Śāntarakṣita's *Madhyamakālaṃkāra* vv. 16-17, as well as Dharmakīrti's *Pramāṇaviniścaya* 1:38. Consciousness is the very opposite of insentience, and this means reflexivity. The activity-agent-action model cannot be applied in the case of a partless unity like reflexive awareness, the very quality of consciousness itself.

In the light of this, Mi pham wants to make it clear that when we speak of 'self-awareness' we do not mean that in addition to an awareness of, say, the table, there is also a further cognitive act directed towards oneself. It is not necessary that in addition to an awareness of the table there is also produced another new action by oneself directed towards oneself *(rang la rang gi byed pa gsar du 'jug mi dgos)*. It is not 'self-awareness' in that sense. *Svasaṃvedana* is the quality of consciousness *qua* consciousness. If there is an act of awareness then in its very being as *awareness* it is also self-aware. In a very real sense the self-awareness *is* the being aware of the table. One can thus show that there is no problem in a transactional convention of self-awareness when applied to consciousness, which is not a hidden object from itself since its very nature is that of luminosity.[13] For consciousness to be luminous by nature (on the model of the lamp) is to know itself in knowing others. This is equivalent to consciousness (which is a knowable) being known, but not requiring another to know it. What we have here

[13] de'i phyir rang la rang gi byed pa gsar du 'jug mi dgos kyang rang nyid gsal ba'i ngo bos rang lkog tu ma gyur par shes pa la rang rig pa'i tha snyad gnod med du 'jug ste /.

is not an explanation of why or how consciousness knows itself, but rather what it is to know itself, what is meant by referring to 'self-awareness'. Mi pham suggests that we take the example of a conventional act of cognizing a referential object in the case of a direct perceptual consciousness of a pot. Why under such circumstances should the opponent hold that a convention of cognizing itself, by its own mind which has arisen in its own mental continuum, in the case of a perceptual consciousness, is so unacceptable?[14] In other words, why should the opponent who will grant that conventionally one cognizes a pot be so concerned when it is added that conventionally one also cognizes in a reflexive sense that one cognizes a pot?

Thus, Mi pham continues, even though there exists in the world quite unmistakably and without error a mere reflexivity, if one were to investigate the conceptually-constructed object according to how it is that it is aware of itself there would not be found anything truly-established but merely unexamined worldly renown.[15] The sort of critical investigation which tries to find out how a basic given datum like reflexivity can possibly be eventually fails. It is not claimed that reflexivity is resistant to that sort of investigation—there is no claim that *svasaṃvedana* is truly established. It exists simply from the perspective of worldly convention, not subject to the sort of ultimate examination familiar in Prāsaṅgika Madhyamaka.

---

14 ji ltar bum pa mngon [204] sum shes pa la yul shes pa'i tha snyad du byed pa bzhin du / rang gi rgyud la gang skyes pa'i blo rang gis mngon sum shes pa la rang shes pa'i tha snyad ci ste mi rung.

15 de bas na rang rig pa tsam 'jig rten na gnod med bslu med du yod kyang des rang ji ltar rig pa'i btags don btsal na ma brtags 'jig rten gyi grags pa tsam las yang dag par grub pa gang yang rnyed par mi 'gyur kyang /.

Therefore, what we mean by self-awareness should be expressed in terms of worldly convention. When we speak of it as 'self-awareness' we call it this because its very own being occurs as the nature of luminosity and awareness. This is said in consideration of the worldly mind which engages in conventional transaction according to appearance, without critical investigation as to whether or not it is established ultimately. In the case of self-awareness, since activity, agent and action are not substantially different *(rdzas gzhan med pas*—i.e., they are the same, self-awareness is reflexive, intransitive), Mi pham explains, we use the conventional expression (i) 'self'. In the case of self-awareness also, since activity, agent and action do exist as imputedly projected by the mind *(blos phar btags pa)*, the convention of (ii) 'awareness' is indeed also appropriate. In other words while self-awareness as such is pure reflexivity where the activity-agent-action model does not apply, a point captured in the use of the term 'self', still it is awareness in that it accompanies the mind's activities and renders them known (i.e., they are not unknown). It is indeed that quality of luminosity which makes the mind's activities what they are, and can thus be appropriately spoken of as 'awareness'.[16]

---

[16] don dam par grub ma grub kyi brtag dpyad med par ji ltar snang ba ltar tha snyad byed pa'i 'jig rten gyi blo'i dpang du na rang nyid gsal rig gi rang bzhin du skyes pa'i phyir rang rig ces dang / de la bya byed las gsum gyi rdzas gzhan med pas na rang zhes pa'i tha snyad dang / de la blos phar btags pa'i bya byed las gsum yod pas rig pa'i tha snyad nges par rung ste . . . Mi pham appears to be saying here that the activity-agent-action model, although inapplicable in the proper sense, as separate things, nevertheless is imputedly projected by the mind onto self-awareness and therefore we can still (analogously or metaphorically perhaps, or in mere language) speak of it as

Happiness and suffering are to be experienced, the mind is the agent which experiences them, and there is the activity of actually experiencing happiness and suffering by the mind. These, Mi pham observes, are fundamental in anyone's system. They form the basic structure of empirical sensory experience, not open to question in itself by anyone, although one could certainly investigate what are the empirical conditions for experience structured in such a way, and one could also carry out an ultimate investigation concerning final coherence, providing one did not create confusion by thinking that the ultimate investigation undermines the givenness as such of the empirical. On the other hand, Mi pham continues dryly, there is a real problem in maintaining that the mind which is the subject is a separate substance from the happiness and so on which are its experiential objects when experiencing happiness etc., and that the happiness and so on which are the objects are separate from that mind.[17]

awareness although it is not awareness in the normal sense, i.e. aware of anything other than itself. We shall return to this issue below.

17 'di ltar bde sdug myang bya yin pa dang / de myong byed blo yin pa dang / blo des bde sdug dngos su myong ba'i bya ba byed pa gsum ni su'i lugs la'ang yod pa gzhir bcas la / bde sogs myong bzhin pa'i blo de la myong bya bde sogs las rdzas gzhan pa'i 'dzin byed kyi blo dang / blo de las tha dad du gyur pa'i gzung bya bde sogs yod par sus khas len dka' ste /. We have seen above (ch. 5) that Mi pham alludes to an argument which can be traced to Dharmakīrti whereby sensations such as happiness which accompany experiences of, for example, strawberries provide evidence for the reflexivity of awareness. In seeing strawberries on a fine spring day I also feel happy, and that happiness is the result of not only seeing strawberries but also as part of the very same act responding to seeing strawberries. I saw strawberries and knew that I saw strawberries. This know-

For Mi pham the reason is clear. If there existed a separate mind which was other than the experience of happiness, it would follow absurdly that it would be a mind without sensation. Correspondingly if there existed happiness, which is what is experienced, as something separate from the mind which apprehends itself, there would be a sensation without consciousness. This, Mi pham observes, is like the positions of Sāṃkhya and Vaiśeṣika, which affirm both inner and outer, happinesses and so on, as insentient.[18] So, even though happiness and the experience

---

ing-that was felt not in thinking 'Ooh, strawberries' but in feeling happy as I saw the strawberries, not as a further act but as part of the very seeing. In such an example it could not be the case that the mind experiencing the strawberries, and the happiness, are two fundamentally different things. Rather the happiness is, in the experience of strawberries, one with the mind enjoying the experience. Thus in happiness one experiences one's own mind. This argument, which is not directly important to Mi pham at this point, would appear at the most to provide an example of absence of difference between the mind experiencing and what is experienced, a possible example of the mind experiencing itself (= self-awareness (i)), rather than an illustration of reflexivity which makes consciousness consciousness (= self-awareness (ii)). This would not be surprising if self-awareness (i) originates with Dignāga and Dharmakīrti, but self-awareness (ii) only became clearly articulated with Śāntarakṣita.

18 bde sogs myong ba de las gzhan pa'i blo yan gar du yod na tshor ba med pa'i blor thal ba dang / rang [205] 'dzin gyi blo de las tha dad pa'i myang bya bde sogs yod na shes pa med pa'i tshor bar 'gyur te grangs can pa dang bye brag pas bde sogs phyi dang nang gi bems por 'dod pa ltar 'gyur ro //. In Sāṃkhya the only sentient thing is *puruṣa,* pure consciousness. All else is *prakṛti,* and insentient. Thus not only are external referents insentient, but so too are all the factors we usually associate with the mind apart from consciousness itself. Since consciousness is pure and in reality quite separate from *prakṛti,* it too does not have sensations. Sensations, on the other hand, are apart from

of it are not separate, nevertheless the existence of a consciousness in the manner of direct perceptual experience of happiness and suffering is renowned to those who hold philosophical tenets as well as the common general world, and it is established by direct perception. This being the case, Mi pham wants to know how is it that one cannot speak of 'self-awareness' there also? He feels that providing we do not confuse this legitimate use of the expression 'self-awareness' with that of, say, Cittamātra, where self-awareness must exist inherently if it exists at all, there should be no problem in accepting both the actuality of self-awareness and the precise appropriateness of this particular term. If it is not affirmed, the opponent should consider whether he or she would wish to accept that happiness and so on are not really experienced at all, or experience too is experienced by another awareness rather than self-awareness. Mi pham has constructed a familiar dilemma. If experience is not itself experienced it would appear to be unexperienced and therefore would be incapable of experiencing anything (but see Matilal (1986) pp. 155 ff.). Experience must be experienced by either itself or another experience. If by itself, then of course, *svasaṃvedana* would be established. There is no middle between self and other. The alternative is that it would have to be experienced by another experience, on the model of referential awareness. This would lead to an infinite regress. The opponent knows per-

consciousness and therefore are insentient. In the case of Nyāya-Vaiśeṣika the self has experiences, but the self is not of the nature of consciousness. Rather, consciousness-terms apply to qualities of the self. Thus both the self which experiences and referents experienced are insentient. This Tibetan picture—at least as regards Nyāya-Vaiśeṣika—is, as it stands, rather a caricature.

fectly well what the answer is here, and Mi pham leaves it for his opponent to draw the conclusion.[19]

In the case of cognitions of various things, Mi pham continues, when we consider that 'I clearly cognize this object as something or other', that which appears as the cognitive referent is designated transactionally from the accusative case (*karman* ('the action'), here *las su bya ba*—that which is done as that which is the direct intentional object of the verbal action itself) or from the isolate of the referential object *(yul ldog)*.[20] What Mi pham is saying here is that for *x*

---

[19] de ltar bde sogs dang de myong tha dad du med kyang bde sdug mngon sum myong ba'i tshul gyis shes pa yod pa ni grub mtha' smra ba dang 'jig rten phal pa thun mongs la grags shing mngon sum gyis grub na // de la rang rig ces brjod pa ji ltar mi 'thad de / de khas mi len na bde sogs dngos su myong ba med zer ram / myong yang gzhan rig gis myong zhes khas len nam bsam par byos shig /. Notice that Mi pham has switched from the non-separation of happiness and the mind which cognizes happiness to the non-separation of happiness and the experience of happiness. One can see how as a Buddhist with a vision of the mind as a series of momentary mental events he is able to do this, but the second formulation appears much less problematic. Indeed it could be tautologous.

[20]The isolate *(ldog pa/vyāvṛtti)* of *x* in a determinate conceptual perception (e.g., our perceptions when *x* is cognised as something or other) is formed from the exclusion of not-*x*, and it indicates that the thing as conceptualized and verbalizable is not or does not involve a real universal but is a construct through exclusion. The object as a conceptualized object is what it is, is identified, simply through the exclusion of all the things it is not. Thus the strawberry as apprehended in a determinate conceptual perception is *qua* conceptual object formed through the exclusion of non-strawberries. The isolate as conceptual object is not the object of direct and immediate perception but the object for thought-construction, or the object for language (see also note 28 below). In the case of Frege's example of the morning star and the evening star, there is one thing but two isolates since that concept formed by the exclusion of not-morning star

to be a referent in a normal everyday determinate and verbalizable cognition is for '*x*' actually or potentially to occupy the grammatical slot of the direct object of a verbal action, or (in non-exclusive disjunction) to stand as an object for conceptual thought. When we ask ourselves *by what* the conceptual referent is cognised the response, Mi pham tells us, must be that it is cognised by one's own mind, and here we have the isolate which is engaging the transactional convention of the (grammatical) agent *(kartṛ)*, a subject *(yul can)* for the referential object.[21] When that subject clearly comprehends the object in a nondual manner, the experiencing is an isolate of the activity (*kriyā;* the actual verbal action itself).[22] Thus we have

---

could not be the same as that concept formed through exclusion of not-evening star. They are understood differently by the conceptual consciousness, as seen in their different modes of formation. Nevertheless, although the isolates are different, and therefore the morning star as conceptual object (isolate) is not the same as the evening star as conceptual object still, in reality, the morning star is the same as the evening star (even if it took many centuries to realize the fact). In a conceptual determinate perception, Mi pham says, the cognitive referent is referred to in normal everyday convention linguistically through the accusative, or as the isolate—the referent as conceptually-created through exclusion. The expression *'karman'* in Sanskrit grammar is used according to Abhyankar and Shukla (1986) to refer to the 'object of a transitive verb, defined as "something which the agent or the doer of the action wants to achieve". The main feature of *karman* is that it is put in the accusative case....Pāṇini has made *karma* a technical term and called all such words "karman" as are connected with a verbal activity and used in the accusative case'.

21 According to Abhyankar and Shukla, *kartṛ* refers to the 'agent of an action, subject; name of a kāraka or instrument in general, of an action, which produces the fruit or result of an action without depending on any other instrument'.

22 The *kriyā* is defined by Abhyankar and Shukla as 'action,

here the grammatical action *(karman),* agent *(kartṛ)* and activity *(kriyā).* How, Mi pham asks, could there be a transactional conventional cognition which is not thus based on the mere isolates of cognitive activity and agent?[23] That is how language operates, in terms of a model supplied by the interplay between subjects, objects and verbal activities. This model also mirrors (or perhaps determines) the structure of our everyday conceptualized cognitions and all too often our understanding but, Mi pham wants to say, the model does not always reflect very accurately even our conventional reality.

We saw earlier that Mi pham had introduced the non-separation of the mind which experiences happiness and the experience of happiness itself. Here we find Mi pham urging that the mind is what experiences, and the experience of happiness is what occurs when the referent, happiness, is clearly experienced *in a nondual manner.* This reference to a nondual manner of experience in this context seems to reinforce the point that it is not a case of a separate mind having a separate something called an experience.

---

verbal activity....The word bhāva many times is used in the same sense as *kriyā* or verbal activity in the sūtras of Pāṇini....Some scholars draw a nice distinction between *kriyā* and *bhāva, kriyā* meaning dynamic activity and *bhāva* meaning static activity'.

[23] de bzhin du gang ji snyed pa'i shes pa yin no cog la bdag gis 'di dang 'di lta bur don 'di gsal par shes so snyam pa'i tshe gang shes par bya ba'i rnam par shar ba de ni las su bya ba'am yul gyi ldog pa nas tha snyad btags pa yin la / gang gis shes snyam du bsam pa'i tshe rang gi blo 'dis so snyam pa ni yul can byed pa po'i tha snyad 'jug pa'i ldog pa yin la / des de gnyis su med pa'i tshul gyis gsal bar rtogs shing myong ba ni bya ba'i ldog pa ste / de 'dra'i shes bya shes byed kyi ldog pa tsam zhig bzhag tu med pa'i 'jig rten gyi shes pa ga la srid cing de 'dra srid ces su zhig gis smra nus te bsam par bya'o //.

The mind having an experience of happiness *is* the mind in what we might call 'happiness-mode'. Nevertheless, in everyday transactional convention we do talk of the mind as that which experiences, and the experience as that which is experienced by the mind. These are, therefore, differences for conceptual thought, although not differences in reality.[24] They are, as Mi pham has shown, different isolates, that is, differences as far as conceptual and therefore conventional transactional thought is concerned. This is reflected in their different positions in the paradigmatic subject-predicate sentence structure. It is likewise in the case of self-awareness; it is possible to make a distinction in terms of (verbal and, therefore, conceptual) isolates between activity, agent and action ('I experience myself') but there is no distinction in reality; it is not really the case that awareness directs an action towards itself. Thus Mi pham indicates that while the activity-agent-action model does indeed reflect the structure of language it is, nevertheless, simply a conceptual construct which represents our ways of speaking and thinking, but is no more than that and does not have legislative function. *Language does not always reflect even conventional reality.* Linguistic structure does not necessarily carry with it even 'relative ontological' implications. While this model necessarily expresses our way of speaking about the reflexive nature of awareness, not only is it singularly unhelpful when trying to think precisely about that reflexiv-

[24] The expression 'reality' here, of course, does not mean ultimate reality. It is a relative form of reality, a reality which is more real in conventional terms as distinguished by conventional transactional investigation. Investigation of the perceptual act here shows that although we make a distinction (isolates) between activity, agent and action, in 'reality' there is no such distinction.

ity, which we refer to with some justification but also perhaps unfortunately as 'self-awareness', but also even when we examine more deeply ordinary everyday referential experiences we find that the activity-agent-action model can distort the actual situation.

Moreover, Mi pham continues, take also the cases of dreams, and illusory objects such as appear in an eye disease, or the generic object *(don spyi)* which occurs in the case of conceptual construction *(rtog pa)*, that is, cases where, in even relative terms, the referents have no actual ontological status.[25] If one considers in such cases a mind which has appeared as it were in the aspect of blue, since there is an occurrence of blue-appearance, a subject which apprehends it, and a comprehending of that blue-appearance by the subject there is respectively objective aspect, subjective aspect, and self-awareness.[26] All these occur

[25] The generic object is related to the isolate, and a result of the process which produces the isolate. The isolate of *x* is produced through the exclusion of not-*x*. The exclusion of not-*x* is presented to conceptual consciousness as a generic object, which is *x* as a universal stripped of all features specific to this or that particular case of *x*. Thus in the case of a strawberry, the strawberry as isolate is not not-strawberry. This is presented as a generic object, a universal, that which is common to all cases of strawberry such that it can be referred to by the term 'strawberry', stripped of any features specific to this particular strawberry. In 'reality', however, strawberries are particular strawberries, and there is no such thing as an abstract strawberry-universal. There is no reality to which the generic object refers. It is the result of conceptual formation through exclusion. In normal conceptualized determinate perception the generic object strawberry is mixed undifferentiably with the actual specific particular object strawberry (see Klein (1991) esp. pp. 127-8; Newland (1992) p. 67) so that what is seen as being 'objectively real' actually involves a considerable degree of conceptual distortion.

[26] Note that Mi pham has now moved from the activity as the ac-

in a consciousness where the object has no reality. In such a case since there is no objective reality involved there must actually be simply consciousness. Even though one can analyze such experiences into objective aspect, subjective aspect and self-awareness, Mi pham points out, it would be unreasonable to hold that actually these occur as separate existents. Since the very consciousness here is mere luminosity in the aspect of blue, it is shown to be truly a case of self-awareness.[27] Thus Mi pham draws attention to the fact that in ordinary conventional referential experiences which are held to be nonveridical there is only

---

tual experiencing of *x* to the self-awareness. This is not surprising, since it is self-awareness as that which demarcates consciousness from non-consciousness which is the experiencing of anything at all. Thus self-awareness in the case of a consciousness apprehending blue *is* the actual experience of blue as *experience* of blue.

[27] [206] de yang rmi lam dang rab rib kyi snang ba dang rtog ngor don spyi la'ang sngon po'i rnam pa lta bur shar ba'i blo la bsams na sngo snang dang de 'dzin dang des de rtogs pa gsum gyi rnam par 'char bas rim pa ltar gzung rnam 'dzin rnam rang rig gsum du phye yang don la de gsum tha dad du yod mi rigs te shes pa nyid sngon po'i rnam par gsal ba tsam yin pas rang rig tu grub pa bzhin no //. Mi pham seems to be shifting rather between self-awareness (i) and self-awareness (ii). In the example of the nonveridical experience we would appear to have a case of self-awareness (i), consciousness experiencing itself. The luminosity which accompanies all consciousness is self-awareness (ii). But Mi pham in fact would hold that these are really just conventional distinctions for a provisional purpose. Consciousness does not really take itself as an object in self-awareness (i). Nevertheless, it seems that there is still some 'real' distinction to be made here between consciousness in *blue-aspect*, where the blue is consciousness appearing under the aspect of blue (self-awareness (i)), and *consciousness* in blue-aspect, where because it is consciousness and has the luminous quality of consciousness there is indeed an experience of blue (self-awareness (ii)).

consciousness where the threefold division using the activity-agent-action model, while no doubt useful, still cannot refer to separate things. Therefore, in such cases, Mi pham wants to say, consciousness does indeed refer to itself, in that the referent is not *different* from that which refers. Just as in the case of our non-veridical experience there is simply consciousness being consciousness (mere luminosity) in the aspect of blue, in the case of all self-awareness there is simply consciousness being itself (the mere luminosity itself) or, better, the being-itself-quality of consciousness. There is no actual division in consciousness; we make practical divisions merely for linguistic and transactional usage.

If it is not understood in accordance with this explanation, Mi pham feels, then take the case of those who are actually not really very bright (*blo rags pa rnams;* 'of gross intellects'), having a very weak understanding. When they look within themselves and consider how it is that the mind itself can be aware of itself, since in such a case that of which one is aware *(rig bya)* and the agent which is aware *(rig byed)* do not appear as two different things, they conclude that there does not exist separately even the mere isolates, not to mention the substantival reality of activity, agent and action. In other words, seeing that in the case of self-awareness subject and object are the same, such rather unintelligent scholars may reason that this means that there cannot even be the separate isolates of activity, agent and action in the case of *svasaṃvedana.* But this does not follow, since the isolate is the result of making a conceptual distinction, and we have different isolates whenever we have different names. As Guy Newland points out, to speak solely of different isolates is to make the minimal conceptual differentiation possible.[28] Thus in the case of something cognizing itself there is certainly still a verbal difference, and therefore a difference of isolate, between activity, agent and action even if there is no substantival differentiation. Because of their misunderstanding of what it is to be an isolate, our rather unintelligent brethren may then, looking at the problem of how it is something can be aware of itself, conclude that it cannot. This, Mi pham thinks, would be altogether too crude. There is no problem at all in *speaking* of self-awareness, awareness aware of itself. Why should there be? There is no contradiction in terms

[28] 1991, p. 60: 'To say that two things are different isolates is to make only the most minimal distinction between them. Since conceptual consciousnesses often operate under the sway of language, things are different isolates as soon as they are given different names—even if those names refer to the same object.' Thus activity, agent and action *must* be different isolates and we can operate with that difference even if they are referring to the same thing, viz. an undivided entity of self-awareness. As different isolates there is no problem in saying that the agent *x* is aware of itself. This is modeled on referential awareness, but it is not the same as referential awareness since in referential awareness *x* is aware of a substantially different thing. There is only a problem in self-awareness if we think that the 'x is aware of *y*' model requires a substantival difference between *x* and *y* in order for an awareness-act to take place. But, Mi pham is saying, while we certainly require some *conceptual* difference between *x* and *y* in order for one to occupy the subject and the other the object slot, this conceptual difference can be quite minimal, represented simply by different name-tokens (in English we can use '*x*' or 'one' in the subject slot, and 'oneself' in the object slot), and that minimal difference only requires different isolates. Different isolates means conceptual difference, not substantival difference. We see here, incidentally, the wonderful and infuriating way in which Mi pham is able to use categories and concepts extremely familiar to the dGe lugs scholars but in an attempt to undermine some key principles of dGe lugs Madhyamaka.

here. Just because of the subject-predicate sentence structure it does not follow that awareness must be split and operating on itself in the way that a knife cuts vegetables. If in this case of putative 'self-awareness' that of which one is aware and the agent which is aware *did* exist as separate substances then there would indeed be problems, since how could this be *self*-awareness at all? Under such circumstances it would in fact be more appropriate to refer to it as a case of 'other-awareness'. That is, it is a condition of self-awareness that subject and object are the same, although it does not follow that they are not different isolates otherwise someone could not refer in language—as they are quite entitled to do without drawing any 'ontological' conclusions—to one as subject and the other as object. Unfortunately, Mi pham tells us, those scholars who are not really very bright do not understand the analysis and therefore how the isolates of activity, agent and action, which are conceptually imputed by worldly transaction onto one consciousness as a substratum having the aspect of such and such a referential object, can exist according to the explanation Mi pham has given above.[29]

---

29 de ltar ma shes par blo rags pa rnams kyis kha nang du phyogs nas blo rang gis rang ji ltar rig ces bltas pa na rig bya rig byed gnyis su mi 'char bas bya byed las gsum gyi rdzas lta ci ldog pa tsam yang tha dad du med pas rang gi rang ji ltar rig ste mi rig go snyam pa shing tu rtsing ste / der rig bya rig byed kyi rdzas tha dad du yod na rang rig ji ltar yin te gzhan rig tu 'os so // yul gang dang gang gi rnam pa can gyi shes pa gzhi gcig la 'jig rten tha snyad kyis btags pa'i bya byed las gsum gyi ldog pa yod pa ni blo rags pas dpyad pa zhugs ma shes pa ste ji ltar yod tshul gong du bstan pa bzhin no //. On *rig bya* 'that of which one is aware' see also my comments below in note 41. It could conceivably mean 'the actual activity of being aware' here, but it seems very unlikely. Tibetan is hampered by the fact that it sometimes chose to translate (in a grammatical context) the

Nevertheless, Mi pham is quick to avoid any possible misunderstanding here. We should not think that Mi pham is constructing an analytic argument for *svasaṃvedana* in response to the Prāsaṅgika critique, that is, an argument entailing *svasaṃvedana* as found under ultimate analysis. His argument is a second-order meta-analysis, an implicit analysis of the nature of a Mādhyamika analysis which entails no denial of the conventional existence of *svasaṃvedana*. The conventional in Prāsaṅgika is the residue of analysis, not in the sense that it is found under analysis but in the sense that the Mādhyamika *qua* Mādhyamika analysis does not negate it. The analysis that clarifies the nature of Mādhyamika analysis is second-order, and what is found by second-order analysis is not inherently-existent since it is not found by that first-order analysis which searches for putative inherent existence. There are different levels of analysis. Not all analysis—even analysis carried out by those who happen to be Prāsaṅgikas—is ultimate analysis. Thus, nevertheless, Mi pham continues, even though this reflexive quality of awareness is validated *(grub pa)* by direct perception, since its ascertainment does not occur through admixture with the sort of critical analytic investigations associated with philosophical tenets, *svasaṃvedana* is only validated as a mere inactive transactional convention of a reflex-

---

Sanskrit *karman* or *āpya* by *bya ba* (literally 'that which is to be done' or 'should be done', the referent of the verbal activity of doing), and sometimes by *las*, the term used in, say, the moral context for *karma*, using *bya ba* also for *kriyā*, the actual verbal activity itself. Here Mi pham seems consistently to use *bya ba* and *las* in the activity-agent-action triplicate for *kriyā* and *karman* respectively, but elsewhere arguably he is less consistent in his usage, employing *bya ba* in contexts of both *kriyā* (activity) and *karman* (action, i.e. referent).

ive awareness.[30] This validation is not the sort which concerns philosophical systems where each seeks to validate something or another as inherently existent, the sort of validation which is subject to the Mādhyamika first-order critique, an ultimate investigation. The validation urged by Mi pham is precisely a second-order validation which, since it is not the result of an ultimate investigation, must be the result of an investigation which is of the conventional transactional type. In other words, *svasaṃvedana* exists conventionally but not ultimately.

If we consider for ourselves how things are in terms of our actual experience, Mi pham wants to maintain that what we mean by 'self-awareness as a direct perception' *(rang rig mngon sum)* in this context—a context in which he is not committed to anything which might be taken to actually contradict the Prāsaṅgika position—is that upon anything whatsoever appearing to one's own consciousness clearly being manifest to oneself, without any requirement of departing from the temporal sequence of experience, there is an indubitability of experience *qua* experience: one cannot doubt *that* an experience is happening when it is happening; one knows that one knows in the very act of knowing (although one can, of course, doubt one's interpretation of that experience).[31] Indubitability upon manifestation—the indubitability of the contents of one's own consciousness

---

30 lar rang rig 'di mngon sum gyis grub pa yin kyang grub mtha'i dpyad pas bslad nas nges pa ma skyes pas rang rig gi tha snyad mi byed pa tsam du zad de /.

31 ji ltar kha nang du phyogs nas bsam na [207] rang gi shes pa la gang dang gang shar ba thams cad dus snga phyi'i res 'jog mi dgos par rang la mngon du gsal zhing the tshom med pa 'di rang rig mngon sum yin no //.

qua contents of one's own consciousness—is for Mi pham a quality which invariably and equally (undifferentiably) accompanies all consciousness in the very occurrence of a consciousness, *as implicated in the actual nature of consciousness itself.* It is related to what makes experience experience (cf. consciousness as luminosity and awareness). Indubitability is indeed a response to the fact that consciousness is self-knowing, reflexive. For Mi pham this is self-evidently how it is, and if reflexivity is understood in this way then whoever says there is no such thing can only be wondered at with an incredulous shake of the head. To deny such reflexivity is patently false. It is, for Mi pham, like a person who is holding onto something very tightly and yet denies she is carrying anything at all.[32] We might add that we are very close here to a version of the Cartesian *cogito.* Mi pham seems to want to say that his dGe lugs opponent's position is more than just absurd, it is also contradictory. I cannot consistently wonder or be unsure whether I am conscious or not.

And yet even though it is established in this way through our own direct perception, still there are those (they appear to be mainly philosophers) who fail to adhere to transactional conventional understanding. For example, Mi pham points out, even though we see through direct perception an ox quite devoid of any generic universal, those who understand incorrectly—such as the Vaiśeṣika Kaṇāda—

---

[32] de ltar yin bzhin rang rig med ces smra ba ni rdzas lag na thogs bzhin bdag gis ma khyer zhes bsnyon 'ding ba lta bur ya mtshan du 'os so //. Mi pham is not clear in context here whether he is saying that the problem with his opponent is contradiction or willful lying. I prefer to dwell on the logical issue of contradiction. So should Mi pham.

accept that an ox is actually present, together with its generic universal. Similarly, even though sensation is experienced through self-awareness (or 'through one's own awareness') as the very essence of consciousness, the followers of Sāṃkhya and so on accept sensation as being of the nature of insentience. Thus there are non-Buddhists too who say that self-awareness is not possible. Once again Mi pham articulates an essential identity of consciousness, sentience, and reflexivity (i.e., luminosity).[33]

One senses that Mi pham feels he really has his opponent on the defensive here. Not only is the opponent accused of denying what is patently obvious in one's own immediate experience, in fact contradicting himself as well as denying in a most un-Prāsaṅgika manner that which is accepted by the 'world', but also Mi pham has aligned the position of his dGe lugs opponent with the speculations of philosophical theorists—indeed, non-Buddhist philosophical theorists. If an attempt is made to insert the Prāsaṅgika's 'transcendental' critique illegitimately into the conventions of the world, it will only deny those very conventions which, *understood as mere conventions,* are usually held (by the dGe lugs pa as well as others) to be safe from violation by the Prāsaṅgika critique and a bastion against nihilism. Such an insertion may also place these 'pseudo-Prāsaṅgikas' among

---

[33] de lta bur don mngon sum grub kyang de'i tha snyad mi sbyor ba gzhan yang yod de / spyi yis dben pa'i ba lang mngon sum mthong yang gzegs zan pa blo gros phyin ci log tu gyur pa dag gis ba lang spyi dang ldan par khas len pa dang / tshor ba shes pa'i rang bzhin du rang rig gis myong yang / grangs can pa sogs kyis bems po'i ngo bor khas len pa yin la / de bzhin du phyi rol pa dag gis rang rig pa mi srid ces smra ba'ang yin no //.

non-Buddhist theorists whose views are not only false but positively unhelpful in the spiritual path.

Mi pham holds that it is clear from all of this that there is no point in either side simply appealing to textual quotations in proof of their thesis. The position has to be demonstrated by reasoning.[34] After all, it would seem that Hindus such as the followers of Sāṃkhya also hold in common with certain Buddhists that there is no such thing as the reflexivity of consciousness, while there are other Hindus and Buddhists who embrace the thesis of reflexivity, yet clearly they do not share authoritative texts in common. Texts have to be put to one side here, and an appeal has to be made to reasoning. In directing attention to the centrality of critical reasoning at this point, perhaps Mi pham also wanted to jar his dGe lugs opponents out of their 'dogmatic slumbers', their routine appeal to set textual quotations and perhaps also set debate structures which, in following the perspectives and arguments of Tsong kha pa, rGyal tshab rje and mKhas grub rje (it could be argued) seemed progressively less capable

---

[34] des na rang rig tha snyad du yod med rigs pas grub bya yin pas na lung kho nas dgag pa'am sgrub par byed pa ni don ci yang med do //. Cf. the comments in 'Mi pham's testament' (Dudjom Rinpoche 1991, pp. 872-3): 'Nonetheless, if I state what may be proven, or disproven, by relying upon the immaculate transmitted precepts of the Sugata and the commentaries on their intention, which are the lamp-like words of the great promulgators of India and Tibet, and by examining for myself, too, what is reasonable, and what is unreasonable, it may still be of some benefit to others, though I have no idea who can benefit whom....Therefore, if those who possess the eye of the doctrine refute me in accord with correct scriptural authority and logic, I should rely upon them like doctors.' Of course, Mi pham *does* make use of authoritative sources in molding his understanding in general, but it is of no use simply to appeal to authoritative sources here in order to settle the issue.

of generating new thoughts or a fresh perspective. Here, Mi pham certainly considered that a new look, a fresh perspective was needed by his dGe lugs opponents, for he felt that they were quite evidently wrong in their denial of the conventional status of *svasaṃvedana,* when *svasaṃvedana* is properly understood.

Mi pham's opponent, it seems, is not really prepared to accept such a radical division between reasoning and authoritative testimony. After all, in appealing to the arguments used by great scholars of the past one accepts the reasoning, but a reasoning which is enhanced precisely by the fact that it was employed by great scholars of the past, those whom we all accept were formidable scholars and practitioners of the Dharma (including, of course, Tsong kha pa, someone who had direct access to Mañjuśrī in order to settle issues of Madhyamaka). Thus Mi pham considers that an opponent may refer us back to the text of Śāntideva's *Bodhicaryāvatāra* itself. Is there not reasoning in that text which shows that there is no need for the existence of *svasaṃvedana*, even conventionally? There is no doubt that Śāntideva reasons against the classic memory argument for self-awareness by arguing that memory, say, of blue can occur on the basis of having previously experienced blue even without having known *that* one experienced blue. The knowing-that does not have to accompany the knowing in order for us now to remember the knowing. The example used by Śāntideva is the strange case of the poisonous rat (or mole—*Bodhicaryāvatāra* 9:24 (Tib. 23)).

An unfortunate person (it is sometimes said to be a poor old bear while hibernating) is bitten by a poisonous rat. He does not know, however, that as well as being bitten he has also been poisoned (perhaps the bear was drowsy with sleep at the time). Much later, in springtime (when the thunder of the spring rains occurs, our bear awakes) our unfortunate person infers from the fact that he does not feel so good and, remembering being bitten by the rat, that actually he must have been not only bitten but also poisoned by the rat. In the case of the poisoning the person is not *remembering* that something experienced occurred. Rather he is inferring the occurrence of something not actually experienced at the time, something which, nevertheless, accompanied an experience of being bitten. What Śāntideva appears to want to say, therefore, is that in a memory of seeing blue I remember blue but infer *seeing* blue, although at the time there was only the experience of blue, not a concurrent experience of seeing blue (i.e., self-awareness as well). In remembering seeing blue I remember blue but infer (if I wish) seeing blue. I am not also remembering {seeing blue}. Memory will not serve to establish *svasaṃvedana*.[35] It is clear from this, Mi

[35] This appears to be the obvious way to take what Śāntideva is saying, and is certainly how he is taken by Tsong kha pa (1970, pp. 26-7), who points out that remembering blue is all there is to it. There is no need for a further factor of 'remembering seeing blue' (although it is of course possible to infer from this that one *did* see blue). A memory of blue is a memory of blue, although if it is a *memory* of blue then that implies seeing blue: sngon po myong ba'i rtags las sngon po rig pa sngon du song bar grub la / sngon po rig par grub pa nyid kyis rig pa tsam du grub zin pa'i phyir / rang rig la sogs pa'i sgrub byed gzhan rtog pa don med do /. As we shall see, this argument misses the point of what Śāntarakṣita or Mi pham would want to say. We can remember blue because we had an *experience* of blue. But (it is claimed) it is a condition of experiences that all consciousness is reflexive. Thus, it is a condition of remembering blue that the original consciousness of blue was reflexive (as Mi pham will put it, had both subject and object). We speak of this as remembering not just blue but remembering also experi-

pham's opponent suggests, that Śāntideva thinks that *svasaṃvedana* is completely unnecessary to memory, including, of course, memory understood as an ordinary conventional transactional phenomenon. Therefore, Śāntideva can indeed be taken as holding that there is no such thing as *svasaṃvedana* even conventionally.[36]

Mi pham wants to make it quite clear that he is far from disagreeing with Śāntideva. He accepts that it looks *as if* there is a refutation of *svasaṃvedana* conventionally in Śāntideva's reasoning here, but Mi pham's appeal would be to the context of the *Bodhicaryāvatāra*—where the refutation is of those who would use memory in order to establish the real inherent existence of *svasaṃvedana*—and also his sense of *svasaṃvedana* as the reflexive nature of consciousness itself, consciousness as consciousness. For memory to occur

encing blue. This is, however, a misleading way of putting it. There were not two *different acts* taking place, one of which could be remembered and the other inferred. Rather, Śāntarakṣita or Mi pham would want to claim, there was one act of seeing blue out of which we can isolate here two components ('blue' and 'seeing'). Thus, if we remember blue it is implicit in that very memory that we saw blue, and therefore in the original experience there was not only blue but also seeing blue, i.e. in order for it to be an *experience* it had to contain both components and since in remembering blue one is remembering an experience of blue so the original experience as a consciousness involves reflexivity. The priority in memory is on a previous *experience* as a condition of memory, not its object.

[36] Mi pham 1975b, p. 207: gal te rang rig med kyang dran pa skye tshul byi bas rmugs pa'i dug la dper byas pa 'dis rang rig tha snyad du bkag pa ji ltar min te / don dam par rang rig med kyang dran pa skye tshul yod ces ni sgrub mi srid la / byi bas rmug pa tsam myong dus dug gtan nas ma myong ba bzhin sngar myong byed rang gis rang gtan ma myong yang [208] phyis sngar gyi myong byed kyi rnam par bzung bar bstan pa min nam zhe na /.

without *svasaṃvedana* in *this* (conventional, transactional) sense would be for memory to occur without there having been any consciousness in the original experience. As Mi pham has pointed out so many times, it simply does not follow that because there is a refutation of an attempt to establish the real ultimate existence of *x*, so there is a repudiation of *x* even conventionally.[37] And in this Mi pham is surely right. If those Indian scholars whom the Tibetan tradition classified as Prāsaṅgikas considered that they were refuting in their Mādhyamika analyses the existence of (certain) conventional possibles from a conventional as well as an ultimate point of view they would surely have said so, or made it reasonably clear that they were doing so. One feels that it never crossed the minds of Prāsaṅgikas prior, quite possibly, to Tsong kha pa himself, that the Prāsaṅgika refutation of *svasaṃvedana* extended to its conventional as well as its ultimate existence.

In actual fact, Mi pham points out, we all agree that there is a mind which experiences, for example, blue as its referential object. That is not a matter of dispute. Now, Mi pham continues, even though there does not exist transactionally in the world another mind (another mental state) which, concurrently with the apprehension of blue, also experiences that apprehension of blue—that is, it is not that there are two mental acts, seeing blue and the apprehension of seeing blue—still through the very experience of blue there does occur (as what it is to have that experience) the

37 de ltar shin tu yang yin te rang rig med kyang dran pa skye tshul tha snyad las 'os med pa yin mod / de 'dra'i sbyor ba de bkod tshod la rang rig tha snyad du 'gog pa ltar snang yang / song tshod la don dam par bkag par song gi tha snyad du kheg mi srid do //.

convention 'apprehension of blue'. Since this is the case it is quite rational to maintain that in the case of a memory of blue (an object) there is memory also of the apprehension of blue, its original subject. At the time of the original experience there were both object and subject. At the time of memory also there is a mere memory of a subject co-ordinated with an object, since in experience subject and object are actually one continuum. In other words, in the very memory of blue, as part of that very memory, there has to be memory of seeing blue. That is what memory is. There is a sense in which the very memory of blue *is* a memory of seeing blue. There cannot be memory of an object (blue) without memory of a subject (seeing blue). The two are not such separate and separable things. For Mi pham all this should be quite obvious to any of us if we examine what it is to have a memory, not in the sense of some sort of putative inherently-existent memory established under critical analysis by holders of non-Prāsaṅgika tenets, but rather what it is to have a memory in our common everyday experience. Since this should be quite obvious to us, it cannot be that memory as implicating consciousness *qua* consciousness, i.e. reflexivity as a conventional transactional phenomenon, is being refuted by Śāntideva here. Thus, for Mi pham, what Śāntideva is actually saying is that if one carries out a critical ultimate examination, other than in the mere mode of unexamined worldly transaction there are not established any memory experiences. What this amounts to is that for Śāntideva's reasoning there exists a mere apprehension of blue, which apprehension is the subject. But there does not exist even conventionally in addition to it a separate subjective aspect which is aware of that or experiences it.[38] Conventional reflexivity is not a separate subjective aspect, but is the nature

[38] ji ltar zhe na yul sngon po lta bu myong ba'i blo ni kun la rtsod med du grub la / sngo 'dzin de yang myong ba'i blo gnyis pa zhig 'jig rten na tha snyad du med kyang sngon po myong ba'i stobs kyis sngo 'dzin zhes tha snyad thob pa de bzhin phyis sngon po dran pa na de'i yul can sngo 'dzin kyang dran rigs te sngar myong dus kyang yul yul can gnyis po de tsam zhig yin la / phyis dran dus kyang yul dang 'brel par yul can dran pa tsam ste rgyud gcig gi dbang du byas pa'i phyir ro // de yang ma brtags pa 'jig rten tha snyad kyi tshul tsam las don dam par brtags na myong dran gang yang mi 'grub ces pa'i don to // des na de 'dra'i ngag sbyor des yul can sngo 'dzin tsam zhig yod kyi slar yang de rig pa'am myong bar byed pa'i 'dzin rnam yan gar ba tha snyad du yang med par dgag pa'i don du song ba yin no //. Note that for Mi pham, therefore, Śāntideva is refuting any notion of a separate subjective aspect experiencing a separate objective aspect, in other words self-awareness (i) as understood by, say, Cittamātra. We have seen already that Mi pham's sense of self-awareness is not self-awareness (i) but rather self-awareness (ii) which, understood correctly as conventional, therefore, does not come within the scope of Śāntideva's argument. We should note also that Mi pham appears to suggest in all of this that (like himself) Śāntideva holds it impossible for there to be memory except on the basis of the conventional existence of *svasaṃvedana*. However, with the example of the rat Śāntideva seems clearly to be arguing that *svasaṃvedana* cannot be proved at all on the basis of the memory argument. That there was an experience of blue is not remembered but inferred on the basis of remembering blue. It is perfectly plausible to argue that Śāntideva's context shows a refutation of attempts to establish *svasaṃvedana* under ultimate analysis through the memory argument, and thus refutes *svasaṃvedana* only ultimately but not conventionally. Śāntideva is unconcerned with (unaware of the issue of) whether *svasaṃvedana* exists conventionally or not. That is up to 'the world' on its own grounds. But for Mi pham's understanding of *svasaṃvedana* as reflexivity, since all consciousness involves *svasaṃvedana* and memory involves consciousness, it is perfectly legitimate for Śāntideva's opponent to argue that if there is memory there must, never-

of consciousness itself. What Śāntideva refutes as not existent even conventionally is a separate (and, by implication, inherently existent) subjective aspect in addition to the primary referential consciousness of blue.

Mi pham's opponent remains thoroughly unconvinced with this as an explanation of Śāntideva's intention. He points out that Śāntideva could not be refuting anyone who held *svasaṃvedana* to be a separate subjective aspect, since that would not be what we mean by 'self-awareness'. A subjective aspect which is actually a separate mental state from that of which it is aware would not be self-awareness at all. Since it would be another conscious state, it would in fact be a form of 'other-awareness', referential awareness. Moreover, it would also be necessary to accept an infinite regress of subjective aspects, since each separate mental state would be a separate consciousness and, if consciousness entails self-awareness and *that* is what we mean by 'self-awareness', each consciousness would require to be known by a further separate subjective aspect *ad infinitum.* There would be many such absurdities and, for this reason, Mi pham's critic points out, among those who hold to Sautrāntika and Cittamātra

theless, be *svasaṃvedana.* The problem is that this is taken as an argument for the inherent existence of *svasaṃvedana.* In spite of his claim that the appeal should be to reasoning and not to the testimony of great scholars of the past, Mi pham is not prepared to countenance that Śāntideva's own understanding is actually anything other than Mi pham's own (i.e., fully correct). Thus Śāntideva cannot be refuting the involvement of *svasaṃvedana* in memory, pure and simple. Rather, he is here refuting any suggestion that there could be memory if there were to be inherent existence. How this relates to the example of our poor invalid (or bear) and his (or her) rat (or mole) is not very clear.

treatises there does not exist a single scholar who accepts that sort of *svasaṃvedana*. In other words, if Śāntideva were here intending to refute *svasaṃvedana* as a separate subjective aspect, he would be refuting a view clearly not held by his doctrinal opponents. The ordinary common folk of the world also do not hold such a view. Thus, such a negation would not relate to anyone.[39] The point of Mi pham's opponent here is that Mi pham cannot possibly be right in thinking that his elaborate interpretation could have been Śāntideva's intention, for if it were, then Śāntideva would have been attacking a view held by no one, and certainly not the view of those non-Prāsaṅgikas who hold *svasaṃvedana* as one of their tenets and who were supposed to be the target of Śāntideva's attack. True to the opponent's reintroduction of textual hermeneutics in reaction to Mi pham's appeal for objective reasoning, whether Mi pham's overall project is coherent or not, he could not be offering a correct interpretation of Śāntideva.

Mi pham's response to all of this is that there is a point which needs to be understood very clearly. If someone affirms self-awareness as truly established, that is as inherently existent, they would not be accepting (as does Mi pham) *svasaṃvedana* as simply a secondary conceptual existent rather than a primary existent.[40] In other words, they would be making the

---

39 gal te 'di snyam du yul can de las blo yan gar ba zhig yin na rang rig kyang min te shes pa gzhan gyis gzhan rig par 'gyur zhing gzhan yang [209] 'dzin rnam thug med du 'dod dgos pa sogs kyi skyon mtha' yas pas na mdo sems kyi gzhung smra ba dag la de 'dra'i rang rig khas len mkhan gcig kyang med la 'jig rten tha mal pas kyang de 'dra khas mi len pas dgag pa de lta bu 'brel pa ci yang med par 'gyur ro snyam na /.

40 'di ni shin tu gsal por go dgos pa'i gnad gcig yin te / gang zhe na rang rig bden grub tu khas len na rdzas su med par btags

strongest possible ontological claim, rather than the weakest possible claim (which is what Mi pham is making) for *svasaṃvedana*. It would follow from this, Mi pham observes, that they would also have to accept activity, agent and action as established from their own side. Under such circumstances, the subjective aspect which is the agent of awareness (*rig byed*) directed towards the apprehension of blue which is the referent of awareness here (or 'that apprehending of blue which is the actual activity of awareness' (*rig bya*)) would necessarily exist as a separate entity. Thus regardless of what the explicit tenets of non-Prāsaṅgika systems are, if they affirm a *svasaṃvedana* as inherently existent and thereby existent in a manner not acceptable to the Prāsaṅgika they must, to be consistent, also affirm *svasaṃvedana* as a separate subjective aspect. It is not surprising that such a separate subjective aspect is found to be incoherent. The point is not whether this is a tenet of Śāntideva's opponents or not. The issue is whether these opponents can be forced into accepting such an unwelcome conclusion. Such a separate subjective aspect does not actually exist, since if a conceptually constructed object *(btags don)* where one acts as an agent on oneself (i.e., self-reference) is critically examined it is not found. In other words a self-referential awareness cannot be found under the sort of critical analysis which searches for putative separate inherent existents. Since such a self-referential awareness is not found under this sort of ultimate analysis, that which is spo-

---

pa tsam gyis ni rang rig gi go mi chod cing /. On the terminology of 'primary existent' for *dravyasat/rdzas yod,* and 'secondary existent' for *prajñaptisat/btags yod* in the context of their original usage in the Abhidharma see my 1981 article.

ken of as 'self-awareness' too is merely a transactional convention. It has no ultimate status.[41]

Mi pham agrees with his opponent that self-awareness would not be possible if it did exist as a separate entity. A separate self-awareness would indeed be a form of other-awareness, not reflexively aware of itself at all. It is this separate self-awareness which is spoken of as not existing even according to transactional convention. Self-awareness must by definition be reflexivity, where that which is aware and that of which it is aware are substantially the same entity.[42] Also, Mi pham adds, what was affirmed by the other side does not exist. If we return the discussion of *svasaṃvedana* to its context within both the *Bodhicaryāvatāra* and the *Madhyamakāvatāra* then we can

---

[41] bya byed las gsum yang rang ngos nas grub dgos pas na rig bya sngo 'dzin de la rig byed kyi 'dzin rnam yan gar du yod dgos te de med par rang gis rang la byed pa 'jug pa'i btags don dpyod na mi rnyed pa'i phyir ro //. On the basis of Mi pham's text earlier (see above, note 8) where *rig bya* clearly refers to the actual activity of awareness, plus the parallel earlier in this sentence with *bya byed las* it is possible to take it that *rig bya sngo 'dzin* here refers to the apprehending of blue which is the activity of awareness. It is more likely, however, that it refers to the apprehension of blue which is the referent of awareness *(bya ba* as *karman (= rig bya'i bya)* rather than *kriyā)*. See above, note 29 for a previous example where *rig bya* must mean the referent of awareness, and also cf. below note 58.

[42] It is clear in context that it is not that the separate self-awareness is an unrealized possible for Mi pham, which could be shown not to exist conventionally by some further form of (conventional) analysis in addition to the Prāsaṅgika's ultimate analysis. Rather, were there to exist such a separate *svasaṃvedana,* it would be inherently existent. Inherently existent entities can only exist ultimately, and therefore if they do not exist they do not exist completely, even conventionally. Thus their conventional existence is refuted implicitly in the Prāsaṅgika ultimate analysis.

see, Mi pham continues, that it is the negation of a truly established self-awareness of that type which is the very basis for criticizing the tenet-system of those who hold as truly established a consciousness which is empty of duality. If there were really an inherently existent reflexive consciousness, then the position of Cittamātra that 'all is mind-only' would be as good as established, since if that were the nature of consciousness then consciousness could indeed know nothing other than itself. In other words, for Śāntideva, and indeed for Candrakīrti, as Prāsaṅgikas, the context of their refutation of *svasaṃvedana* is one of refuting an inherently-existent self-aware consciousness for which *svasaṃvedana* provides a crucial support. It is nothing to do with an issue of the conventional status of consciousness. If one critically examines as something postulated as true, and not merely a conceptual construct, both *svasaṃvedana,* which is the means for proving such a consciousness, and the self-luminous consciousness which is what is to be proved, then such reasoning would show what is in fact a conceptually constructed object as not established. Under such conditions there could be no such thing: an inherently existent *svasaṃvedana* and self-luminous consciousness simply do not exist. It is in this way also, Mi pham tells us, that we should understand the discussions in other texts where reasoning refuting *svasaṃvedana* is given.[43]

[43] ma rnyed na rang rig ces pa'ang tha snyad tsam du 'gyur gyi don dam par mi 'gyur ro // yang gar du yod na'ang rang rig par mi 'thad la de 'dra tha snyad du'ang med cing pha rol gyis khas blangs kyang med pa de ltar rang rig bden grub bkag pa de kho nas gnyis stong gi rnam shes bden grub tu smra ba'i grub mtha'i lugs la gnod pa brjod pa'i gtso bo yin te / rnam shes kyi sgrub byed rang rig dang bsgrub bya rang gsal gyi shes pa gnyis ka btags pa tsam las yang dag par dpyad na btags

Mi pham turns next to the common example of the inability of a sword to cut itself, an example used in the sūtras against the possibility of self-awareness. Of course, he says, if one considers this example then clearly it is the case even from a conventional transactional perspective that a sword cannot cut itself. Thus one might think that the use of such examples indicates that even from a conventional perspective consciousness also cannot be aware of itself. But this does not follow. The mere use of such an example does not necessarily indicate that its subject is nonexistent *even conventionally*. The example of a sword shows that consciousness cannot refer to itself. The fact that there is *also* no such thing even conventionally as a sword that can cut itself does not necessarily entail for Mi pham that there is no self-awareness even conventionally. Otherwise, when one mentions the son of a barren woman and so on as examples for the nonorigination of such things as a pot it would follow that the pot does not exist even conventionally. Take the argument: 'A pot does not originate from itself, from other, from both or from no cause at all—as in the case of the son of a barren woman'. It does not follow that because the son of a barren woman does not originate at all, even conventionally, so a pot also does not originate at all, even conventionally. Clearly, conventionally a pot does originate, and this is a point important to the dGe lugs perspective on Madhyamaka and its wish to preserve at all costs the conventional as conventional. The use of an example is proportionate only to its context and purpose and should not be applied in order to draw wider conclusions. If we did take the example of

don ma grub par rigs pa de kho nas gtan la phab pa yin no // [210] de dang rigs mthun par rang rig 'gog pa'i rigs pa gzhung gzhan las gsungs pa dag kyang de ltar shes par bya'o //.

the sword to mean that there is no self-awareness even conventionally, Mi pham continues, then it would follow that there would not exist, even conventionally, direct perceptual consciousness by oneself of one's own mind, which is quite absurd; Mi pham intends to return to this point later as well.[44]

Therefore, even though—when subjected to an examination of it as something postulated as true, or inherently existent—what is referred to as self-awareness is not established, nevertheless Mi pham is quite clear there is no harm done to the Prāsaṅgika perspective by a *svasaṃvedana* that is conceptually constructed in dependence upon the isolate. This self-awareness is not a separate reality, but the nature of consciousness itself as reflexivity, luminosity. Nevertheless, it can be distinguished in discourse, and it is therefore conceptually constructed as an entity in dependence upon the isolate. This does not contradict anything essential to the Prāsaṅgika and should thus be no cause for worry to a follower of Prāsaṅgika tenets. On the other hand it does not follow from the fact that *y* is not incompatible with *x* that *x* includes *y*. Still, for Mi pham not only is *svasaṃvedana* not incompatible with Prāsaṅgika Madhyamaka, but the Prāsaṅgika (perhaps within the wider context of system building or practice) would positively benefit from understanding the conventional existence of reflexive self-awareness. It is 'like a medicine which be-

[44] de'i phyir ral gri'i dpe la sogs pa la bsams na ral gri rang gis rang tha snyad du gcod pa med mod kyi / de tsam gyis dpe can tha snyad du yang med mi dgos te bum sogs skye med kyi dper mo gsham bu sogs bkod pa bzhin no // de lta min na rang blo rang gis mngon sum shes pa tha snyad du yang med par 'gyur te 'og tu yang 'chad par 'gyur ro //.

stows benefit' *(phan byed kyi sman ltar 'gyur te)*.[45] Thus, while Mi pham seems to hold in general that the Prāsaṅgika does not *negate* the conventional existence of *svasaṃvedana,* he wants to urge the positive counterpart: that, conventionally, consciousness is indeed characterized by reflexivity and there are positive benefits to be gained by the Prāsaṅgika as much as anyone else in realizing this fact and incorporating it into one's system. For a full understanding the Prāsaṅgika perspective needs to be supplemented. Clearly *svasaṃvedana* is necessary to experience, and therefore to a comprehensive system which will fully validate conventional life as a basis for the spiritual path. But one feels that not least among the benefits of acknowledging conventional *svasaṃvedana* for Mi pham must be the importance of the self-luminous reflexive nature of consciousness as such in rDzogs chen and Mahāmudrā meditation (see next chapter).

The ontological status of reflexivity as something conceptually constructed through language, in dependence upon the isolate, Mi pham continues, is in this respect similar to cases where there are worldly linguistic conventions such as 'the head of Rāhu'. In the case of the Indian myth of Rāhu, Rāhu managed to drink the gods' elixir of immortality but was beheaded by Viṣṇu for his impertinence. Rāhu is now a star, an immortal disembodied head which chases the sun and moon, swallowing them at eclipses. The sun and moon reappear after passing through the neck of Rāhu. When we speak of 'the head of Rāhu' the implication might be that there is an attached body

---

45 de'i phyir rang rig ces pa yang dag par dpyad na ma grub kyang ldog pa la brten nas rang rig tu btags pa de 'dra ni thal 'gyur ba'i lugs la gnod pa med par ma zad phan byed kyi sman ltar 'gyur te.

referred to as 'Rāhu' for which this is the head. But the expression 'the head of Rāhu' is simply a worldly convention (and there is nothing wrong with that). It should not be taken to have existential implications. Any implications are simply the results of linguistic structure. There is in fact really only a head there. Likewise, when we speak of self-awareness it is not that consciousness really knows itself, in the way consciousness might know Archibald or turnips. There is really only consciousness, a consciousness which precisely has the luminous and aware nature of consciousness. That luminous and aware nature is its reflexivity. A suitability to posit the transactional conventions of activity and agent in accordance with the world, Mi pham points out, is in fact a dimension of the position of the Prāsaṅgika Candrakīrti not held in common with other systems. Thus, for the Prāsaṅgika of all people, there should be no problem in accepting as merely conventional whatever are the linguistic isolates familiar in worldly discourse. There need be no ontologically unacceptable implications, and under these circumstances and the interpretation which he has given, Mi pham feels there need be no difficulty for the Prāsaṅgika in actually accepting *svasaṃvedana* as it is patently understood in transactional convention. In the world, even in the case of someone like an old man, when he experiences through direct perception a pot and so on, there is an error-free experience in which he clearly experiences his own mind. Thus the contention that one knows one's own mind by oneself is also well-known as admitted in the world.[46]

---

46 gang gis na sgra gcan gyi mgo zhes sgra gcan ni sngon dus su mgo bcad de bdud rtsi 'thungs pa'i stobs kyis ma shi bar 'jig rten na rgyu zhes 'dod pa las de la mgo las gzhan pa'i lus med

Having responded with hermeneutics and critical reasoning to an opponent who wished still to have recourse to authoritative testimony, Mi pham too introduces textual support for his perspective. One perfect source for Mi pham's purposes (as yet untraced) tells us that happiness and so on are indeed experienced. The apprehension of happiness does not occur to some other person. Therefore, it is understood that 'the mind is aware of itself', and this is also exactly the way it is according to worldly transactional convention. In other words, 'self-awareness' is to be understood structurally as meaning that one's experiences are not experienced, not known, by someone else, and yet they are still experiences, still acts of consciousness. Therefore, we have *self*-awareness. That is all. For Mi pham this should be obvious to everyone, and

---

kyang 'jig rten na de 'dra'i tha snyad byed pa dang / de bzhin du mchig gu'i lus zhes pa la sogs pa yan lag dang yan lag can gyi tha snyad de dag ming gis btags pa tsam gyis bzhag pa la'ang 'jig rten gyi ngor bya byed kyi tha snyad 'jog rung bar dpal ldan zla ba'i bzhed pa thun mongs min pa yin pa'i phyir na / de 'dra'i tha snyad kyi rnam bzhag rung ba de la rang rig gi tha snyad de [211] ltar mi rung ba ci yang med la / 'jig rten rgan pos kyang bum sogs mngon sum myong ba bzhin rang blo gsal por myong ba'i nyams myong bslu med 'di las rang sems rang gis shes zhes kha len par yongs su grags pa'ang yin pa'i phyir ro //. As regards this last comment, one should remember that for Mi pham (following Dignāga and Dharmakīrti, and indeed Śāntarakṣita) 'one directly experiences one's own mind' is equivalent to 'in one's own cognitive act *x* one's own mind is not unknown and it is not necessary for another mental act to be employed in order to know one's own mind'. That in our normal everyday experience another mental act is not required in order to know one's own mind is quite obvious to anyone. It is error-free *(bslu med)* since we cannot be in doubt or mistaken as to whether we are experiencing our own minds or not. It is for such reasons that Dignāga in his *Pramāṇasamuccaya* included *svasaṃvedana* under direct perception.

not controversial.[47] Thus, Mi pham comments (with a certain degree of humor) that if *svasaṃvedana* is accepted in this way on the grounds of mere unexamined conventional transaction, in conformity with the world, then for a system such as this there would occur great happiness! Mi pham quotes also from a rather Cittamātra portion of the *Ghanavyūha Sūtra.* All the manifold appearance is actually one's own mind. The mind does indeed see itself although it is not realized. This claim provides an ideal quote for Mi pham to counter the often-quoted scriptural reference to the mind being unable to see itself 'as a knife cannot cut itself'. Mi pham gives also a tantric source, the *bDe mchog 'byung ba sogs sngags kyi rgyud* which follows Śāntarakṣita in maintaining that since it is not insentient, the mind is aware of its own nature.[48]

---

[47] If there is an experience of happiness it makes no sense to wonder if the experience of happiness is experienced. Part of what it is to have an experience of happiness is that it is not {not-experienced}. Thus the experience of happiness is indeed an *awareness.* Moreover, if I have an experience of happiness it also makes no sense to ask whether it is happening to me or to another. It is not {not-me}. The awareness and awareness *by me* are not additional factors to the experience of happiness. They are involved in what it is to be an experience of happiness, and the appeal here is to our own everyday experience. Thus we can speak of the experience of happiness as involving 'self-awareness'. End of the matter.

[48] des na // gang phyir gang gis yul myong gyur de las // zhes sogs gsungs pa bzhin du / gang phyir bde sogs nyams su myong de las // 'dzin pa 'di gzhan nga la yod min pa // de phyir rang sems rig ces rtogs 'gyur te // 'di yang 'jig rten tha snyad tshul lugs yin // ces 'jig rten pa dang mthun par ma brtags tha snyad tsam gyi dbang du rang rig khas blangs na'ang lugs de la shin tu bde bar 'gyur zhing / rgyan stug po bkod po'i mdo las / sna tshogs snang ba rang sems te // lus can rnams kyi bdag nyid gnyis // phyi dang nang dang thams cad du // gzung dang 'dzin pa lta bur gnas // sems kyis sems ni

Mi pham had promised earlier to return to the issue of the relationship between self-awareness and the way by which we know our ordinary everyday experiences. While the Prāsaṅgika is not *necessarily* committed *qua* Prāsaṅgika to an acceptance of *svasaṃvedana* conventionally (although he or she is for Mi pham committed to not denying it conventionally), nevertheless we have seen that Mi pham holds there are benefits to be derived from its acceptance. An acceptance of conventional transaction as what it is—conventional transaction and no more—would appear to be a central part of Candrakīrti's system, and in order to be fully coherent and consistent Mi pham considers that the Prāsaṅgika should within the wider context positively accept the conventional existence of the reflexive nature of consciousness. After all, the Prāsaṅgika too is part of the ordinary conventional world and holds whatever is held by the ordinary conventional world (inasmuch as it is held conventionally by the conventional sources most qualified to judge). In fact even those who hold to the Prāsaṅgika system have to admit that either (i) one knows one's own mind by direct perception or (ii) one's mind is not so known.[49] If one knows one's own

---

mthong yin yang // khong du mi chud dus pa rnams // kha gnyis sems de lus can gyi // yin yang shes par ma gyur pa // bdag gir byed pa'ang de bzhin byed // yul lta bur yang rab tu snang // rdza ma la sogs gzugs su gnas // rdza la sogs pa'ang yod ma yin // 'di yi don la thub pa dag // [212] rnal 'byor nyam chung rnam par myos // zhes dang / bde mchog 'byung ba sogs sngags kyi rgyud las kyang / bems po min phyir bdag nyid rig // ces gsungs so //.

49 Note that Mi pham would consider this investigation to be an example of using a conventional type of reasoning to establish conventional truths. The conventional is not *irrational,* it only fails to be founded when subjected to ultimate analysis

mind by direct perception, then either (a) one's mind is known as self-illuminating or (b) it is known because there is, on the one hand, the consciousness which is the cause to be known and, on the other, there exists a separate substance as a verifying consciousness which knows it.

In the case of (i)(a), of course, we have in fact (conventionally) established self-awareness. In the case of (i)(b) then necessarily either (I) that verifying consciousness is simultaneous with that mind which is the cause to be known; or (II) the mind to be known is known by something which occurs after it. Supposing it is suggested that the verifying consciousness is *not* simultaneous with the mind which is to be known (i.e., (II)). Under such circumstances, Mi pham argues, it is difficult to see how it could be direct perception when it is of a referential object which at that time does not exist. Moreover, it would also be necessary to deal with such problems as whether the consciousness of something seen outwardly and that of something seen inwardly are mixed or not. Perhaps one can reconstruct the argument here as follows: Supposing one sees a strawberry and also feels happiness at the sight. If the verifying consciousness which is (according to Dharmakīrti involved and expressed in) feeling happy at the sight occurs after the experience of the strawberry has ceased, then there is a real problem concerning our actual experience of seeing the strawberry *and* feeling happiness at the sight,

---

which searches for inherent existence. Mi pham is perfectly aware of Prāsaṅgika arguments aimed against similar trains of reasoning which as far as he is concerned seek to establish *svasaṃvedana* as an inherently-existent reality found under ultimate analysis. Cf. here also Tsong kha pa (1973b, pp. 177-9; Thurman trans. pp. 320-1) and mKhas grub rje's *sTong thun chen mo* (text pp. 420, 424 ff; Cabezón pp. 347, 350 ff.).

which appear not only to be simultaneous but also to be, as it were, mixed in one experience. If they are mixed in one experience then obviously the consciousness of happiness could not occur after the experience of the strawberry has ceased. On the other hand the other option that there exists a separate verifying consciousness which is simultaneous with each consciousness (option (I)) is also not a viable alternative. By whom (or what) is such a second mind cognised as existing? Mi pham's point here is probably both an empirical one—that we all know from our own experience that we simply do not have a separate additional consciousness which accompanies every consciousness and makes it known to us—and also (far more vicious) the problem of an infinite regress which Mi pham will highlight next. Moreover, it is scarcely satisfactory to try to maintain as another option the existence of a separate simultaneous verifying consciousness for each conscious act even were such a verifying consciousness not actually apprehended at all! Thus, Mi pham explains, if each mind or consciousness-event *(blo)* has a further different consciousness-event which is its apprehending subject there would occur innumerable faults, such as a vicious infinite regress of consciousness-events. If even a single separate subjective aspect is not possible, how much less likely would be the case with many of them![50]

---

50 de ltar min na thal 'gyur ba'i lugs 'dzin pa de dag gis rang gi blo rang gis mngon sum gyis shes par khas len nam mi shes par khas len / shes so zhe na rang gsal du shes pa yin nam shes par bya rgyu'i shes pa dang shes byed rdzas gzhan du yod pas shes pa yin / dang po ltar na rang rig grub pa la // gnyis pa ltar na shes par bya rgyu'i blo de dang dus mnyam pa'i shes pa'am de'i rjes su skyes pa gang gis shes dgos / dus mi mnyam na yul da lta med pa la mngon sum ji ltar yin tshul dang kha

On the other hand, if we adopt option (ii) and take it that there in no way exists another apprehending subject for each cognitive act—in other words consciousness cannot *in any sense* be said to know itself—then, even though the eye might see a pot and so on it would not be able to see itself. Thus, one's own mind would indeed become an object hidden from oneself. Since, for Mi pham (as indeed for his dGe lugs critics), to be is to be a knowable, one's own mind is also a knowable and thus when it is occurring in an act of consciousness it, as well as the object, should be known. Otherwise, Mi pham implies, there would occur the paradoxical situation that although the object may (hypothetically) be known, one's own mind could only be known in the way that hidden objects are known, through inference (inference based on what previous experience?), and thus at the time the object is known the present mind knowing that object not only is not known but could never be known *as present mind*. Quite absurdly, one's own mind could never be known directly, in its very occurrence (and therefore as present). One's own mind as a present event would thereby in fact cease to be. It would always be past mind. All Mi pham's position on the conventional existence of reflexivity requires is a denial of this, a denial that one's mind as present is hidden from itself. If not only the object is known but also the mind actually knowing that object is not an object hidden to itself, i.e. not {not-known}, Mi pham has es-

---

phyir bltas dang nang bltas kyi shes pa spel mar skye ba yin min sogs sgrub dgos la / dus mnyam na'ang de 'dra'i blo gnyis yod par gang gis shes te / ma bzung bar yang yod ces bya mi rung // zhes gsungs pa bzhin no // gal te blo thams cad la'ang 'dzin byed kyi blo gzhan re yod na blo thug pa med par 'gyur ba sogs skyon tshad med la 'dzin rnam yan gar ba gcig cig kyang mi srid na du ma lta ci smos pa'i phyir ro //.

tablished his position. He requires here absolutely nothing more, and it seems to him not only obvious, but also entailed by the dGe lugs position that to be is to be a knowable (Hopkins 1983, pp. 214-5).

Supposing one's own mind were an object hidden from oneself. In that case it could be known only through an inference. But such an inference would be impossible. Take the case of the inference, 'I have a consciousness, because I apprehend a strawberry'. First, Mi pham wants to say, there could be no possibility of the logical sign *(rtags)* 'because I apprehend a strawberry'. The consciousness directly perceiving that the conceptualized cognition *(kun rtog)* of what occurred in one's own mind was or was not like this or that, is under the circumstances of one's own mind being an object hidden from oneself simply not possible. In other words, even if hypothetically a direct perception of a strawberry did occur, since we do not know at the very same time *that* there has been any perception at all, how could there be the conceptualizing or constructing activity (such as blending with a generic image: see Klein 1986, ch. 4) which is necessary to everyday perceptual and conceptual discourse? We could never have the conceptualized cognition 'I apprehend a strawberry', and it is difficult to see how there can be an inference of one's own mind when there can be no logical sign on which to base the inference.[51] One cannot infer or derive *y* from *x* if

[51] 'dzin byed gzhan med na mig gis bum sogs mthong bar byed kyang rang mthong bar byed mi nus pa ltar rang blo rang ngor lkog tu gyur nas rang sems la gang skyes pa'i kun rtog [213] 'di dang 'di 'drar gyur ma gyur ces mngon sum shes mi srid na'ang rang la blo ji 'dra skyes pa de ni rtags la ltos mi dgos pa rang gis nges pa 'di ci zhig gis yin dpyad nas smra dgos so //. I have unpacked and reconstructed what I think is a plausible version of a very compressed argument here. Perhaps

one has no awareness of (the occurrence of) *x*. If one's own mind is an object hidden from oneself and is therefore not directly perceived then, with the failure of inference, by what could it be ascertained by oneself?

The opponent seems to want to suggest here that all this critical investigation of a hypothetical conventional *svasaṃvedana* is in some sense at variance with the project of Prāsaṅgika Madhyamaka. Perhaps it is not necessary to engage so minutely in such examination. For Mi pham, however, even if I am a Prāsaṅgika it is reasonable that I reply to the question of whether one's own mind is known by oneself or not. These are matters of conventional transactional experience. It is not a question of some sort of putative ultimate existence which might be negated by the Prāsaṅgika's ultimate investigation. The Prāsaṅgika can indeed claim that *qua* Prāsaṅgika he or she has no views on the matter, but he or she must be required to adopt some stance (if only implicitly) within the wider context of transactional activity, and even as a Prāsaṅgika—inasmuch as the Prāsaṅgika on these issues adopts conventionally whatever is held by the world providing it does not contradict the Prāsaṅgika perspective—he or she cannot evade the question of whether one's own mind is known by oneself or not.[52] If the answer is no, various unwelcome conclu-

there are other equally or more plausible versions—which is not to say that under such circumstances Mi pham would not have rather liked this one as well.

52 Note that in adopting conventionally whatever is accepted by the world providing it does not contradict the Prāsaṅgika perspective, it seems to me the Prāsaṅgika is not committed to the *final truth* of whatever is adopted, even conventionally. For example, in the Middle Ages the (Western) 'world' accepted as true (for the sake of argument) the Aristotelean cosmological

sions follow for the Prāsaṅgika as for anyone else. If the answer is yes—and for Mi pham there is absolutely no reason on Prāsaṅgika grounds why it should not be, once it is understood just what is and what is not entailed in the positive response—then the conventional existence of *svasaṃvedana* in Mi pham's sense will, in fact, be granted. For the Prāsaṅgika also cannot evade, if required, at least a minimal involvement with a further question, which is the manner by which consciousness knows itself *(shes tshul ji ltar yin)*? It is reasonable that even the Prāsaṅgika should respond to this question if asked.[53] It does not follow

vision. A Prāsaṅgika in Medieval Paris could accept the Aristotelean cosmology without being committed to the impossibility of any subsequent scientific falsification. In fact a Prāsaṅgika with his or her notion of the conventional as relative *may* be more open to the mutability of what counts as truth in the 'world' and the progressive yet ever-open non-finality of scientific truth. A scientist who is also a Prāsaṅgika could indeed engage in the enterprise of experimental falsification and thus perhaps change what the 'world' considers to be true. This need not be thought to contradict the acceptance of whatever is held to be true by the world, for (perhaps a Mi pham might argue) a Prāsaṅgika scientist can accept whatever is held to be true by the world *in the way whatever is held to be true by the world is accepted by a scientist,* that is, among other things, open to experimental falsification. How this falsification might come about and the conditions under which it could occur are conventional matters but are not incompatible with Prāsaṅgika Madhyamaka, although equally neither are they necessarily the concern of the Prāsaṅgika as such.

53 The mention of this point shows that Mi pham does not consider the fact that the Prāsaṅgika adopts conventionally whatever is accepted by the world to mean that the Prāsaṅgika is prevented from carrying out conventional investigation into the conventional grounding, explanation or coherence of the conventional. In other words, from the fact that one is a Prāsaṅgika it does not follow that one has to simply accept naively the everyday perspective of the 'person-in-the-street' (join

that the Prāsaṅgika normally has to go so far as to introduce arguments like the absence of any distinction in the manner of determination of the minds of oneself and others without the reflexivity of one's own awareness; in other words, the Prāsaṅgika does not *qua* Prāsaṅgika have to positively argue for the conventional existence of *svasaṃvedana.* Nevertheless, since conventionally we have seen that consciousness must know itself, the Prāsaṅgika cannot and does not actually negate the conventional existence of self-awareness.[54]

This is indeed how it is conceived by Dharmakīrti, who is in Buddhism, Mi pham tells us, the very crest-jewel of all those who declare conventional transactional awareness. The dGe lugs tradition, as is well-known, much admired Dharmakīrti and integrated Dharmakīrti's epistemology into their understanding and application of *inter alia* Prāsaṅgika Madhyamaka. Here once more Mi pham attempts to outdo the dGe lugs pas in what they themselves would see as their own area of expertise. In terms of epistemology—from the Prāsaṅgika point of view a conventional transactional concern—Dharmakīrti, the

---

Wittgenstein in his garden) and leave it at that. One *can* still investigate on the conventional level, and there are more or less satisfactory conventional explanations. Science is still possible.

[54] gal te de 'dra'i dpyad pa zhib mor gzhug mi dgos so snyam na rang sems rang gis shes sam mi shes zhes dri ba la thal 'gyur ba yin kyang lan 'debs rigs la / shes tshul ji ltar yin zhes dri na yang brjod par rigs pas na rang rig med na rang gzhan gyi blo gcod tshul khyad med du 'gyur ba sogs dgos med kyi dgag pa ma yin te /. The argument for reflexivity based on the absence of any distinction in the manner of determination of the minds of oneself and others can be found in Mi pham's commentary to *Bodhicaryāvatāra* 9, treated in chapter 5 above.

greatest of all epistemologists, accepts *svasaṃvedana*.[55] Indeed, Mi pham continues, *svasaṃvedana* is the very essence of Dharmakīrti's position. It is perfectly reasonable to ask that those who go round negating *svasaṃvedana* transactionally, maintaining that this very essence of Dharmakīrti's position is on the same footing as the son of a barren woman, should have to respond to the question of by what means consciousness knows itself.[56] For my part, Mi pham declares, I too am a Prāsaṅgika. As such, I would not normally need to give reasoning to show the conventional existence of *svasaṃvedana*. However, it is not rational that someone should go round expounding the view that self-awareness is proved to be nonexistent (even con-

---

[55] As we have seen, Mi pham follows Śāntarakṣita in seeing *svasaṃvedana* as reflexivity, the very nature of consciousness as consciousness. Śāntarakṣita himself often followed Dharmakīrti on issues of epistemology, but it seems likely that to take *svasaṃvedana* as the reflexive nature of consciousness itself is an innovation by Śāntarakṣita. If so, then Dharmakīrti's understanding of *svasaṃvedana* would presumably differ in certain rather important respects from that of Śāntarakṣita and Mi pham.

[56] It is worth noting Mi pham's point here. If self-awareness as taught by great Buddhist teachers like Dharmakīrti and Śāntarakṣita is not the case even conventionally then it is a complete fiction, and is no more real than the son of a barren woman (actually a logical contradiction). Is this really what the Prāsaṅgika wants to say? Actually Candrakīrti would appear to have no problem with declaring the tenets of great non-Prāsaṅgika teachers complete fictions (see *Madhyamakāvatārabhāṣya* on 6:26). After all, inherent existence is a complete fiction, yet it is taught one way or another, according to Prāsaṅgikas, in the tenet-systems of all but Prāsaṅgika Madhyamaka. Nevertheless, Mi pham feels not only that reasoning does not negate the conventional existence of *svasaṃvedana*, but reasoning and experience can actually demonstrate it.

ventionally) because such has been merely asserted, simply on the strength that it is a tenet.[57]

There is another point. Someone could still argue that even though one might conceive of self-awareness through the isolate of the subjective aspect, this is not acceptable since actually, in the case of self-awareness, activity and agent do not exist separately. That is (if we generalize the principle), there simply could not be a case where two things occur as separate for conceptual thought (different isolates) but are not actually separable (one entity). Were one to adopt this approach, Mi pham points out, there would be serious problems not least for certain important strategies within the dGe lugs perspective itself. If one denies the different isolates-one entity model, then one would have to deny also the single-nature relationship *(bdag gcig 'brel)* transactionally, since the same principle is operative both in the case of a relationship of something to its own nature and of self-awareness of one-

[57] sangs rgyas gyi bstan pa 'di la tha snyad kyi rig pa smra ba kun gyi gtsug gi nor bur gyur ba dpal chos kyi grags pas de ltar brtag pa mdzad pa yin na de'i bzhed pa'i snying po rang rig dang mo gsham gyi bu mgo mnyam par tha snyad du dgag pa smra ba rnams kyis de la lan tshul bzhin du bstan par rigs kyi / nged thal 'gyur ba'i lugs 'dzin pa yin pas rigs pa ma smras kyang grub mtha'i dbang gis rang rig med par dam bcas pa tsam gyis 'grub bo zhes brjod par ni mi rigs so //. What Mi pham appears to be saying with this last point is that normally the Prāsaṅgika would not need to give arguments to show the conventional existence of *svasaṃvedana.* However, the dGe lugs pa is saying that there is no *svasaṃvedana* even conventionally, and apparently has no compelling reason for this apart from the fact that it is given as a tenet of the Prāsaṅgika. It is, therefore, necessary for Mi pham to set forth the reasoning which shows that even for a Prāsaṅgika there is no objection to the conventional existence of self-awareness.

self.[58] If the single-nature relationship is not acceptable then there would be dramatic repercussions for the dGe lugs vision of Madhyamaka, since it would also follow that there would not exist even conventionally two truths, one entity.[59] Moreover, cognition of a referential object by nondual gnosis *(gnyis snang med pa'i ye shes)* would not be appropriate, since clearly for Mi pham subject and object in nondual gnosis are also

---

[58] gzhan yang 'dzin rnam gyi ldog pa nas rang rig tu btags kyang don la bya byed so sor med pas mi 'thad na bdag gcig 'brel yang tha snyad du med par kha len dgos te / bdag rang la rang 'brel ba dang rang gis rang rig pa gnyis [214] tshul 'dra ba'i phyir ro //. The expression *bya ba* as used here in 'activity and agent' *(bya byed)* would seem better suited to the *object* of the verbal action (referent, 'action'; *karman)* than the actual activity *(kriyā)* itself. The word *bya ba* is sometimes used in this way in Sanskrit grammar in Tibet, and we have also seen an example above (note 8) where *byed pa* appears to be used by Mi pham for *kriyā* (see Verhagen 1994, p. 339). Mi pham certainly does not always seem to keep *bya ba* and *las* separate. A single-nature relationship occurs when two 'things' are related inasmuch as they both have the same nature. If the one were not to exist, the other could not exist. It is employed in dGe lugs discussions of the two truths, for example. See the treatment in mKhas grub rje (text p. 439-40; Cabezón, pp. 363-4: 'Therefore, the two truths are of the same nature but have different opposites *(ngo bo gcig la ldog pa tha dad)*, having a single-nature relationship such that if one did not exist neither could the other *(med na mi 'byung ba'i bdag gcig 'brel)* just like production and impermanence.'), and also a reference to Tsong kha pa in Newland (1992), pp. 62-3. See Newland for an extensive discussion of the dGe lugs arguments against the two truths as either the same or different from each other. Among other things, one thing has a single nature relationship to itself. Of course, this involves one entity, different isolates—just as in the case of *svasaṃvedana*.

[59] On the use of the one entity-different isolates model in order to show the relationship between the two truths see Newland (1992), ch. 4.

one entity and two isolates.[60] Thus a Buddha, for example, would not see conventional objects. This is because in nondual gnosis either one cognizes in conformity with the nonappearance *dualistically* of object

---

60 The dGe lugs view of the Buddha's omniscience and nondual gnosis would seem to hold that the Buddha apprehends objects correctly, although still as objects. See mKhas grub rje (text p. 466; Cabezón p. 383): 'When, in this way, the Buddha's gnosis enters into emptiness, like water mixing with water, that gnosis directly and simultaneously understands conventional phenomena in such a way that they appear as dual, that is, as distant from the [consciousness] itself. Even though this dualistic appearance exists, however, it need not involve the error of dualistic appearance.' The question for Mi pham, however, is whether the dGe lugs pa accepts that in the Buddha's nondual gnosis objects are apprehended as one entity with the perceiving consciousness. If not, then this is not really nondual gnosis. If, however, objects are one entity with the perceiving consciousness then short of the single-nature relationship/different isolates-one-entity model the Buddha would not see conventional objects. See also Newland, ch. 12. On the rNying ma view, cf. Dudjom Rinpoche (1991), p. 215: 'In ultimate reality, all things should be known as the great sameness of reality, naturally without divisions and [the need for] clarification....all things subsumed by the relative and ultimate truths should be established as naturally indivisible, in the great pure sameness free from conceptual elaborations, the original natural expression of the buddhas.' Cf. also the contemporary bKa' brgyud lama Tshul khrims rgya mtsho Rinpoche (1986), pp. 77-8: 'From the Shentong *[gzhan stong,* q.v.] point of view, the luminous self-aware *[rang rig]* non-conceptual mind that is experienced in meditation, when the mind is completely free from concepts, is Absolute Reality...When the luminous, self aware, non-conceptual mind that is Wisdom Mind (Jnana) is realized by the supreme wisdom (prajna) there is no seeing and seen aspect, no realizing and realized aspect to the realization. This is called the Transcendence of Supreme Wisdom (Prajnaparamita). It is none other than the non-conceptual Wisdom Mind (Jnana) itself.' For further discussion see the next chapter.

and subject (i.e., one entity-different isolates in a single-nature relationship), or in such gnosis the appearance directly of object to subject is simply not appropriate at all (i.e., there is just one simple entity), and thus in nondual gnosis there is no appearance of subject and object and therefore no cognition of conventional objects. In other words, in a true *nondual* gnosis either one apprehends an object nondualistically—in which case subject and object must be one entity even though they are subject and object (different isolates)—or the object cannot be cognised at all. One has examined critically already how there can be agency by oneself directed towards oneself. Just as some would hold *svasaṃvedana* to be unacceptable because of an unwillingness to consider as one partless thing that which appears threefold (as activity, agent and action), so if one examined critically a mind which is without object and subject it, therefore, could not occur in the aspect of an objective referent *(gzung bya)*. That is, if the opponent is unwilling to consider in the case of self-awareness that one partless entity can have a threefold aspect in terms of isolates, he or she will certainly be unwilling to accept in the case of the Buddha's nondual gnosis that one partless nondual entity can have a twofold aspect as subject and object in terms of isolates. Thus the Buddha could not cognize conventionalities. Under such circumstances, if a referential object were to be apprehended as existing within the purview of appearance, then it could not be without object and subject, and thus it could not be nondual gnosis.[61] Therefore, Mi pham is

---

[61] bdag gcig 'brel mi 'thad na bden gnyis ngo bo gcig pa'ang tha snyad du med par 'gyur zhing / yang gnyis snang med pa'i ye shes kyis yul rtogs pa'ang mi 'thad par 'gyur te yul yul can gnyis su mi snang bzhin du nges de rtogs pa'i byed pa 'jug

saying, if one does not consider that one partless thing can appear as if diverse through the strategy of different isolates, then either (i) nondual gnosis would not have an object; or (ii) if it did have an object, it would not be nondual. Granted that the Buddhas, for example, do by definition have nondual gnosis, it follows that their minds would be completely contentless, for they would not perceive any conventional objects at all.

With this, Mi pham completes his lengthy justification of why the conventional existence of reflexivity is not at variance with the position of Prāsaṅgika Madhyamaka. Just as with reflexive awareness, he continues, it is certainly not necessary for the conventional existence of the substratum *(ālaya)* to be positively affirmed in Prāsaṅgika Madhyamaka. Nevertheless, in Prāsaṅgika there does not appear to be reasoning which refutes it transactionally. Mi pham, who has nearly finished his reply to bLo bzang dpal ldan bstan 'dzin, does not intend to go into the refutation ultimately of the *ālayavijñāna*, and he tells us he does not plan to devote an extensive discussion to the subject at all. I, too, have said quite enough for the time being.[62]

---

pa'am de la de mngon sum du snang ba mi 'thad pa mtshungs par 'gyur ba'i phyir dang / rang la rang gi byed pa 'jug pa la ji ltar dpyad kyang gsum du snang gi cha med gcig tu 'char mi btub pas rang rig mi 'thad par brjod pa ltar gzung 'dzin med pa'i blo la ji ltar dpyad kyang gzung bya'i rnam par mi 'char la / de la snang ngor yul yod par bzung na gzung 'dzin med par mi 'char ba yang de bzhin no //.

62 kun gzhi yang thal 'gyur ba'i lugs la khas len mi dgos mod / de tha snyad du 'gog pa'i rigs pa mi snang la don dam par 'gog pa ni smos ma dgos so // 'on kyang de'i tshul rgyas par mi spro'o //.

CHAPTER 8

Concluding Note — Why All The Fuss?

In his original commentary to *Bodhicaryāvatāra* 9, while discussing the substratum (*ālaya*), but implicitly also *svasaṃvedana,* Mi pham had asked his opponents why they were so concerned with the issue of the conventional existence of the *ālaya* and *svasaṃvedana*: 'If the substratum is not accepted as truly established, what harm is there to Madhyamaka through someone having accepted it transactionally' *(kun gzhi bden grub tu khas ma blangs na tha snyad du khas blangs pas dbu ma'i tshul ci zhig nyams)*? Structurally, Mi pham bases his appeal here on a claim that the concern of the Mādhyamika (at least the Prāsaṅgika) is with issues of putative inherent existence, not whether or not something exists as such conventionally. It seems that Mi pham can appeal for support to Śāntideva himself, since it is Śāntideva who tells us (*BCA* 9:26) that '[one] reverses the construction of truth, which is the cause of suffering'. In other words, the concern of the Madhyamaka is with overcoming reification into inherent existence, because it is that conception of inherent existence and our actions based on such a conception which leads to *duḥkha*. I have suggested that within this context Śāntideva is saying *(modus tollendo tollens)* that if we are to overcome suffering we have to overcome the conception of inherent existence. Nothing more. Since inherent existence is an equivalent in Prāsaṅgika Madhyamaka to ultimate existence or being truly established, it follows that Śāntideva does not see the concern of Madhyamaka to be with whether or not *x* exists conventionally as such (assuming *x* is a possible conventional), *whatever that thing may be.* The cases cited by Śāntideva of '[something] as seen, heard or cognised' are cited as merely examples of everyday sensory experience, structurally distinguished here not from self-awareness but from conceptions of inherent existence.

Thus, it seems to me that Mi pham, operating within the framework supplied by his commentary to Śāntideva, is right in asking why it is that his opponent is so concerned with whether or not the *ālaya* and *svasaṃvedana* exist conventionally. *Prima-facie* it does not seem that these two doctrinal categories need necessarily involve inherent existence, even if their discussion does arise within the context of a consideration of Cittamātra. For Mi pham it is precisely because—within this context of a discussion of Cittamātra—the substratum-consciousness and self-awareness are urged as inherently existent in order to support the Cittamātra perspective of an inherently existent nondual consciousness stream, that they are opposed by the Mādhyamika at all. Thus the Mādhyamika attack is solely on the substratum-consciousness and self-awareness as inherently existent and as bases or arguments for further inherent existence, not on their conventional existence as such. On the other hand, since for Mi pham also (no doubt following Śāntideva) the sole concern of Madhyamaka is with overcoming suffering, and therefore attacking inherent existence, it is also not a concern of Madhyamaka *as such* whether or not some sort of *ālaya* and *svasaṃvedana* do exist from merely the conventional transactional point of view, although within a wider context of concern with the conventional as well as the ultimate (manifested in part in the completeness of one's Buddhist system embracing all teachings of the Buddha) we can know, Mi pham wants to say, that interpreted correctly the substratum and reflexive nature of consciousness appear to be appropriate understandings of how (of course, conventionally) the world is.

Mi pham had asked why his opponents felt so strongly about their understanding that the *ālaya* and *svasaṃvedana* do not exist even conventionally, that—like the son of a barren woman—they have a completely fictional status. Perhaps many reasons for this debate emerge from within the respective visions of Madhyamaka and its role within their systems held by Mi pham, the rNying ma practitioner of rDzogs chen and adherent to a perspective known as 'Great Madhyamaka', and the dGe lugs pa with his vision of emptiness, the ultimate truth, as a nonaffirming negation *(prasajyapratiṣedha)*.[1] For this dGe lugs perspective

1 'Great Madhyamaka' *(dBu ma chen po)*, in *this* context seems to be a perspective broadly of a *gzhan stong* ('emptiness of other') type involving emptiness as an affirming negation *(ma yin dgag/paryudāsapratiṣedha)* which implies a positive albeit nonconceptual ultimate reality. An appropriate expression for this nonconceptual ultimate reality according to Mi pham is 'a mere gnosis which is reflexive awareness' (*so so rang rig pa'i ye shes tsam/pratisvasaṃvittijñānamātra*—see e.g. Mi pham 1975a, p. 28), or Mi pham's *dBu ma'i lta khrid zab mo.*

emptiness is a mere negation, a complete absence (it is indeed equivalent to absence, absence pure and simple, of inherent existence), and that absence itself is also empty of inherent existence. There is no implication in emptiness of any positive or true reality, non-conceptual or otherwise. Emptiness is, nevertheless, the ultimate truth in that it is what is ultimately true about its basis *(gzhi)*, the *x* which is empty of inherent existence. For this view, espoused by the dGe lugs pa, emptiness in the sense of absolute negation of inherent existence applies to all things without exception.

Three, perhaps four, particular reasons why Mi pham's dGe lugs rivals so opposed his understanding of *svasaṃvedana* immediately spring to mind.

(i) We have seen already that there is a view found in dGe lugs circles that if a consciousness is not only aware of the object, but also incontrovertibly and directly aware of itself as well, it should follow that the consciousness (or specifically *svasaṃvedana* itself) is inherently existent (see above, ch. 6). In other words, consciousness as involving *svasaṃvedana* is not a possible conventional reality such that it can fall within Mi pham's principle that the Prāsaṅgika is neither concerned with nor involved in the existence or otherwise of conventional realities. Rather, since if there is *svasaṃvedana* consciousness would inherently exist, then—in spite of what Mi pham says—consciousness as involving *svasaṃvedana* is like the God of the theists, the permanent universal, or inherent existence itself which can only exist ultimately, and it is thus very much the concern of the Prāsaṅgika as a source of suffering. Such a consciousness involving *svasaṃvedana* is in fact a complete fiction like the son of a barren woman. Certainly the clearest and perhaps the most plausible reason for this dGe lugs understanding appears to be that if consciousness incontrovertibly and directly is aware of itself it also validates its own existence. If it can validate its own existence then, contrary to a very old Buddhist axiom, consciousness does not exist in dependence upon its intentional object. If an act of consciousness exists, it is self-validated (see the quote from Newland in ch. 6 above). Thus it follows that a reflexively aware consciousness does not exist dependently and therefore is inherently existent.

That this reasoning might occur in dGe lugs circles I do not doubt. I have argued above, however, that it is unconvincing (on either plausible interpretations of the opponent's argument). It is true that if consciousness is incontrovertibly and directly aware of itself it is self-validating. In other words, we cannot be mistaken in wondering whether we are having acts of consciousness or not. It does not follow, however, that our acts of consciousness no longer exist in dependence upon their causes. The issue of self-validation and the issue of causation are not the same. It can still be argued that a perceptual act of awareness of blue has as its cause *inter alia* the blue patch which is its intentional referent as well as the preceding moment in the consciousness stream (and no doubt many other causes as well). These can be taken as causes in the good old Buddhist sense of 'this being, that occurs; with the non-occurrence of this there is the non-occurrence of that'. If there were no blue referents there could be no perceptions of blue. The issue of the self-validation of consciousness, that the existence of an act of consciousness is known in the very occurrence of that consciousness itself, is quite a different issue from one of the cause of an act of consciousness. Since it is clear that consciousnesses still have causes even if they are self-validating, it simply does not follow that with the acceptance of *svasaṃvedana* consciousness must be inherently existent. Nor, on the other plausible interpretation of the dGe lugs argument (cf. ch. 6 above), does it follow that specifically *svasaṃvedana* must be inherently existent—even if either or both might be the direction of arguments for *svasaṃvedana* as used in Cittamātra.

(ii) The fact that the refutation of *svasaṃvedana* in Madhyamaka sources always occurs within the context of a refutation of Cittamātra is due to the close relationship between self-awareness and arguments for the mind-only perspective. This includes not only one argument for an inherently existent consciousness continuum but also, notably in the hands of the Yogācāra-Svātantrika Mādhyamika Śāntarakṣita and his followers, reflexivity provides a particular argument for the substantial identity of consciousness as subject and its referential object. *Svasaṃvedana* also provides a means and an example by which those who adhere to the mind-only perspective can explain the possibility of consciousness taking itself as a referent. Thus the close association of self-awareness with arguments for mind-only, definitely not the view of Prāsaṅgika Madhyamaka, might be taken perhaps as inclining Mi pham's Prāsaṅgika opponents towards little sympathy for his attempt to justify *svasaṃvedana*. Indeed, given dGe lugs doxography, Mi pham's enthusiasm for the conventional existence of the *ālaya(vijñāna)* and *svasaṃvedana* and the clear influence of Śāntarakṣita upon his thinking would immediately suggest to his rivals and opponents that Mi pham himself, for all his protestations that he is a Prāsaṅgika, should in fact be numbered among those who follow the Yogācāra-Svātantrika Madhyamaka. This classification would be preferable to any suggestion that the borders of scholastic affiliation and allegiance might be blurred. Such an immediate categorization in the Tibetan context would also serve to dismiss Mi pham from serious consideration as a Mādhyamika rival were it not partly because Mi pham was familiar with the dGe lugs framework of tenet and argumentation and able to employ it in his very attack upon dGe lugs Madhyamaka, but primarily because Mi pham insisted on basing his interpretation of Prāsaṅgika Madhyamaka on a close reading of Śāntideva's *Bodhicaryāvatāra* (not to mention Mi pham's considerably less interesting commentary to the *Madhyamakāvatāra)*, a work classed as Prāsaṅgika by dGe lugs writers and a work in which they had for centuries, and with justification, claimed considerable expertise and had more or less determined what they considered to be the correct framework of interpretation.

We have seen already how it is possible to argue from the position that *svasaṃvedana* characterizes consciousness to a position of mind-only, whether that position of mind-only is understood in Yogācāra terms or in Madhyamaka terms, as occurs in what Tibetan doxographers refer to as Śāntarakṣita's Yogācāra-Svātantrika Madhyamaka. There can be no doubt that *svasaṃvedana* was seen both by its proponents and its opponents as intimately related to the mind-only thesis, and it is arguable that this very close connection—particularly when it is related to the doxographers' project of reifying Buddhist philosophy into distinct schools—tended to discourage a perspective on *svasaṃvedana* which might separate its mind-only uses from its possible coherence and explanatory value as conventional occurrence.[2] The

[2] Cf. here the comment by the late dGe lugs lama Padma rgyal

uses of self-awareness in generating a mind-only thesis are various. First, self-awareness provides an example where, it is argued, awareness takes as its referent something which is not substantially different from awareness itself. In other words, in a case where an opponent might argue that the consciousness of blue and its referent cannot be mind-only because the referent of a consciousness cannot itself be a consciousness, *svasaṃvedana* provides an example of an awareness where subject and object are the same substance *(ekadravya)*. Here *svasaṃvedana* is used simply for its *exemplary* function. Second, *svasaṃvedana* is used by mind-only theorists to explain *what is actually going on* when a consciousness is aware of its referent. Consciousness is actually aware of consciousness, for there is mind-only (as in the case of a dream), and therefore all consciousness is actually self-aware. The use of *svasaṃvedana* here is a use which relies on the model I have called 'self-awareness (i)'—awareness takes an object, a referent, and that referent turns out to be itself. Third, there is an argument for mind-only based on the self-awareness (ii) model, the model we find employed by Śāntarakṣita and Mi pham, and actually used by the Yogācāra-Svātantrika Mādhyamika Śāntarakṣita in order to establish his position of mind-only as a conventional truth. This is the argument called by Matilal 'the veil of ideas'.[3] As an argument for mind-only, what this amounts to is a claim that consciousness by its very nature is the exact

---

mtshan Rinpoche in the second volume to his commentary to the *Madhyamakāvatāra* (1984/5 p. 60): de ltar na shes pa gzhan dbang de nyid rang bzhin gyis grub pa la de'i sgrub byed rang rig sgrub dgos na'ang de ma grub pas gzhan dbang rang bzhin gyis grub pa 'di mi rigs zhes dgag pa mdzad do //.

[3] See Matilal (1986, p. 159)—quoted above ch. 2, n. 19.

opposite of that which is insentient. Here consciousness is said by its very nature to be reflexive (*svasaṃvedana*); its objects are not. The problem, however (a problem felt in a different but not dissimilar context by Descartes in trying to relate the soul as pure unextended knowing subjectivity with the physical brain), is how to explain the connection between a consciousness which by nature is reflexive, with referents which by nature are not. In fact, it is claimed, two such different orders of reality could not interact—there has arisen the 'veil of ideas', consciousness cannot reach beyond itself to insentience. From which it should follow that we do not have any experiences of insentient referents at all. Since we clearly do experience objects, the final stage in the argument is that subjects and objects must be of the same order. They cannot both be insentient, for under such circumstances there would be no sentience, no experiences, at all. Thus they must both be sentience—hence 'mind-only'. From self-awareness (ii) one can in following this reasoning conclude also self-awareness (i), awareness that takes referents which are of the nature of awareness.

Mi pham as a Mādhyamika, indeed a self-confessed Prāsaṅgika, is not committed to any of these mind-only strategies even though he would accept the initial premisses of the last argument. Mi pham has Prāsaṅgika arguments against mind-only and, notwithstanding that, all of these arguments occur within the context of ultimate analysis. According to his own vision of Madhyamaka, as a Prāsaṅgika Mi pham will not argue against the conventional existence of whatever is conventionally accepted by those in the world best qualified to know. The world does not hold to a conventional mind-only position, and thus Mi pham does not either. But as we have seen, Mi pham does want to hold that the reflexive nature of awareness is something accepted (more often implicitly than explicitly) in the world. Neither he nor the world need adopt the veil of ideas and its argued implications, for, as a Prāsaṅgika, Mi pham is not required to seek for complete systematic coherence in what *the world* holds, the conventional, and the world itself is perfectly capable of holding both that awareness must be reflexive (self-awareness (ii)) and at the same time that objects of awareness patently are not of one substance with consciousness (i.e., denying self-awareness (i)). The close connection between *svasaṃvedana* and arguments for mind-only is not, for Mi pham, a necessary connection. It is possible, under a framework probably derived by Mi pham largely from Śāntarakṣita's treatment of the issue, to separate *svasaṃvedana* from *cittamātra,* and from Yogācāra. When there is no longer a case for the ultimate, inherent existence of *svasaṃvedana,* Mi pham wants to say (following Śāntideva), the conventional existence of *svasaṃvedana* ceases to be a concern of the Prāsaṅgika. Nevertheless, Mi pham considers that he has good arguments for *svasaṃvedana*'s conventional existence, and in establishing this conventional existence Mi pham is moving outside the scope of Prāsaṅgika Madhyamaka as he understands it.

The deep disagreement with dGe lugs scholars on these issues, however, arising out of Mi pham's commentary to *Bodhicaryāvatāra* 9, is not due just to the fact that dGe lugs scholars failed to realize the contingent and not necessary connection between *svasaṃvedana* and Yogācāra arguments for mind-only. It is true, as we have seen, that the idea of a Prāsaṅgika not opposing the conventional existence of *svasaṃvedana* appears to upset a carefully-constructed dGe lugs doxography. It is arguable that dGe lugs scholars—through centuries of a progressively more formalized debate—had perhaps lost the ability to generate new thoughts, to take a new and critical look at what had become their orthodoxy. All of these factors may have contributed to the fierceness, the vigor, with which Mi pham's perspective on Madhyamaka appears to have been opposed. But there are perhaps other reasons why Mi pham wanted to establish the status of conventional *svasaṃvedana* as the characteristic of consciousness, and why its acceptance might be thought to cause problems for the dGe lugs vision of Madhyamaka. These reasons are connected with Mi pham's position as a rNying ma pa, a rDzogs chen pa, and a leading exponent of the *ris med* movement.

(iii) Attention has been drawn recently, not least through the oral teachings of His Holiness the Dalai Lama, to the importance of the interpretation and use of the *Bodhicaryāvatāra* among certain non-dGe lugs nineteenth and twentieth century Tibetan teachers of the *ris med* ('non-partiality'or 'non-sectarian') movement (see Dalai Lama 1994, pp. 1, 7-8; Khenchen Kunzang Palden and Minyak Kunzang Sönam 1993, pp. xv-xvi). Particularly influential in this context was dPal sprul Rinpoche, O rgyan 'jigs med chos kyi dbang po (1808-87), who is indeed held to have been an emanation or reincarnation of Śāntideva, no doubt due to his interest and learning in the *Bodhicaryāvatāra*. dPal sprul Rinpoche was a teacher not only of Mi pham himself but also of even a dGe lugs lama like Thub bstan chos kyi grags pa (Mi nyag Kun bzang bsod nams), although Thub bstan chos kyi grags pa's own commentaries to the *Bodhicaryāvatāra* seem to have been written from within the dGe lugs perspective.[4] For his part, Mi pham was perhaps the most brilliant philosophical writer associated with the *ris med* movement, and certainly the most brilliant *ris med* philosophical writer to be willing to take on the tradition of dGe lugs exegesis on their own ground through writing rival commentaries to a whole range of great Indian treatises. With his characteristic modesty, Mi pham himself claims not to have studied much, but he mentions specifically that he was taught *Bodhicaryāvatāra* 9 by dPal sprul Rinpoche. dPal sprul Rinpoche appears not to have written any commentaries to this text, and it was left to Mi pham, therefore, to write a detailed commentary to the ninth chapter of the *Bodhicaryāvatāra,* clearly establishing a reading of Śāntideva's Prāsaṅgika Madhyamaka expressed in terms and within the framework recognized by the dGe lugs tradition but rather different from it in certain important respects.[5] Thus Mi

[4] The present Dalai Lama is proud of holding a lineage of interpretation of the *Bodhicaryāvatāra* which passes through dPal sprul Rinpoche, who was also held to be an emanation of Avalokiteśvara. See Dalai Lama (1994) p. 1. In spite of the influence of the largely non-dGe lugs *ris med* movement on the reading and use of the *Bodhicaryāvatāra,* however, there seems to have been in certain dGe lugs circles a dislike of resorting at least to rNying ma lamas for meditation instruction. See Pabongka Rinpoche 1991, p. 86. For perhaps understandable doctrinal reasons the dGe lugs tradition has always felt some suspicion of the *ris med* approach.

[5] Note that although Mi pham produced a commentary to only the ninth chapter of the *Bodhicaryāvatāra* (itself suggesting his intention of producing a vision of Prāsaṅgika philosophy to rival that of his opponents), Mi pham's pupil Kun bzang dpal ldan commented on the whole text (1989). For the ninth chapter see also Khenchen Kunzang Palden and Minyak Kunzang Sōnam (1993). In treating the ninth chapter Kun bzang dpal ldan appears to follow Mi pham very closely, almost word for word. Thus *one* possibility is that in his commentary on the

pham's commentary to *Bodhicaryāvatāra* 9 can perhaps be read as the response of the *ris med* movement in terms of familiar scholastic dogmatics and debate to the dGe lugs vision of Madhyamaka, particularly Prāsaṅgika Madhyamaka. Understood in this way within the Tibetan context, perhaps it is not actually surprising that Mi pham's commentary and perspective produced such hostility from dGe lugs writers.[6]

---

other chapters, too, Kun bzang dpal ldan is following an oral commentary by Mi pham to those chapters on which Mi pham himself did not write a commentary. Anyway, in this commentary we are likely to have a text which also does not differ from Mi pham's intentions on the other chapters.

[6] Mi pham himself claims not to have written his commentaries in order to attack other traditions, or dispute with them. He was asked to write 'some textbooks according to our own tradition' (see 'Mi pham's testament' in Dudjom Rinpoche 1991, p. 873) by the great *ris med* master 'Jam dbyangs mkhyen rtse dbang po (1820-92). Mi pham claims that at the time there was very little study or understanding of the philosophical position of the rNying ma tradition. In fact 'there are few who even consider and inquire as to just what are the essential points of our tradition's philosophical system; rather, most simply imitate other traditions.' Thus, as he points out, Mi pham's primary motivation was in order to fulfill his teacher's request, and to revive an understanding of the rNying ma philosophical position among fellow rNying ma pas. 'But [the adherents of] the other philosophical systems took them to be refutations and later many critical essays and so forth arrived from all quarters.' In typical fashion, Mi pham disclaims any originality. Yet the philosophical position of the rNying ma is not for Mi pham one option among other options each in all respects equally good. Mi pham actually says that 'when I looked at them, I saw that all the profound essential points were only to be found in the doctrinal traditions which had been transmitted through the precious lineages of the Ancient Translation School [rNying ma]; so especially great certainty was born within me' (*ibid.*, p. 872). Mi pham considers the rNying ma position (on *svasaṃvedana,* for example) to be correct, and there-

We have seen already that one feature of Mi pham's commentary to *Bodhicaryāvatāra* 9 is his use and approval of the expression 'Great Madhyamaka' *(dbu ma chen po)*, in its classical form a term associated particularly with the Jo nang pas, involving a *gzhan stong* ('emptiness of other') perspective probably originally derived from the *Ratnagotravibhāga*. This perspective holds to a true Ultimate Reality which is empty of adventitious defilements which are other than it *(gzhan stong)* but not empty of its own inherent existence (not *rang stong)*.[7] An important feature of this

---

fore *inter alia* the dGe lugs position on *svasaṃvedana* to be incorrect. In establishing the rNying ma philosophical position Mi pham *is* debating with others. It is clear from what Mi pham says subsequently ('I never felt, even in dreams, such motivations as hostility towards other traditions, or self-congratulatory pride...') that Mi pham wants to stress the pure intentions which motivated his philosophical enterprise. But one can enter into genuine debate with pure motivation and a helpful spirit, and *pace* what Mi pham says, the adherents of other traditions were right and proper to treat Mi pham's texts as refutations and respond with their own replies. It is perhaps a sad testimony to the actual practice (rather than principle) of the Tibetan debate tradition (at least between *schools)* that Mi pham appears to equate genuine doctrinal dispute and debate with other schools with hostility towards other traditions and self-congratulatory pride.

[7] For the Great Madhyamaka in a rNying ma and also *ris med* context see Dudjom Rinpoche (1991), pp. 169 ff., where there are many quotations from the *Ratnagotravibhāga* in particular. On the superiority of Great Madhyamaka and its differences from Cittamātra and Prāsaṅgika ('the inconceivable pristine cognition has been illustrated, and through the vision of its nature the ultimate truth is perceived. It is wrong to refer to the mere emptiness, which is nothing at all [i.e., the Prāsaṅgika absence of inherent existence], as the ultimate truth' (p. 185)). See *ibid.*, ch. 4, and on the two truths in Great Madhyamaka, ch. 7. On the relation of all this to rDzogs chen see pp. 896 ff. Really, Dudjom Rinpoche says, *when they are understood properly*

true Ultimate Reality, which is often identified with 'a mere gnosis which is reflexive awareness' (*so so rang*

---

the Prāsaṅgika *rang stong* and Great Madhyamaka *gzhan stong* perspectives come to the same essential point (p. 208, but note his comment above on the *wrongness* of the Prāsaṅgika vision of what constitutes ultimate truth). This 'same point' involves the transcendence of conceptuality. But whether this does mean they amount to the same, or are really saying the same thing, is debatable. Either there is a positive, really existing Ultimate Reality or there is not. It is not enough to say 'is or is not' amount to the same thing when we are dealing with an Ultimate Reality which is nonconceptual. The question is whether there *is* (or is not) such a nonconceptual Ultimate Reality. The dGe lugs tradition (with justification) would not agree that in nonconceptuality there is no difference. The putative nonconceptual Ultimate Reality is not the same as a nonconceptual state of consciousness enjoying a nondual experience of the ultimate truth, which is a mere absence of inherent existence. The fact that both would be experienced in nonconceptual states would not be enough to dissolve all difference. For a dGe lugs pa there cannot be a nonconceptual state experiencing a true Ultimate Reality, since there is no such thing as an Ultimate Reality of that sort. It is necessary to settle first (quite conceptually) whether there can be such a thing, before one can talk of experiencing it. On the perspective of the Great Madhyamaka cf. also the contemporary bKa' brgyud lama Tshul khrims rgya mtsho Rinpoche (1986), p. 76: 'They consider themselves to be the Great Madhyamikas because their system involves not only recognizing freedom from all conceptual contrivance, but also the realization of the Wisdom Mind (Jnana) that is free from all conceptual contrivance. This non-conceptual Wisdom Mind is not the object of the conceptualizing process and so is not negated by Madhyamaka reasoning. Therefore, it can be said to be the only thing that has absolute and true existence. It is important to understand that this true existence does not mean that it can be conceptualized. If it were even the most subtle object of the conceptual process, it could be refuted by Prasangika reasoning....So what is this non-conceptual Wisdom Mind? It is something that one realizes through means other than the conceptual process. One experiences it directly just as it is...For this realization a Guru is absolutely necessary.'

rig pa'i ye shes tsam / pratisvasaṃvittijñānamātra), is that it is beyond all conceptuality and therefore not open to the Mādhyamika critique of ultimacy, which can only touch an ultimate which has been conceptualized. It is arguable that it was around such a nonconceptual Ultimate Reality that the scholars associated with the *ris med* movement hoped to be able to bring together conflicting Tibetan theoretical systems. The Ultimate Reality would harmonize with certain Indian root texts, and an Ultimate Reality as a mere gnosis which is reflexive awareness would not only fit with Tantric texts but also provide a bridge between Mahāyāna exoteric thought *(sūtrayāna)* and the Tantras. On the other hand, the Prāsaṅgika critique of all ultimacy, a critique of even the ultimate reality of emptiness itself, could be portrayed as, first, a clearing away of what does *not* exist, and, second, a critique of any *conceptualized* absolute. Thus, Prāsaṅgika Madhyamaka has its legitimate place as the overcoming of all concepts, and transcends itself when its function has been fulfilled. Anyone who would see this Prāsaṅgika Madhyamaka perspective itself as having the final word has become attached to the concepts of Madhyamaka and, therefore, attached to a mere tool. The emptiness referred to in Prāsaṅgika texts is certainly a pure negation, a negation of inherent existence, but it is necessarily a conceptualized emptiness. In direct nonconceptual gnosis a true Ultimate Reality is revealed in one's own nondual experience, an Ultimate Reality which could also be spoken of as an 'emptiness' for which the Mādhyamika negations paved the way. The conceptualized and relative emptiness known in Prāsaṅgika negations is a 'nonaffirming negation' *(med dgag / prasajyapratiṣedha),* a mere negation which does not in itself affirm any positive reality. The emptiness known in direct nonconceptual awareness, on the other hand, is an 'affirming negation' *(ma yin dgag / paryudāsa-pratiṣedha)*, an emptiness which affirms a true nonconceptual Ultimate Reality—an Ultimate Reality which, if it has to be conceptualized, can be spoken of as 'a mere gnosis which is reflexive awareness'. This is the Great Madhyamaka and, its adherents claim, the final position of both Nāgārjuna and Asaṅga. In its movement from conceptual to nonconceptual, portrayed also as a movement from doctrinal elaboration and debate to direct experience, it was hoped by the enthusiasts for the *ris med* approach that this Great Madhyamaka could bring together in their correct places all the different Buddhist doctrinal systems, perspectives and practices. It was viewed with suspicion and sometimes bitterly opposed by dGe lugs scholars who already had their own holistic framework and saw themselves as defending the system of Nāgārjuna and Candrakīrti, a position felt to be completely at variance with any claim of ultimate inherent existence, a position where all things without exception, including the ultimate truth itself, are empty of their own inherent existence *(rang stong)*.[8]

[8] Perhaps I should say a little more here about my association (if cautious and tentative) of Mi pham with a teaching of Ultimate Reality and even a version of the *gzhan stong* position. This latter in particular will be thought controversial. Geoffrey Samuel is not alone, for example, when he states that '. . . Mip'am, the most important Nyingmapa scholar of the late nineteenth century and a prominent member of the Rimed movement . . . argued for a Madhyamaka interpretation of the Nyingmapa teachings, in this respect opposing the tendency of other Rimed teachers such as the Kagyüdpa lama Jamgön Kongtrul to employ more positive (*shentong*) phraseology' (1993, p. 465). There is no doubt that Mipham argued for a Madhyamaka interpretation of rNying ma pa philosophy; the question is what his understanding of Madhyamaka was, taken as a whole

with its place beside Tantric and rDzogs chen theory and praxis. For example, take Mi pham's *dBu ma'i lta khrid zab mo:* Having explained the process of Madhyamaka analysis to discover emptiness of things, absence of inherent existence, Mi pham comments that 'while empty, appearing; while appearing, empty; one should contemplate appearance and emptiness in the manner of an illusion—this is the metaphoric (*rnam grangs;* verbal; conceptual) ultimate' (stong bzhin snang la snang bzhin stong // snang stong sgyu ma'i tshul du bsgom // 'di ni rnam grangs pa'i don dam //). This ultimate—emptiness, absence of inherent existence, the ultimate of a Prāsaṅgika like Candrakīrti or Tsong kha pa, the status of things which exist due to dependent origination—is the same ultimate that Mi pham speaks about in his commentary to *Bodhicaryāvatāra* 9:140 as a *nyi tshe ba'i stong pa [nyid],* a limited or relative, i.e. not truly ultimate, ultimate. This expression is used disparagingly of false claims to real ultimacy in the *Laṅkāvatārasūtra* and *Samādhirājasūtra,* and in those sūtras the Buddha says that the *nyi tshe ba'i stong pa nyid* is to be abandoned (see Williams 1983b, pp. 133ff, which treats Mi bskyod rdo rje's similar use of *nyi tshe ba'i rnam grangs pa'i stong nyid* in attacking Tsong kha pa's understanding of the ultimate as emptiness. For Mipham's use, see also Williams (forthcoming)). Use of such an expression—employed critically for the wrong view in the sūtras—clearly indicates an ultimate which is not at all the final true ultimate. In his comments on *BCA* 9:140 (p. 86) Mi pham explicitly links *rnam grangs pa* such as absence of a pot, or empty [emptiness] of a pot with the *nyi tshe ba'i stong pa [nyid]* as both finally delusory since the entities which they negate are delusory, although true to his use of Prāsaṅgika thought, Mi pham does hold that these negations *are* true relatively/conventionally, and thus emptiness is true as far as things which come within its range are concerned. Thus it is clear that for Mi pham the Prāsaṅgika emptiness put forward by, say, Tsong kha pa—a nonaffirming negation (*med dgag*)—is not a true ultimate, nor is it *the* true ultimate, since Mi pham is prepared to speak of an actual ultimate (a *rnam grangs min pa'i don dam*) which must therefore be different from this emptiness. In his *dBu ma'i lta khrid zab mo,* for example, Mi pham continues with the caution that with the previous emptiness, (the *rnam grangs pa'i don dam [stong pa nyid]*), since one has not passed beyond conceptual construction (*kun tu rtog*) there is no seeing the true nature (*chos nyid*) which is free from verbal differentiations (*spros bral*) (kun tu rtog las ma brgal phyir // spros bral chos nyid mthong ba min //). Note that Mi pham does not use the expression *chos nyid* here for the emptiness which is a mere negation, mere absence of inherent existence. The emptiness which is a mere negation is not the highest, final emptiness. This is not because of the way it is seen, or the fact that in speaking about it it has been conceptualised. It is something to do with what it actually *is*. Absence of inherent existence *is*, in its very nature, by definition, a pure negation. And as a pure negation it *is*, as Mi pham knew from *Bodhicaryāvatāra* 9:140, in its very nature, by definition, relative to the negandum—in this case, fictitious inherent existence. Thus absence of inherent existence, emptiness, is in its very nature, by definition, according to Śāntideva, ultimately delusory and, for Mi pham, is in its very nature, by definition a *nyi tshe ba'i stong pa nyid*. As a negation, absence of inherent existence is relative to its counterpositive. For Mi pham this makes it a conceptual emptiness, a conceptual (*rnam grangs*) ultimate. Thus it is clear, I think, that for Mi pham if there is a *rnam grangs min pa'i don dam* it cannot be the same as mere absence of inherent existence, and it cannot therefore be a mere nonaffirming negation (*med dgag*). In the *dBu ma'i lta khrid zab mo* Mi pham refers to this *rnam grangs min pa'i don dam* as the true nature (*chos nyid*) of all dharmas (*chos*). And although it is free from affirmations of existence, nonexistence and so on (*yod med la sogs khas len bral*) and has a meaning (or referent) which is strictly unutterable (*brjod med don*) Mi pham is also unequivocal in referring to it as 'gnosis (*ye shes/jñāna*) which is nonconceptual absorption, known as reflexive awareness (cf. the 'mere gnosis which is reflexive awareness' (*so so rang rig pa'i ye shes tsam*) of rDzogs chen: de ni chos kun chos nyid [9a] de // rnam grangs min pa'i don dam ba // so sor rang gi rig bya ba // mnyam gzhag mi rtog ye shes yin //). Thus a *ye shes*—an expression which must have primary mentalistic usage—is said to be the *rnam grangs min pa'i don dam*. We have seen that absence of inherent existence is defective because it is a relative ultimate and comes within the range of conceptualisation. Nondual *ye shes* is either truly ultimate or it is not. Since it is a consciousness of some sort it is clearly not a pure negation. This, apart from anything else, is why Mi pham elsewhere (in 1976b, for example) can deny that the *rnam grangs min pa'i don dam* is a mere nonaffirming negation, a pure negative bound up with duality. If absence of inherent existence is (with Candrakīrti and Tsong kha pa) the only ultimate then a *ye shes* no matter how exalted should be a conventional truth and there could be no true ultimate at all. The only ultimate would be an ultimate said by Mi pham and others to be a relative *nyi tshe ba'i stong pa nyid.* But clearly for Mi pham this nondual *ye shes* is not only an ultimate, but *the* finally true nonconceptual ultimate, beyond the *nyi tshe ba'i stong pa nyid,* and an affirming negative (*ma yin dgag*). But the ultimate of, say, Tsong kha pa, the emptiness which is a mere negation of inherent existence, is a thoroughly uncompromising ultimate. Anything both existing and other than absence of inherent existence itself is, for Tsong kha pa, a conventional truth, and anything which is putatively both said to exist and not to come within the range of absence of inherent existence would be a true, inherently existent ultimate truth. According to Śāntideva in *Bodhicaryāvatāra* 9:140, followed by Mi pham, the relative (= *rnam grangs*) emptiness is delusory, *as is that which is empty* (its basis). Thus if the nonconceptual *ye shes* were empty of inherent existence, that relative emptiness alone would be the only ultimate, while nonconceptual *ye shes* (= the *rnam grangs min pa'i don dam*) would become delusory. I do not think this is what Mi pham wants. The only alternative is that he considers the nonconceptual *ye shes,* as nonconceptual, not to come within the range of absence of inherent existence and for that very reason to be truly ultimate. However the key to understanding Mi pham's position lies in his appeal to true nonconceptuality. Thus it is a condition of the existence of a truly nonconceptual entity that one cannot say that it exists. Nevertheless it is also a condition of praxis and therefore the philosophical system which supports certain sorts of praxis that one can, one must, *indicate* that the nonconceptual entity exists. Thus Mi pham, in denying that the true ultimate can be a mere negation, and denying that it can be a nonaffirming negative, in fact indicates a true ultimate which really—dare I say, inherently—exists, exists in the fullest possible sense. However because it is nonconceptual it must be beyond both existence and nonexistence. The view that Mi pham does not hold to a *gzhan stong*-type position is I suspect largely the result of Mi pham's criticisms of the Jo nang pa *gzhan stong* Absolutism in his *bDe gshegs snying po'i stong thun chen mo Seng ge'i nga ro.* The problem with any *gzhan stong* position which is based on the nonconceptuality of the Ultimate is that there is a sense in which it contradicts itself in speaking. The Ultimate has to be shown to exist while at the same time the claim to existence has to be withdrawn in order that one is not accused of falling within the conceptual dichotomy of existence and nonexistence. There are perhaps radically different types of *gzhan stong* position in Tibetan thought, and indeed not all those who hold such a position would want to use this expression for it. The Jo nang pa tradition had for centuries provided Tibetan thinkers with an example of a philosophy which apparently contradicts nonconceptuality by affirming the *existence* of the ultimate. Irrespective of whether other thinkers in fact hold substantially the same position on ontology or ontological primacy as the Jo nang tradition, any thinker who wishes to clarify his (or her) adherence to true nonconceptuality will in Tibet need to refute someone for falling into the wrong view of existence, and someone for falling into that of nonexistence. The Jo nang tradition supplies the first, and for many critics Tsong kha pa *et al.* provide the second. The Jo nang pas have contradicted themselves in speaking of their nonconceptual Ultimate. The more they speak and systematise, the more they contradict themselves. Thus it is perfectly possible to argue that the problem for the Jo nang pas is not *what* they say, but the fact that they are saying it at all (plus—I would want to add—any difficulties which might result from the very coherence of nonconceptual entities, let alone mentioning them). The problem for their critics however, is that short of accepting a third value which would equal the fourth member of the *catuṣkoṭi* (i.e. the ultimate neither is nor is not), to deny that the ultimate is a mere negation, mere absence of inherent existence—and indeed to relativise that negation—must logically entail that the ultimate, if it is to be an actual ultimate reality at all, *is* something which does inherently exist—even if one is then going to retreat by saying that since it is beyond all conceptuality we cannot actually say that it exists. In refuting both the Jo nang tradition on the one hand for adhering to existence, and Tsong kha pa *et al.* on the other for adhering to nonexistence, however, it seems to me that Mi pham also in true *ris med* fashion wants to be able to incorporate both their contributions. Thus Tsong kha pa, for example, is right in that anything which can be conceptualised, i.e. can be spoken about, can be analysed with ultimate analysis and shown to be empty of inherent existence, merely conventional. Any ultimate which can be spoken about also comes within the range of refutation through ultimate analysis. Thus it is also correct to say that for Mi pham properly speaking one cannot refer to anything which resists ultimate analysis. But of course, anything which can be spoken about for Mi pham comes within the range of conceptualisation (= *rnam grangs*), and its ultimate also is a *rnam grangs pa'i don dam*. The *rnam grangs min pa'i don dam* is precisely unutterable and thus cannot be refuted by ultimate analysis. How could it? And the Jo nang pas are, I suggest, right for Mi pham in indicating that the true ultimate is beyond any emptiness which is a mere negation, and cannot be refuted by conceptual (or any other) means. In the *dBu ma'i lta khrid zab mo* Mi pham refers to the praxis which finally understands the *rnam grangs min pa'i don dam* as he has explained it as the 'Great Madhyamaka yoga' (*dbu ma chen po'i rnal 'byor yin*). Mi pham frequently refers to the true position in such contexts as the Great Madhyamaka (see, for example, Williams 1992b, and Williams, forthcoming; cf. Khenchen Kunzang Palden 1993, p. 114 following Mi pham's commentary to *Bodhicaryāvatāra* 9:140 exactly: 'To abide in that Primal Wisdom in which all concepts have subsided—this is indeed the Great Madhyamaka, the Great Middle Way free from all assertions.'). The expression 'Great Madhyamaka' has a very venerable ancestry in Tibetan thought (see van der Kuijp 1983, pp. 37 ff; Hookham 1991, *passim*, but esp. pp. 157-9). Basically it has one of two meanings. On the one hand it can be used to refer simply to Prāsaṅgika Madhyamaka, or the particular understanding of Madhyamaka held as finally correct by thinker *X*. This way of using the term tends to be earlier and with reference to earlier thinkers. But the term had for centuries, and especially in more recent centuries, been used particularly as a technical term for the *gzhan stong* position—very often associated with the Jo nang pas—and it had become a key expression among *ris med* thinkers precisely for an approach which, in its stress on a nonconceptual Ultimate which thereby transcends ultimate analysis was, I suggest, important to the *ris med* project of harmonising traditional doctrinal rivalries. Van der Kuijp refers in this context to Kong sprul blo gros mtha' yas (1813-99), an older contemporary of Mi pham and very much part of the same circle and movement: 'it is useful to realise how one of the greatest founders and exponents of the nineteenth century 'non-partial' (*ris-med*) movement, which was the direct cause for a renewed interest in this 'Great *madhyamaka*', thought about the antecedents of a way of thinking he felt so close to' (p. 40). It is indeed possible that Mi pham intended by his use of this expression nothing more than the Prāsaṅgika position of absence of inherent existence as the only ultimate. But I very much doubt it, particularly in the light of the discussion above. The term 'Great Madhyamaka' was very much part of his *ris med* environment as a term for a form of *gzhan stong*. Had Mi pham wanted to use it in a completely different way he would surely have made the point very clear. Mi pham was no fool. Perhaps I can also make one final *ad hominem* point. The suggestion that Mi pham (and others) did not advocate a form of Ultimate Reality, or even *gzhan stong*, sometimes looks as if it is animated by the perspective that would see the whole history of Buddhist thought as a series of footnotes to Nāgārjuna (and Candrakīrti?), plus the feeling that somehow Nāgārjuna is *right*. Perhaps this is partly because a number of scholars of Buddhism are also practitioners of various forms of Buddhism, and Nāgārjuna's thought—liberally interpreted—has certain features which appeal to the relativistic streak of late-twentieth century scientific and moral thought. Thus whichever is our favorite Buddhist thinker has to be defended from having contradicted Nāgārjuna and particularly from having taught any form of unfashionable (quasi Neoplatonic or Hegelian?) Ultimate Reality. Sometimes we even see it stated that such an interpretation must be wrong *because* it contradicts Nāgārjuna. But Buddhist thought over more than two thousand years is much more complicated than this, as ages change thought changes and it is quite possible that some subsequent Mahāyāna thinkers paid no more than lip-service to Nāgārjuna while continuing their own way. Moreover I doubt Nāgārjuna is the final word in philosophy. For all I know *gzhan stong* thought may indeed be true, although the history of philosophy suggests that we tend not to find truth as such but rather some jolly fascinating mistakes. Still, whether Mi pham really teaches a form of nonconceptual Ultimate Reality or not requires consid-

(iv) I introduced earlier in passing the problem of whether a Buddha's direct nondual and nonconceptual omniscient awareness can know itself or not, and we saw then some suggestion that, for 'Jam dbyangs bzhad pa at least, there may be an inclination to accept the reflexivity of awareness under such circumstances. But as 'Jam dbyangs bzhad pa was only too aware, the omniscient consciousness of a Buddha can be portrayed an an exceptional case (see Newland (1992) p. 103); and Mi pham would want to say that the reflexivity of consciousness necessitated by the Buddha's knowing everything, knowing all knowables—among which one has to include his own consciousness (a form of self-awareness (i)?)—is not the same reflexivity we are talking about when we understand consciousness as being reflexive through its very nature as consciousness (self-awareness (ii)). Take the case, however, of a direct nonconceptual and nondual awareness of the ultimate truth, emptiness. For dGe lugs theorists, emptiness is what is discovered through analysis when searching to find if *x* has ultimate, inherent existence or not. In other words under ultimate analysis *x* is simply not there, it is not found, and *x* is thus discovered to lack, to be empty of, inherent existence. That lack of inherent existence is an emptiness, and that emptiness is the ultimate truth concerning *x*. An emptiness is held to be a pure negation, albeit a negation of a particular type of thing in that it is a negation of *x*'s own inherent existence. An

---

erable further research. No doubt the sources are capable of alternative interpretations. The fact still remains that Mi pham clearly does hold to a nonconceptual *ye shes* which is characterised by *so so rang rig pa* and which has some sort of primacy and importance and is not completely divorced from conventional consciousness.

emptiness is also a nonaffirming negation in that as a negation it does not in itself imply the positive existence of anything else. Thus, in the nonconceptual awareness of emptiness, which occurs in a meditative absorption focused on the ultimate truth, the referent *(artha)* is an ultimate truth and a pure nonaffirming negation. As a nondual and nonconceptual experience there should be no positive thing and also no conventional truth contained or implied in that experience itself.

An awareness is a consciousness, and a consciousness is not an emptiness. Thus an awareness is not an ultimate truth since, in dGe lugs Prāsaṅgika Madhyamaka, only emptinesses are ultimate truths. Moreover, a consciousness is patently a positive thing and not a negation. In a nondual meditative absorption focused on the ultimate truth there should be known only an ultimate truth, which is a pure negative. Therefore, this meditative absorption should not also know itself, a consciousness. It is here in particular that dGe lugs theorists must have felt some concern about the memory argument for *svasaṃvedana*. Apart from Buddhas, other practitioners emerge from their nondual absorption on emptiness and in the post-absorption state see conventionalities, but conventionalities now characterized with the emptiness they remember from their nondual absorption. According to the memory argument for *svasaṃvedana,* it should follow that in the original nondual, nonconceptual absorption there was both (i) an experience of emptiness and (ii) an experience of the experience of emptiness. This second experience takes as its object an awareness, which as a consciousness is both a positive and a conventional entity. Even without the memory argument for *svasaṃvedana,* if all consciousness is reflexive by nature then in the very nondual experience of the ultimate truth there should also be present a positive phenomenon, the consciousness itself. Not only might it be argued that such a nondual experience, *qua* experience, directly involves or implies the consciousness (a positive phenomenon) itself and therefore emptiness ceases to be a nonaffirming negation, but someone might also argue that in the experience of discovering emptiness as a result of a search for putative inherent existents one also *finds* a consciousness. Thus not only is emptiness an ultimate truth, but so is the consciousness itself. Alternatively, in the direct nondual nonconceptual absorption on emptiness two things are actually experienced: an ultimate truth that is a negation—emptiness—and a conventional truth that is a positive phenomenon—the experiencing consciousness.

Mi pham was a follower of the *ris med* movement, a rNying ma pa and a practitioner of rDzogs chen. He does indeed hold, I think, that there is a positive Ultimate Reality which is implied and present in the experience of emptiness. Moreover, this Ultimate Reality is mentalistic in that although it is nonconceptual it can be indicated using terms which are drawn from consciousness-vocabulary. It is spoken of as 'a mere gnosis which is reflexive awareness'. The rDzogs chen Ultimate Reality is also said to be the very nature of all consciousness itself, consciousness *qua* consciousness.[9] This is not something which is brought into existence or attained at enlightenment. Rather it

---

[9] This is the very essence or nature of mind *(sems nyid)* itself. As Ultimate Reality, according to Samten Karmay (1988, pp. 175 ff.) it is described in rDzogs chen texts as the true nature of mind *(sems kyi chos nyid* or *sems kyi rang bzhin)*, or significantly as reflexivity *(rang gi rig pa)*. It is the primordial basis *(gdod ma'i gzhi)*.

has always been present. There can be little doubt at all that although dGe lugs sources are keen to distinguish completely the use of 'reflexive awareness' *(rang rig)* as a characteristic of all consciousness in tenet systems such as Cittamātra or Yogācāra-Svātantrika Madhyamaka, from its specific use in the context of nondual, nonconceptual gnoses attained during the path, in his defense of reflexivity as a feature of all awareness as such Mi pham does not in fact want to distinguish these senses of *'rang rig'*.[10] For Mi pham, I suggest, the fact that all consciousness is reflexive by nature is necessary but by no means sufficient for the

---

[10] On the dGe lugs distinction see Padma rgyal mtshan Rinpoche (1984/5), pp. 60-1: 'phags pa rnams kyi rgyud la mnyam gzhag zag med kyi ye shes skad cig snga ma'i byed pa la ma ltos par skad cig phyi ma rnams kyang rang stobs kyi yul gzigs pas so sor rang rig ces bya la / de bzhin du 'jig rten pas rang gis rang mthong ba la rang rig ces pa dang yang mi 'dra bar shes par bya'o //. In his detailed criticism of Mi pham's Madhyamaka (p. 180), the dGe lugs lama bLo bzang rab gsal points out that if the gnosis which is reflexive awareness were the same as the mundane reflexive awareness argued for by some other tenet-systems then the gnosis would know itself. Under such circumstances that gnosis would become an ultimate truth (so so rang rig pa'i ye shes rang rig na rang nyid rig par 'gyur la / de lta na ye shes de nyid don dam par 'gyur zhing). This must be because since nondual gnosis takes as its referent the ultimate truth, and it knows itself through direct and incontrovertible perception, it should itself be an ultimate truth, indeed an ultimate truth as a mentalistic positive reality. This would be a serious and unwelcome conclusion for a dGe lugs pa, but would in fact appear to be perfectly welcome to Mi pham. Nevertheless, it would seem that Mi pham's opponent's argument here rests on a misunderstanding, on taking 'self-awareness' in the sense of self-awareness (i). On this basis, ultimate gnosis would take itself as a referent. But Mi pham's self-awareness is self-awareness (ii). Here, ultimate gnosis does not take *itself* as a referent, but it is nevertheless reflexive because it is a gnosis (i.e., a consciousness).

demonstration of 'a mere gnosis which is reflexive awareness', and for the further rDzogs chen identification of this mere gnosis with consciousness as such *(sems nyid)* and, therefore, its presence through even everyday unenlightened consciousness.

One suspects that Mi pham may also have been interested in the possibility of arguing from the conscious presence of awareness itself in a direct nondual, nonconceptual absorption on emptiness, to emptiness as an affirming negation. At least he might want to argue that any such awareness of emptiness cannot get rid of the awareness-factor itself, an awareness factor which as something nonconceptual cannot be touched by the Prāsaṅgika negations. He may have even wanted to go further and link this with showing that not only is emptiness discovered as an ultimate truth about *x* when *x* is subjected to ultimate analysis, but necessarily the awareness itself in a nondualistic experience becomes an ultimate truth. It is certainly possible to see why dGe lugs scholars were so concerned about any attempt—particularly by a follower of a *gzhan stong* rDzogs chen perspective—to defend the acceptability to Prāsaṅgika Madhyamaka (held by dGe lugs scholars, as by most Tibetans, to be the highest and, therefore, the finally true tenet-system) of the conventional reflexivity of consciousness. Mi pham had asked with reference to the *ālaya* (and *svasaṃvedana)* 'what harm is there to Madhyamaka through someone having accepted it transactionally?' The answer from the dGe lugs side is that apart from any other problems there might be, to concede the conventional existence of these may lead to a slippery slope whereby eventually there will emerge the 'absurdities' of a *gzhan stong* mentalistic absolutism.

Eventually—for *if* Mi pham were to try and argue for a mentalistic absolutism based solely on the reflexive nature of consciousness, on the model suggested above, he would face some problems. It seems to me that it need not follow that because the nondual, nonconceptual awareness of emptiness is reflexive, emptiness becomes an affirming negation. Nor need it follow in any vicious sense that the direct experience of emptiness, the ultimate truth, is mixed with an experience of a conventionality. And it certainly need not follow from any of this (should Mi pham wish it to do so) that nondual awareness need become an ultimate truth. Emptiness itself, in the Prāsaṅgika sense as understood by dGe lugs scholars like Mi pham's opponents, is a simple negation. It is simply an absence of inherent existence. There is no implication in this of a positive phenomenon. If all consciousness were reflexive then it would be tautologous to say that in experiencing emptiness the awareness of emptiness is also aware of itself. This is simply to say that it is an awareness. It does not follow from any of this that the emptiness itself is not a pure nonaffirming negation. *Of course*, in the experience of emptiness there is also a positive phenomenon, and, of course, in the experience of emptiness, an ultimate truth, there is also present a consciousness, a conventional truth. That is because it is an *experience* of emptiness as well as emptiness itself. It is clear that the experience of emptiness is not the same as emptiness. To think that reflexivity requires an awareness of two things, the object and the consciousness itself, is still to misunderstand the self-awareness (ii) nature of reflexivity. Reflexivity is the nature of consciousness *qua* consciousness. Therefore, it is argued that if there is an awareness of emptiness, there must also be reflexivity. Nothing follows from this about either the nature of emptiness or the ontology of consciousness. This is the case notwithstanding the fact that emptiness is here experienced nondualistically and nonconceptually. These expressions are to do with *the way emptiness is experienced,* not emptiness itself. If I experience emptiness nondualistically in an experience which as an experience is reflexive, and I do not distinguish between the emptiness experienced and the experiencing consciousness, still it does not follow that emptiness is anything other than a nonaffirming negation, and it also does not follow that the consciousness itself has been found through ultimate analysis and is, therefore, an ultimate reality (or Ultimate Reality). Nor does it follow incidentally that because the consciousness is experienced as nonconceptual it is beyond the reach of Prāsaṅgika negation. One can certainly conceptualize that which is experienced nonconceptually, otherwise it would not be possible to know that such an experience had occurred, or what it signified. A completely unconceptualizable Ultimate Reality would be without meaning and neither 'Ultimate' nor a 'Reality'. The Prāsaṅgika analysis can reach anything of which there is speech, in other words, it can reach anything which can be inserted into the analysis. That too is a tautology.[11] It was not the consciousness experiencing this particular emptiness which was searched for through our ultimate analysis. Thus we cannot claim that this consciousness is found under ultimate analysis when we fail to find the inherent existence of *x*, since what is found under such analysis is directly related to what is being searched for. If someone (a Mi pham?) wants to argue that the consciousness experiencing emptiness (whether it is nonconceptual or not) inherently exists, then it is possible for, say, the dGe lugs Prāsaṅgika to switch the

---

[11] For more on nonconceptual experiences and some Tibetan debates, see Williams (1992a).

analysis to that consciousness. The Prāsaṅgika claim is that for all *x*, *x* lacks inherent existence. If the opponent responds that nevertheless the analysis has not negated his or her putative Ultimate Reality, since that Reality is nonconceptual and the analysis has only failed to find a conceptualized Ultimate, then the opponent too cannot make sense of such a nonconceptual Ultimate Reality, and cannot urge it (put it forward in discourse/debate) against the Prāsaṅgika's analysis. To do so would be to try and have one's cake (or perhaps one's mo-mo) and eat it as well.

The issue of the conventional status of *svasaṃvedana* in this particular Tibetan debate turns out to be closely linked with other issues such as the nature of Prāsaṅgika Madhyamaka and Tibetan disputes concerning the *rang stong* and *gzhan stong* perspectives on ultimate reality. These disputes have further ramifications concerning also the nature of practice (the role of conceptual analysis versus allowing the 'natural primordially present nonconceptual yet reflexive nature of the mind' to shine forth, for example), and where doctrinal differences are reflected in differences in practice it is likely that there may well also be differences in what is considered to be the goal. I have suggested that in India and also in Tibet for many centuries the particular vision of Madhyamaka, at least as represented by the *Bodhicaryāvatāra* and its commentaries, did not embrace the idea that when the Madhyamaka negates *svasaṃvedana,* it also negates *svasaṃvedana* even conventionally. What does or does not exist conventionally was of no concern to the Mādhyamika.[12] Mi pham is, I think, right

[12] It may or may not turn out that this is Candrakīrti's perspective too. If there is convincing evidence that Candrakīrti definitely did negate *svasaṃvedana* as understood in its most in-

in drawing our attention to this and in posing the question, what concern it is to the Mādhyamika whether *svasaṃvedana* exists ultimately? It is clear, of course, that his dGe lugs opponents were very concerned with such a suggestion. For Mi pham's own wider rDzogs chen involvement also it appears to be important to him that all consciousness has this reflexive quality. If it does not, then it is no use incorporating reflexivity into the Ultimate Reality, the gnosis which is consciousness or mind as such *(sems nyid)*. He may, indeed, have hoped to be able to reason for a nonconceptual *gzhan stong*-type perspective from his treatment of *svasaṃvedana,* and that was no doubt one major source of dGe lugs concern. Yet I have argued Mi pham could not draw *gzhan stong* Great Madhyamaka conclusions from his treatment of *svasaṃvedana* alone, and I do not believe that the dGe lugs tradition had anything to be afraid of in accepting the conventional status of reflexivity when understood in the sense urged by Mi pham.

One last point. How original was Mi pham in his approach to *svasaṃvedana* in his *Bodhicaryāvatāra* commentary and response to his critics? Much of Tibetan Madhyamaka literature remains unavailable and unknown. I began this monograph by pointing out that there were a number of previous writers who argued that the Prāsaṅgika accepts *svasaṃvedana* conventionally. Mi pham himself states that he received direct teachings on *Bodhicaryāvatāra* 9 from dPal sprul

nocuous (Mi pham) sense even conventionally, then one response would be to examine more closely whether it makes any sense to think of Śāntideva and Candrakīrti as both members of the same subschool of Madhyamaka. Perhaps someone should do this anyway, and also examine much more carefully than has been the case so far the forces and factors which molded the Tibetan vision of Indian doctrinal 'schools'.

Rinpoche, and, as we have seen, Mi pham disclaims any great originality. Nevertheless, Mi pham's *Bodhicaryāvatāra* commentary produced a fierce response from dGe lugs critics, which suggests some originality, and I do not know of another treatment of *svasaṃvedana* for length, approach or sophistication like that found in Mi pham's reply to bLo bzang dpal ldan bstan 'dzin. I doubt that this reply and its detailed arguments were learnt from dPal sprul Rinpoche, who seems not to have written a commentary to the *Bodhicaryāvatāra* and was presumably not over-interested in the complexities and niceties of scholastic Madhyamaka philosophy. Many of Mi pham's commentaries (to the *Madhyamakāvatāra* for example) are fairly pedestrian word-commentaries. In terms of Mi pham's Madhyamaka commentaries by far the most important are those to *Bodhicaryāvatāra* 9 and the *Madhyamakālaṃkāra*. I have argued that Śāntarakṣita's treatment of *svasaṃvedana* in the *Madhyamakālaṃkāra* is central to Mi pham's own approach, and relatively the *Madhyamakālaṃkāra* appears to have been a text neglected by Tibetan commentators. It seems to me that in formulating an approach to *svasaṃvedana* found in Mi pham's commentary to *Bodhicaryāvatāra* 9, the *Madhyamakālaṃkāra* was crucial. There is no mention of Mi pham studying Śāntarakṣita with dPal sprul Rinpoche. I do not know of another major Tibetan commentator on both the *Madhyamakālaṃkāra* and the *Bodhicaryāvatāra* from whom Mi pham could have derived this approach. *He* is the one who wrote two great commentaries to these works, and it is in Mi pham's own direct response to his critics that we find the most elaborate explanation of his treatment of *svasaṃvedana*. I want to be cautious about this, but at the moment I incline towards the view that in developing his defense of the conventional existence of the reflexive nature of awareness, Mi pham was engaging in some original and creative thinking which, within the scholastic framework of his day and tradition, might be considered to be quite radical and exciting. Mi pham's thought on *svasaṃvedana* is clever, still stimulating in its perspective on Madhyamaka (a perspective different in some ways from the dGe lugs approach more well-known in the West) and in certain respects perhaps convincing. It is all the more welcome in that such creative thought which tries to question and if necessary break out of the framework and strictures of established boundaries appears to be rather rare in the commentarial Tibetan Madhyamaka of the past few hundred years.

APPENDIX 1

Some Tibetan Texts

I have reproduced here for those who read Tibetan the full texts of Mi pham's *Nor bu ke ta ka* commentary to *Bodhicaryāvatāra* 9:26 (25), together with bLo bzang dpal ldan bstan 'dzin's critical observations and Mi pham's response as contained in his *Sher 'grel brgal lan nyin byed snang ba*. These are not critical editions. They are simply romanised versions of the received texts contained in volume 13 of the *Collected Writings of 'Jam mgon 'ju Mi pham rgya mtsho*, reprinted by Sonam Topgay Kazi, Ngagyur Nyingmay Sungrab Series, Gangtok, 1975, and have not been compared with any other versions. The print quality of this edition of Mi pham's *Collected Writings* makes it generally very legible. Apart from romanising the texts the only alterations have been to insert in square brackets the number of the Tibetan folio side as given in volume 13, to offer in italics one or two obvious textual changes, to separate-out for ease of reading bLo bzang dpal ldan bstan 'dzin's criticisms from Mi pham's reply, and to underline for clarity the root verse of *Bodhicaryāvatāra* 9:25 in Mi pham's commentary, and the text of Mi pham's commentary as quoted by bLo bzang dpal ldan. Nearly all the material contained in these sections from Mi pham's works has been given in footnotes above and discussed in the main body of the monograph.

(I) MI PHAM'S *sPYOD 'JUG SHES RAB KYI LE'U'I TSHIG DON GO SLA BAR RNAM PAR BSHAD PA NOR BU KE TA KA* ON *BODHICARYĀVATĀRA* 9:26 (TIBETAN 9:25)

[21] de la rnam rig smra ba na re / shes pa nyid gsal zhing rig pa min na rang mi gsal bas gzhan yang gsal mi nus la / de ltar na mig gis mthong ba dang / rna bas thos pa dang / yid kyis shes pa'i tha snyad thams cad rgyun chad par 'gyur te / 'di kun gsal rig gi shes pa la brten nas rnam gzhag bya dgos kyi gzhan du mi srid pa'i phyir zhe na / ji ltar mthong thos dang shes pa 'di dag ma brtags nyams dga' ba tsam gyi dbang du byas te brjod na ni / 'dir dgag pa min te de dgag mi nus la dgag kyang mi dgos pa'i phyir / 'o na ci zhig 'gog ce na / 'dir sdug bsngal gyi rgyur gyur pa dngos po kun la de bzhin gyi bden par rtog pa bzlog bya yin no // 'dir mthong ba mngon sum dang / thos pa gang zag gzhan nam lung las dang / shes pa rjes dpag tshad ma'i sgo nas bzhag pa'i tha snyad la 'grel pas bshad do // mdor na rang rig pa 'gog pa ni don dam par 'gog pa yin gyi bem po las log tsam la [22] tha snyad du rang rig par 'dogs pa'i tshul de 'gog pa ma yin te /de bkag na rang blo rang la lkog tu gyur par khas len dgos pas rang gzhan gyi blo shes pas gcod tshul la khyad med du thal ba dang rang rgyud la blo yod pa'i sgrub byed mi rigs pa dang / mthar don rig gi tha snyad kyang rgyun chad par 'gyur ba sogs rig pa'i dbang phyug gis ji skad gsungs pas gnod cing / rang rig 'gog pa'i rigs pa ji snyed pa thams cad phung sogs 'gog pa'i rigs pa bzhin du don dam par 'gog gi tha snyad du bkag pa'i gtan med ma yin par shes dgos shing / lugs 'dir tha snyad du'ang rig kun gzhi khas mi len zer yang

'dir tha snyad du ni dgag pa'ang med la sgrub pa'ang med kyi don dam par bkag pa kho na yin no // de la kha cig gis dbu ma pa yin na kun gzhi khas len par mi bya ste / kun gzhi ni rnam rig pa'i lugs yin zer yang legs par ma brtags pa ste / kun gzhi bden grub tu khas ma blangs na tha snyad du khas blangs pas dbu ma'i tshul ci zhig nyams / tha snyad du khas len mi rung ba ni tha snyad dpyod byed kyi tshad mas gnod pa spyi rtag pa la sogs pa lta bu yin gyi / don dam pa'i rigs pas bkag tshad khas mi len na phung khams skye mched kyang gten med du khas blang dgos so // de phyir thal 'gyur ba'i gzhung du kun gzhi don dam par bkag gi tha snyad du mi 'gog kyang de'i rnam gzhag mdzad de sgrub pa'ang min no // de bzhin du rang rig tha snyad du khas len pa ni rtog ge'i bag chags goms pa'i dbang gis yin gyi khas blang bar mi bya zer ba'ang gyin ste / don dam pa gtan la 'bebs pa la rang rig dang kun gzhi mi dgos mod / tha snyad kyi rnam bzhag dpyod pa la med du mi rung zhing tha snyad dpyod pa'i tshad mas grub na de tha snyad du med ces 'gog pa'i rigs pa ni med do // [23] gal te rigs pa ci ste med / zla grags zhi lhag *[omit 'g']* la sogs pa'i gzhung na ji snyed cig bshad pa 'di ma mthong ngam zhe na / de don rig la'ang mtshungs so // mi mshungs te don rig ni tha snyad du mi 'gog go zhen na / bde sogs rang gis nyams su myong ba yang tha snyad du ji ltar 'gog ste mi 'gog go // des na sems bden grub tu 'dod pa la rang rig pa mi thad kyang bden med du 'dod pa la rang rig pa'i tha snyad shin tu 'thad par yang shes par bya ste ji bzhin rtogs pa ni sngar yang nyung ngo //

(II) MI PHAM'S *SHER 'GREL BRGAL LAN NYIN BYED SNANG BA*

bLo bzang dpal ldan bstan 'dzin:

[198] slar yang sprul pa'i sku gang gi zhal nas / 'dir deng sang gi spyod 'jug ṭī ka byed pa kha cig gis / mdor na rang rig pa 'gog pa ni / don dam par 'gog pa yin gyi bem po las [199] log tsam la tha snyad du rang rig par 'dogs pa'i tshul de 'gog pa ma yin te /de bkag na rang blo rang la lkog tu gyur pa dang rang rgyud la blo yod pa'i sgrub byed mi rigs pa dang // mthar don rig gi tha snyad kyang rgyun chad par 'gyur ba sogs rig pa'i dbang phyug gis ji skad gsungs pas gnod ces dang / lugs 'dir tha snyad du'ang rang rig dang kun gzhi khas mi len zer yang / tha snyad du ni bkag *[Mi pham: dgag]* pa'ang med la sgrub pa'ang med mod kyi don dam par bkag go zhes smra ba'ang rang gi nang cha bstan pa tsam du zad de / lugs 'dir don dam du ma zad tha snyad du'ang rang rig bkag pa yin pa'i phyir te / dpal ldan zla bas 'jug 'grel du / 'on te 'jig rten tha snyad kyi dbang du yin na ni / de lta na'ang rang rig pa'i rgyu can gyi dran pa mi srid pa nyid du / zhes gsal bar gsungs pa'i phyir dang // gzhan yang tha snyad du rang rig bkag pa ma yin na tha snyad du bya byed las gsum po de rang ngos nas grub par thal ba'i thal ba bzlog tu med pa'i phyir /rang blo rang la lkog tu gyur pa dang / don rig gi tha snyad rgyun chad par 'gyur ba sogs dgos med kyi dgag pa rnams kyang 'dod du rigs te / gong *[gang?]* du rang rig med kyang dran pa skye ba 'chad pa la dgos pa yod cing / grub mtha' gong 'og gi lugs [200] rnams so so nas ma 'dres par 'chad dgos pa'i phyir ro //de bzhin du kun gzhi'i rnam shes pa'ang tha snyad du yod ces smra ba ga la rigs te de ltar na lugs 'dis phyi rol gyi don yang 'gog dgos par 'gyur la / des na mdo sde sa bcu pa dang de'i dgongs 'grel sogs las phyi don 'gog tu mi rigs par

gsungs pa sogs don med pa nyid du thal bas 'dod du ga la nus te mi nus so // gzhan yang khyod kyi 'grel pa 'dir 'khogs bshad kyi tshig phreng 'di dang rigs mthun pa mang du mchis kyang re re nas dgag tu ma langs mod / 'on kyang 'dir gnod pa'i lung rigs kyi sgo tsam bstan la 'di rnams la zhib tu dpyad na phal cher 'gog par yod pas zhib mo'i blos go bsdur mi dman re mdzod / rgyal gsung dri med gser gyi lhun po ni // khungs ldan lung rigs rin chen phras mdzes shing // dgag sgrub rta bdun 'od kyi zer 'khyud pa // 'di yang rgyal bstan mdzes pa'i dpyid du grub // ces pa'i bar gyis sun 'byin par mdzad do //

Mi pham's reply:
de la lan mdo tsam brjod na / spyir dbu ma thal 'gyur ba'i lugs la rnam shes tshogs drug tu bzhed pa dang / rang rig gi rnam bzhag sogs ma mdzad pa ni rang gzhung na gsal mod / der tha snyad du zhal bzhes med pa tsam zhig gis tha snyad du med nges su go dgos [201] pa'i nges pa ga la yod de / dper na thal 'gyur ba'i lugs la gnyug sems dang bde ba chen po sogs kyi tha snyad sbyor don med kyang de dag tha snyad du mi 'thad pa ma yin pa bzhin no //de dang ga la 'dra ste rang rig la dgag pa nan tan mdzad par dngos su gsal bas tha snyad du med par 'gog pa de thal 'gyur ba'i khyad chos su 'jog go zhe na / dbu ma'i gzhung na rang rig nan gyis bkag pa yod mod kyi / de dag gis don dam par bkag par 'gyur gyi tha snyad du mi khegs te dper na gzhan rig bzhin no //ci'i phyir mi khegs snyan [*snyam?]* na tha snyad du yang med ces 'gog na rtag pa'i sgra dang dbang phyug byed pa po la sogs pa bzhin du tha snyad dpyod byed kyi tshad mas gnod pa dngos su yod pa dgos na 'di la de mi srid pa'i phyir ro // de'i phyir 'jig rten tha snyad kyi dbang du'ang rig pa'i rgyu can gyi dran pa mi srid pa nyid du zhes sogs gsungs pa ni / rang rig

pa ni grub la rag mod kyi / de lta'ang dran pas dran par rigs min te / gzhan phyir ma shes rgyud la skyes pa bzhin / zhes gsungs pa ltar snga phyi'i shes pa rang mtshan gyis grub pa'i so so ba la sngar rang gis rang myong du chug kyang da lta dran mi srid par ston pa'i rigs par 'dug gi / 'jig rten tha [202] snyad du rang rig yod pa la gnod nges kyi rigs pa gang yang mi 'dug na de tsam zhig brjod pas ci yang mi 'grub bo // rigs pa yod de gong du brjod pa ltar tha snyad du rang rig yod na bya byed las gsum rang ngos grub par thal ba bzlog tu med do zer na 'di rgyu mtshan ma nges pa'i tshig tsam ste / rang ngos nas grub pa zhes pa dbu ma'i skabs 'dir don dam dpyod pa'i rigs pas dpyad bzod la brjod pa yin la / des rang rig ma grub par ni 'dod cing tha snyad du rang blo rang gis rig na bya byed las gsum rang ngos nas grub dgos pa'i rgyu mtshan rdul tsam med de don rig bzhin no // gal te 'di'i skabs kyi bya byed las gsum zhes pa rig bya rig byed rig pa'i bya ba gsum tha dad du med pa la / rig pa'i tha snyad kyang mi thob cing / rang gis rang la byed pa 'jug pa la dpyad na yul yul can tha dad du yod na'ang rang rig tu mi 'gyur te gzhan rig tu 'gyur ro // tha dad du med na'ang byed pa mi 'jug ste bya byed las gsum gcig tu 'gyur bas ral gris rang gis rang mi gcod pa bzhin no snyam na // de ltar yin mod de dper na sngo 'dzin shes pa dang sngon po gnyis bar bcas pa dang ma bcas pa'am snga phyi ji ltar yin dpyad na gang ltar kyang des de 'dzin pa mi srid mod kyi dpyad pa de dag don dam dpyod [203] par song gi 'jig rten tha snyad du sngon po nyams su myong ba'i shes pa gtan med par mi 'gro ba bzhin du / rang rig la'ang bya byed las gsum tha dad du med kyang rang blo nyid skyes tsam nas lkog tu ma gyur par myong ba gsal rig gi ngo bor skyes pa la rang rig ces brjod la de 'jig rten tha snyad du yod de tha snyad du rang rgyud kyi blo rang gis dngos su rig pa'am mi rig pa gnyis su kha tshon chod pa las mi rig par 'dod na rang blo rang la lkog gyur du khas len pa las 'os med do // des na dpal ldan chos kyi grags pa'i zhal nas / blo yis nyams myong bya gzhan med // de yi myong ba'ang gzhan yod min // gzung dang 'dzin pa gnyis med phyir // de ni de ltar rang nyid gsal // zhes dang / dbu ma rgyan las / rnam shes bems po'i rang bzhin las // bzlog pa rab tu skye ba ste // bems min rang bzhin gang yin pa // de 'di bdag nyid shes pa yin // gcig pa cha med rang bzhin la // gsum gyi rang bzhin mi 'thad phyir // de yis rang gis rig pa ni // bya dang byed pa'i dngos por min // zhes gsungs pa bzhin no // de'i phyir rang la rang gi byed pa gsar du 'jug mi dgos kyang rang nyid gsal ba'i ngo bos rang lkog tu ma gyur par shes pa la rang rig pa'i tha snyad gnod med du 'jug ste / ji ltar bum pa mngon [204] sum shes pa la yul shes pa'i tha snyad du byed pa bzhin du / rang gi rgyud la gang skyes pa'i blo rang gis mngon sum shes pa la rang shes pa'i tha snyad ci ste mi rung / de bas na rang rig pa tsam 'jig rten na gnod med bslu med du yod kyang des rang ji ltar rig pa'i btags don btsal na ma brtags 'jig rten gyi grags pa tsam las yang dag par grub pa gang yang rnyed par mi 'gyur kyang /don dam par grub ma grub kyi brtag dpyad med par ji ltar snang ba ltar tha snyad byed pa'i 'jig rten gyi blo'i dpang du na rang nyid gsal rig gi rang bzhin du skyes pa'i phyir rang rig ces dang / de la bya byed las gsum gyi rdzas gzhan med pas na rang zhes pa'i tha snyad dang / de la blos phar btags pa'i bya byed las gsum yod pas rig pa'i tha snyad nges par rung ste 'di ltar bde sdug myang bya yin pa dang / de myong byed blo yin pa dang / blo des bde sdug dngos su myong ba'i bya ba byed pa gsum ni su'i lugs la'ang yod pa gzhir bcas la / bde sogs myong bzhin pa'i blo de la myong bya bde sogs las rdzas gzhan pa'i 'dzin byed kyi blo dang / blo de las tha dad du gyur pa'i gzung bya bde sogs yod par sus khas len dka' ste / bde sogs myong ba de las gzhan pa'i blo yan gar du yod na tshor ba med pa'i blor thal ba dang / rang [205] 'dzin gyi blo de las tha dad pa'i myang bya bde sogs yod na shes pa med pa'i tshor bar 'gyur te grangs can pa dang bye brag pas bde sogs phyi dang nang gi bems por 'dod pa ltar 'gyur ro // de ltar bde sogs dang de myong tha dad du med kyang bde sdug mngon sum myong ba'i tshul gyis shes pa yod pa ni grub mtha' smra ba dang 'jig rten phal pa thun mongs la grags shing mngon sum gyis grub na // de la rang rig ces brjod pa ji ltar mi 'thad de / de khas mi len na bde sogs dngos su myong ba med zer ram / myong yang gzhan rig gis myong zhes khas len nam bsam par byos shig / de bzhin du gang ji snyed pa'i shes pa yin no cog la bdag gis 'di dang 'di lta bur don 'di gsal par shes so snyam pa'i tshe gang shes par bya ba'i rnam par shar ba de ni las su bya ba'am yul gyi ldog pa nas tha snyad btags pa yin la / gang gis shes snyam du bsam pa'i tshe rang gi blo 'dis so snyam pa ni yul can byed pa po'i tha snyad 'jug pa'i ldog pa yin la / des de gnyis su med pa'i tshul gyis gsal bar rtogs shing myong ba ni bya ba'i ldog pa ste / de 'dra'i shes bya shes byed kyi ldog pa tsam zhig bzhag tu med pa'i 'jig rten gyi shes pa ga la srid cing de 'dra srid ces su zhig gis smra nus te bsam par bya'o // [206] de yang rmi lam dang rab rib kyi snang ba dang rtog ngor don spyi la'ang sngon po'i rnam pa lta bur shar ba'i blo la bsams na sngo snang dang de 'dzin dang des de rtogs pa gsum gyi rnam par 'char bas rim pa ltar gzung rnam 'dzin rnam rang rig gsum du phye yang don la de gsum tha dad du yod mi rigs te shes pa nyid sngon po'i rnam par gsal ba tsam yin pas rang rig tu grub pa bzhin no // de ltar ma shes par blo rags pa rnams kyis kha nang du phyogs nas blo rang gis rang ji ltar rig ces bltas pa na rig bya rig byed gnyis su mi 'char bas bya byed las gsum gyi rdzas lta ci ldog pa tsam yang tha dad du med pas rang gi rang ji ltar rig ste mi rig go snyam pa shing tu rtsing ste / der rig bya rig byed kyi rdzas tha dad du yod na rang rig ji ltar yin te gzhan rig tu 'os so // yul gang dang gang gi rnam pa can gyi shes pa gzhi gcig la 'jig rten tha snyad kyis btags pa'i bya byed las gsum gyi ldog pa yod pa ni blo rags pas dpyad pa zhugs ma shes pa ste ji ltar yod tshul gong du bstan pa bzhin no // lar rang rig 'di mngon sum gyis grub pa yin kyang grub mtha'i dpyad pas bslad nas nges pa ma skyes pas rang rig gi tha snyad mi byed pa tsam du zad de / ji ltar kha nang du phyogs nas bsam na [207] rang gi shes pa la gang dang gang shar ba thams cad dus snga phyi'i res 'jog mi dgos par rang la mngon du gsal zhing the tshom med pa 'di rang rig mngon sum yin no // de ltar yin bzhin rang rig med ces smra ba ni rdzas lag na thogs bzhin bdag gis ma khyer zhes bsnyon 'ding ba lta bur ya mtshan du 'os so // de lta bur don mngon sum grub kyang de'i tha snyad mi sbyor ba gzhan yang yod de / spyi yis dben pa'i ba lang mngon sum mthong yang gzegs zan pa blo gros phyin ci log tu gyur pa dag gis ba lang spyi dang ldan par khas len pa dang / tshor ba shes pa'i rang bzhin du rang rig gis myong yang / grangs can pa sogs kyis bems po'i ngo bor khas len pa yin la / de bzhin du phyi rol pa dag gis rang rig pa mi srid ces smra ba'ang yin no // des na rang rig tha snyad du yod med rigs pas grub bya yin pas na lung kho nas dgag pa'am sgrub par byed pa ni don ci yang med do // gal te rang rig med kyang dran pa skye tshul byi bas rmugs pa'i dug la dper byas pa 'dis rang rig tha snyad du bkag pa ji ltar min te / don dam par rang rig med kyang dran pa skye tshul yod ces ni sgrub mi srid la / byi bas rmug pa tsam myong dus dug gtan nas ma myong ba bzhin sngar myong byed rang gis rang gtan ma myong yang [208] phyis sngar gyi myong byed kyi rnam par bzung bar bstan pa min nam zhe na / de ltar shin tu yang yin te rang rig med kyang dran pa skye tshul tha snyad las 'os med pa yin mod / de 'dra'i sbyor ba de bkod tshod la rang rig tha snyad du 'gog pa ltar snang yang / song tshod la don dam par bkag par song gi tha snyad du kheg mi srid do // ji ltar zhe na yul sngon po lta bu myong ba'i blo ni kun la rtsod med du grub la / sngo 'dzin de yang myong ba'i blo gnyis pa zhig 'jig rten na tha snyad du med kyang sngon po myong ba'i stobs kyis sngo 'dzin zhes tha snyad thob pa de bzhin phyis sngon po dran pa na de'i yul can sngo 'dzin kyang dran rigs te sngar myong dus kyang yul yul can gnyis po de tsam zhig yin la / phyis dran dus kyang yul dang 'brel par yul can dran pa tsam ste rgyud gcig gi dbang du byas pa'i phyir ro // de yang ma brtags pa 'jig rten tha snyad kyi tshul tsam las don dam par brtags na myong dran gang yang mi 'grub ces pa'i don to // des na de 'dra'i ngag sbyor des yul can sngo 'dzin tsam zhig yod kyi slar yang de rig pa'am myong bar byed pa'i 'dzin rnam yan gar ba tha snyad du yang med par dgag pa'i don du song ba yin no // gal te 'di snyam du yul can de las blo yan gar ba zhig yin na rang rig kyang min te shes pa gzhan gyis gzhan rig par 'gyur zhing gzhan yang [209] 'dzin rnam thug med du 'dod dgos pa sogs kyi skyon mtha' yas pas na mdo sems kyi gzhung smra ba dag la de 'dra'i rang rig khas len mkhan gcig kyang med la 'jig rten tha mal pas kyang de 'dra khas mi len pas dgag pa de lta bu 'brel pa ci yang med par 'gyur ro snyam na / 'di ni shin tu gsal por go dgos pa'i gnad gcig yin te / gang zhe na rang rig bden grub tu khas len na rdzas su med par btags pa tsam gyis ni rang rig gi go mi chod cing / bya byed las gsum yang rang ngos nas grub dgos pas na rig bya sngo 'dzin de la rig byed kyi 'dzin rnam yan gar du yod dgos te de med par rang gis rang la byed pa 'jug pa'i btags don dpyod na mi rnyed pa'i phyir ro // ma rnyed na rang rig ces pa'ang tha snyad tsam du 'gyur gyi don dam par mi 'gyur ro // yang gar du yod na'ang rang rig par mi 'thad la de 'dra tha snyad du'ang med cing pha rol gyis khas blangs kyang med pa de ltar rang rig bden grub bkag pa de kho nas gnyis stong gi rnam shes bden grub tu smra ba'i grub mtha'i lugs la gnod pa brjod pa'i gtso bo yin te / rnam shes kyi sgrub byed rang rig dang bsgrub bya rang gsal gyi shes pa gnyis ka btags pa tsam las yang dag par dpyad na btags don ma grub par rigs pa de kho nas gtan la phab pa yin no // [210] de dang rigs mthun par rang rig 'gog pa'i rigs pa gzhung gzhan las gsungs pa dag kyang de ltar shes par bya'o // de'i phyir ral gri'i dpe la sogs pa la bsams na ral gri rang gis rang tha snyad du gcod pa med mod kyi / de tsam gyis dpe can tha snyad du yang med mi dgos te bum sogs skye med kyi dper mo gsham bu sogs bkod pa bzhin no // de lta min na rang blo rang gis mngon sum shes pa tha snyad du yang med par 'gyur te 'og tu yang 'chad par 'gyur ro // de'i phyir rang rig ces pa yang dag par dpyad na ma grub kyang ldog pa la brten nas rang rig tu btags pa de 'dra ni thal 'gyur ba'i lugs la gnod pa med par ma zad phan byed kyi sman ltar 'gyur te / gang gis na sgra gcan gyi mgo zhes sgra gcan ni sngon dus su mgo bcad de bdud rtsi 'thungs pa'i stobs kyis ma shi bar 'jig rten na rgyu zhes 'dod pa las de la mgo las gzhan pa'i lus med kyang 'jig rten na de 'dra'i tha snyad byed pa dang / de bzhin du mchig gu'i lus zhes pa la sogs pa yan lag dang yan lag can gyi tha snyad de dag ming gis btags pa tsam gyis bzhag pa la'ang 'jig rten gyi ngor bya byed kyi tha snyad 'jog rung bar dpal ldan zla ba'i bzhed pa thun mongs min pa yin pa'i phyir na / de 'dra'i tha snyad kyi rnam bzhag rung ba de la rang rig gi tha snyad de [211] ltar mi rung ba ci yang med la / 'jig rten rgan pos kyang bum sogs mngon sum myong ba bzhin rang blo gsal por myong ba'i nyams myong bslu med 'di las rang sems rang gis shes zhes kha len par yongs su grags pa'ang yin pa'i phyir ro // des na // gang phyir gang gis yul myong gyur de las // zhes sogs gsungs pa bzhin du / gang phyir bde sogs nyams su myong de las // 'dzin pa 'di gzhan nga la yod min pa // de phyir rang sems rig ces rtogs 'gyur te // 'di yang 'jig rten tha snyad tshul lugs yin // ces 'jig rten pa dang mthun par ma brtags tha snyad tsam gyi dbang du rang rig khas blangs na'ang lugs de la shin tu bde bar 'gyur zhing / rgyan stug po bkod po'i mdo las / sna tshogs snang ba rang sems te // lus can rnams kyi bdag nyid gnyis // phyi dang nang dang thams cad du // gzung dang 'dzin pa lta bur gnas // sems kyis sems ni mthong yin yang // khong du mi chud dus pa rnams // kha gnyis sems de lus can gyi // yin yang shes par ma gyur pa // bdag gir byed pa'ang de bzhin byed // yul lta bur yang rab tu snang // rdza ma la sogs gzugs su gnas // rdza la sogs pa'ang yod ma yin // 'di yi don la thub pa dag // [212] rnal 'byor nyam chung rnam par myos // zhes dang / bde mchog 'byung ba sogs sngags kyi rgyud las kyang / bems po min phyir bdag nyid rig // ces gsungs so // de ltar min na thal 'gyur ba'i lugs 'dzin pa de dag gis rang gi blo rang gis mngon sum gyis shes par khas len nam mi shes par khas len / shes so zhe na rang gsal du shes pa yin nam shes par bya rgyu'i shes pa dang shes byed rdzas gzhan du yod pas shes pa yin / dang po ltar na rang rig grub pa la // gnyis pa ltar na shes par bya rgyu'i blo de dang dus mnyam pa'i shes pa'am de'i rjes su skyes pa gang gis shes dgos / dus mi mnyam na yul da lta med pa la mngon sum ji ltar yin tshul dang kha phyir bltas dang nang bltas kyi shes pa spel mar skye ba yin min sogs sgrub dgos la / dus mnyam na'ang de 'dra'i blo gnyis yod par gang gis shes te / ma bzung bar yang yod ces bya mi rung // zhes gsungs pa bzhin no // gal te blo thams cad la'ang 'dzin byed kyi blo gzhan re yod na blo thug pa med par 'gyur ba sogs skyon tshad med la 'dzin rnam yan gar ba gcig cig kyang mi srid na du ma lta ci smos pa'i phyir ro // 'dzin byed gzhan med na mig gis bum sogs mthong bar byed kyang rang mthong bar byed mi nus pa ltar rang blo rang ngor lkog tu gyur nas rang sems la gang skyes pa'i kun rtog [213] 'di dang 'di 'drar gyur ma gyur ces mngon sum shes mi srid na'ang rang la blo ji 'dra skyes pa de ni rtags la ltos mi dgos pa rang gis nges pa 'di ci zhig gis yin dpyad nas smra dgos so // gal te de 'dra'i dpyad pa zhib mor gzhug mi dgos so snyam na rang sems rang gis shes sam mi shes zhes dri ba la thal 'gyur ba yin kyang lan 'debs rigs la / shes tshul ji ltar yin zhes dri na yang brjod par rigs pas na rang rig med na rang gzhan gyi blo gcod tshul khyad med du 'gyur ba sogs dgos med kyi dgag pa ma yin te / sangs rgyas gyi bstan pa 'di la tha snyad kyi rig pa smra ba kun gyi gtsug gi nor bur gyur ba dpal chos kyi grags pas de ltar brtag pa mdzad pa yin na de'i bzhed pa'i snying po rang rig dang mo gsham gyi bu mgo mnyam par tha snyad du dgag pa smra ba rnams kyis de la lan tshul bzhin du bstan par rigs kyi / nged thal 'gyur ba'i lugs 'dzin pa yin pas rigs pa ma smras kyang grub mtha'i dbang gis rang rig med par dam bcas pa tsam gyis 'grub bo zhes brjod par ni mi rigs so // gzhan yang 'dzin rnam gyi ldog pa nas rang rig tu btags kyang don la bya byed so sor med pas mi 'thad na bdag gcig 'brel yang tha snyad du med par kha len dgos te / bdag rang la rang 'brel ba dang rang gis rang rig pa gnyis [214] tshul 'dra ba'i phyir ro // bdag gcig 'brel mi 'thad na bden gnyis ngo bo gcig pa'ang tha snyad du med par 'gyur zhing / yang gnyis snang med pa'i ye shes kyis yul rtogs pa'ang mi 'thad par 'gyur te yul yul can gnyis su mi snang bzhin du nges de rtogs pa'i byed pa 'jug pa'am de la de mngon sum du snang ba mi 'thad pa mtshungs par 'gyur ba'i phyir dang / rang la rang gi byed pa 'jug pa la ji ltar dpyad kyang gsum du snang gi cha med gcig tu 'char mi btub pas rang rig mi 'thad par brjod pa ltar gzung 'dzin med pa'i blo la ji ltar dpyad kyang gzung bya'i rnam par mi 'char la / de la snang ngor yul yod par bzung na gzung 'dzin med par mi 'char ba yang de bzhin no // kun gzhi yang thal 'gyur ba'i lugs la khas len mi dgos mod / de tha snyad du 'gog pa'i rigs pa mi snang la don dam par 'gog pa ni smos ma dgos so // 'on kyang de'i tshul rgyas par mi spro'o //

Appendix 2

I am reprinting here my 1983 paper 'On *rang rig*', which was originally given as a conference paper in Austria and published in Ernst Steinkellner and Helmut Tauscher ed., *Contributions on Tibetan and Buddhist Religion and Philosophy* (Wien: Arbeitskreis für Tibetische und Buddistische Studien Universität Wien, Wiener Studien zur Tibetologie und Buddhismuskunde Heft 11, pp. 321-32). I have made no alterations to the paper except to bring it more closely into line with the typographic style of the present work, to correct one or two obvious misprints, and insert in square brackets the page references to the original printing. I have however incorporated the paper's bibliography into the final Bibliography below. I have made no alterations to my translations of technical terms in this paper in order to correspond with those in the monograph. Although I am now no longer sure I would agree with some of the things said here, and I would phrase matters differently with hindsight, still the paper can serve as an introduction to the present work and it does treat some issues which are taken up at greater length, and make some points which I have chosen not to address further, in the present volume.

ON *RANG RIG*

It is well known that Candrakīrti, in his discussion of the two *satyas* in the *Madhyamakāvatārabhāṣya*, placed under *mithyāsaṃvṛtisatya* the philosophical views of his opponents. That is, all the philosophical activity of those thinkers who aren't Prāsaṅgika Mādhyamika is incorrect even from the conventional everyday point of view, without beginning to consider its pretensions to revealing ultimate truth.[1]

In his commentary on the *Madhyamakāvatāra* (the *Dwags brgyud grub pa'i shing rta)*, however, Mi bskyod rdo rje, the eighth Karma pa, tells us that there were many earlier commentators who understood Candrakīrti's refutation of the substratum consciousness *(ālayavijñāna)*, self-referring consciousness *(svasaṃvitti)*, the external object and the person *(pudgala)* to be only a refutation from the ultimate point of view, and not conventionally *(tha snyad du)*.[2] Tsong kha pa

---

1 See Candrakīrti's *Madhyamakāvatārabhāṣya* on *Madhyamakāvatāra* 6:26. See also Atīśa's *Satyadvayāvatāra* 70a: dang po gnyis te chu zla dang/ grub mtha' ngan pa'i rtog pa'o /

2 *Dwags brgyud grub pa'i shing rta* p. 457: go shāk sogs bod kyi 'jug 'grel byed pa mang pos slob dpon zla grags kyi bzhed par gzhung 'dis tha snyad du rang lugs la rang rig yod pa yin par sgrub po / zhes dang / de bzhin kun gzhi rang rig phyi don gang zag rnams lugs 'dis tha snyad du 'gog pa min kyi / dpyad bzod du grub pa'i kun gzhi sogs 'gog par byed pa yin lo /

certainly held that the Prāsaṅgika Madhyamaka accepts conventionally the external object and the person, when these are understood correctly.[3] But Mi bskyod rdo rje singles out for particular mention the Sa skya lamas Go ram pa bSod nams seng ge and Shākya mchog ldan, and I want to look briefly at two things: First, the issues involved in urging the acceptance or otherwise of self-referring, reflexive consciousness; and second, some philosophical dimensions of the dispute between Go ram pa bSod nams seng ge and Mi bskyod rdo rje.

[322] Mi pham, in his lucid commentary on Śāntarakṣita's *Madhyamakālaṃkāra* explains that for Śāntarakṣita consciousness in its occurrence is in all important respects the exact reverse of insentient phenomena. Consciousness has as its nature luminosity and awareness, 'whatever is by nature not dead, not insentient, is conscious of its very self, self-aware, self-luminous'.[4] Self-consciousness is what distinguishes sentience from insentience, in the case of consciousness, and uniquely in the case of consciousness, there is self-reference, self-consciousness in the very same act. By 'self-consciousness', Mi pham explains, is

---

[3] For Tsong kha pa's acceptance of the conventional existence of the external object see, for example, his *rTsa ba shes rab kyi dka' gnas chen po brgyad kyi bshad pa* pp. 15 ff. On the status of the person see the same text pp. 40 ff.

[4] See Mi pham' s *dBu ma rgyan gyi rnam bshad 'jam dbyangs bla ma dgyes pa'i zhal lung* (Mi pham 1976a(ii)) pp. 141 ff: de ltar bem po min pa'i rang bzhin gang yin pa de lta bu 'di ni bdag rang nyid shes pa'am rang rig rang gsal zhes pa yin no / This is an expansion of Śāntarakṣita's *Madhyamakālaṃkāra* v.16bc: bem min rang bzhin gang yin pa / de 'di bdag nyid shes pa yin //, given in the Sanskrit text of the *Tattvasaṃgraha,* v.1999b: iyam evātmasaṃvittir asya yā'jaḍarūpatā //and also quoted in the *Bodhicaryāvatārapañjikā (BCAP)* on *Bodhicaryāvatāra (BCA)* 9:20.

meant that in one nature *(ngo bo gcig)* there is both awareness of object and of subject.[5] Śāntarakṣita and his commentators assert emphatically that consciousness is unitary and partless, and cannot be judged on the model of unconscious beings, 'chariots, a wall and so on'.[6] It is pointless to argue in the case of self-consciousness that an act cannot be directed towards itself. Act, agent, object, knowing, knower, knowable—none of these categories applies in the case of a partless consciousness which is in its very nature, and not as an additional act, self-conscious.[7]

There is an argument, familiar in the West from Aristotle's *De Anima* and, more recently, the work of

---

[5] *dBu ma rgyan gyi rnam bshad* pp. 141-142: de'ang gzung char snang ba'i rnam pa de'ang shes pa yin / de 'dzin pa'ang shes pa yin cing de gnyis ngo bo gcig yin...An opponent is here raising an objection that if this were the case then act and agent would be the same thing. Śāntarakṣita, and Mi pham, go on to explain that this in fact doesn't follow.

[6] Ibid. p. 142: 'di ltar gzhal bya sna tshogs pa snang ba'i yul dang / de 'dzin pa'i yul can so sor yod pa lta bu'i snang tshul gyi dbang du byas te gzung rnam dang 'dzin rnam zhes bzhag kyang don la rnam par shes pa gang zhig shing rta dang rtsig pa la sogs pa bem po'i rang bzhin gsal rig dang bral ba dag las bzlog pa gsal zhing rig pa'i mtshan nyid can du rab tu skye ba ste /. I am grateful to Tom Tillemans and Achok Rinpoche for correcting a misreading of this verse. This incorporates *Madhyamakālaṃkāra* v. 16ab: rnam shes bem po'i rang bzhin las / bzlog pa rab tu skye ba ste //, which equals *Tattvasaṃgraha* v. 1999a: vijñānaṃ jaḍarūpebhyo vyāvṛttam upajāyate /, and is also quoted in the *Bodhicaryāvatārapañjikā* on 9:20.

[7] See the *dBu ma rgyan gyi rnam bshad* pp. 142-143 on *Madhyamakālaṃkāra* v. 17: gcig pu cha med rang bzhin la / gsum gyi rang bzhin mi 'thad phyir / de yi rang gis rig pa ni / bya dang byed pa'i dngos por min // This equals *Tattvasaṃgraha* v. 2000: kriyākārakabhāvena na svasaṃvittir asya tu / ekasyānaṃśarūpasya trairūpyānupapattitaḥ //, and this verse is also quoted in *BCAP* on *BCA* 9:20.

Franz Brentano and Jean-Paul Sartre, to the effect that if consciousness isn't conscious, that is, conscious of [323] itself as well as conscious of the object, then, being unconscious, there could be no conscious awareness.[8] Thus far Śāntarakṣita. Self-consciousness is the very nature of consciousness, if consciousness isn't self-conscious then it is *bem po, jaḍa,* dead. If luminosity isn't luminous, says Kamalaśīla in his *Madhyamakālaṃkārapañjikā,* then it cannot apprehend other objects.[9] It is worth noting that the (misleading) metaphor of light for consciousness, a metaphor which reoccurs here in the example of light illuminating itself in the very same act of illuminating others, has been traced by the philosopher Gilbert Ryle to the Protestant need to know the state of his soul without recourse to confessors and scholars—thus the God-given 'light' of conscience.[10] Whether there is any conceptual similarity here with Buddhism I leave to a different occasion, but it is clear that the image of light for consciousness was very old in India and had no need of Protestants for its revelation!

If consciousness is known in another, reflective rather than reflexive, act of consciousness then we face an infinite regress, since the second act would

---

8 See Aristotle, *De Anima* III:2, Franz Brentano's *Psychology from an Empirical Standpoint* (English trans.), pp. 121 ff, and Sartre's *Being and Nothingness* pp. lix-lxvii (English trans.) and *The Transcendence of the Ego, passim.* For an influential criticism of consciousness, self-consciousness and this argument in particular, see Gilbert Ryle, *The Concept of Mind* pp. 148-189, especially pp. 150-156.

9 *Madhyamakālaṃkārapañjikā* f. 98b: gsal ba yang gsal ba ma yin na ni gsal ba gsal ba ma yin pa'i phyir mi gzhan gyi mngon sum bzhin du mdun na rnam par gnas pa'i don kyang mngon sum du mi 'gyur ro /.

10 See *The Concept of Mind* pp. 152-153.

have to be known in the same way as the first, and so on. Or, Tsong kha pa points out in his commentary on *Madhyamakāvatāra* 6:73a (the *dBu ma dgongs pa rab gsal),* representing the *pūrvapakṣa,* if the second act doesn't require to be itself illuminated by another act, then why is it necessary for the first to be so illuminated?[11] But what is wrong with an infinite regress? The problem, Tsong kha pa notes, is that in the case of an infinite regress the initial perception of, say, blue, is never founded, never established.[12] Moreover if an infinite regress of consciousness were required in order to found one consciousness then there could be no progression beyond the first attempt at objective knowledge. For Tsong kha pa, clearly, to complete an infinite series requires an infinite time. There could be no delimitation of other objects, [324] forms, sounds and so on.[13] Thus, to quote Brentano, 'The presentation of the sound and the presentation of the presentation of the sound form a single mental phenomenon.'[14]

Now, it's not clear to me this train of argument is valid or even coherent. To deny that consciousness is conscious of itself at the same time as it is conscious of objects is not necessarily to claim that it is unconscious, anymore than to deny that whiteness is itself white is thereby to claim that whiteness is black, or indeed any other colour. It is to deny that a category is

---

[11] *dBu ma dgongs pa rab gsal* p. 285: de la de 'jal byed kyi shes pa don gzhan dgos sam mi dgos / mi dgos na shes pa snga la yang mi dgos par 'gyur la /.

[12] *Ibid.:* thug med du song na ni sngo 'dzin dang po la myong ba mi 'grub pa'i skyon yod do /.

[13] *Ibid.:* gnyis pa yul gzhan yongs su mi gcod par thal ba ni / shes pa snga ma phyi mas gcod na ni gzugs sgra la sogs pa'i yul gzhan mi gcod pa dang / de la mi 'pho bar 'gyur te /.

[14] *Psychology from an Empirical Standpoint* p. 27.

necessarily applicable to itself. The negation of 'conscious' is not 'unconscious' but rather 'not conscious'. If I claim to be conscious of blue but not conscious of being conscious of blue I am not thereby claiming that I am unconscious. Moreover we might anyway choose to deny, with Tsong kha pa, that saying 'I am conscious of seeing blue' adds anything to saying 'I see blue'.Whether something is nevertheless lost in this analysis, a distinction perhaps between being conscious *of x* and conscious *that x* is, of course, a different issue.[15]

There is another argument used by Buddhists in support of self-referring, reflexive consciousness which I am not familiar with from any Western context. This is the argument from memory. Put by Tsong kha pa in its simplest form, the argument runs as follows: When I remember that I sensed blue at a former time the sensation is a cause, although not the only cause, of the memory. In remembering—and in the Buddhist discussion of memory I think we can see an example of a particular case of *reflective* awareness, awareness taking as its object another awareness which has occurred previously—the awareness

[15] See Tsong kha pa's *dKa' gnas chen po brgyad* pp. 26-27: sngon po myong ba'i rtags las sngon po rig pa sngon du song bar grub la / sngon po rig par grub pa nyid kyis rig pa tsam du grub zin pa'i phyir / rang rig la sogs pa'i sgrub byed gzhan rtog pa don med do / This argument is used by Tsong kha pa in the context of the 'memory argument' which will be dealt with subsequently. Its generalization seems to be in keeping with Tsong kha pa's overall position. A similar argument may be indicated by Wittgenstein's treatment of pain in his *Philosophical Investigations,* paras. 416 ff. That self-consciousness is indicated in the distinction between being conscious of *x* and conscious that *x* is persuasively argued by Pratima Bowes in her book *Consciousness and Freedom.* Among the views she treats in this book are two Indian views, Sāṃkhya and Advaita Vedānta.

which serves as the referent of the memory act is seen to have both subjective and objective elements. That is, Tsong kha pa explains, when we remember, the memory image is seen [325] to be composed of 'formerly *this* was seen' and 'it was seen *by me*.[16] Or, as Tsong kha pa expressed it elsewhere, when I remember that I truly saw blue there is a memory of blue and a memory of seeing blue. Thus in the original act there must have been the sensation of blue and also the sensation of seeing blue.[17] These two formulations of the same argument are worth noting, for they indicate that reference in the first formulation to perception *by me* is intended to indicate self-consciousness in the sense of reflexive consciousness of *its*elf, not consciousness of *a* self, perception *by* a self. That these two issues are different is seldom sufficiently realised in Western philosophy, their confusion was fatal for Descartes, who concluded from the argument that consciousness in being conscious is conscious of being conscious, reflexive self-consciousness, to the existence of a substantial Self.[18]

---

[16] See Tsong kha pa's *Drang nges legs bshad snying po* (1973b) p. 175: de yang sngar 'di mthong ngo zhes yul dang ngas mthong ngo zhes yul can dran pa yod pas sngar gyi sngo 'dzin gyi shes pa lta bu de la myong ba yod do /.

[17] In his *dKa' gnas chen po brgyad* p. 5: bye brag tu ngas sngon po yang dag par mthong ngo snyam du dran pa'i tse sngon po dran pa dang / sngon po'i mthong ba dran pa / dran pa'i 'dzin stangs la yod la / des dpag par bya ba'i sngon po nyams su myong byed dang / sngon po mthong ba myong byed gnyis yod par grub pas /.

[18] See, in particular, Descartes' *Discourse on Method* 4, where he concludes, from the fact of doubting, his own existence—'I think, therefore I am' and sees this as equivalent to being 'a substance, of which the whole essence or nature consists in thinking'. That this inference is problematic was noted at length by Kant, *Critique of Pure Reason* (Kemp-Smith transl.),

But it is at least debatable whether a reflection on consciousness, introspection, can establish what is actually present to consciousness in lived experience. The presence of a number of elements in the verbal formulation of a reflective awareness 'I saw blue' doesn't indicate that these elements correspond to epistemological elements in the original experience. As Kant pointed out, there is an 'I think' which is capable of accompanying all my mental acts, but the only significance of this is that all my mental acts are *mine*.[19] It is not quite clear what it would be for me to have someone else's mental acts, and thus the 'I saw blue' carries with it no implications as to the status of self-consciousness or a self. Tsong kha pa points out that one can infer simple sensation from memory, but one is unable to infer self-consciousness. On the basis [326] of sensing blue one can conclude in memory that formerly there was the awareness of blue, but this only allows the establishment of simple awareness, not self-awareness. On the other hand if there is a memory of simple awareness of blue it is unnecessary to postulate self-consciousness.[20] That is, if I remember seeing blue, and I am remembering the objective part, 'blue', this is sufficient for memory. It is possible, but not necessary, to add on top of this an addi-

---

pp. 330 ff.

[19] *Critique of Pure Reason* pp. 152 ff. Cf. Strawson's *The Bounds of Sense* p. 165: 'It would make no sense to think or say: *This* inner experience is occurring, but it is occurring to me?...Again, it would make no sense to think or say: I distinctly remember *that* inner experience occurring, but did it occur to me?' Tsong kha pa makes more or less the same point in his *Drang nges legs bshad snying po* (1973b) p. 176: rang lugs kyis rang rig med kyang dran pa skye ba mi 'gal ni // gang phyir gang gis yul myong gyur de las / dran pa 'di gzhan nga la yod min pa /.

[20] See the *dKa' gnas chen po brgyad,* quoted in n.15 above.

tional awareness that it was *me* who saw blue but, apart from Kant's contentless 'I think', the memory of seeing blue itself doesn't require this additional awareness and therefore will not indicate a self-consciousness present in all consciousness. If I remember seeing blue, through a memory of blue, Tsong kha pa wants to claim, then if I am mistaken and I didn't see blue this is not a case of memory but of imagination. And if I really did see blue then in remembering blue it would be absurd to say that there is for me a memory of blue but not a memory of seeing blue or indeed that *I* saw blue. How could my memory of blue pertain to anyone or anything else? And thus the simple memory of blue is sufficient; to say 'I saw blue' adds nothing to this simple awareness, it doesn't allow us to infer self-consciousness as an aspect of the initial experience.

I want now to look at some aspects of Go ram pa bSod nams seng ge's portrayal of Candrakīrti's position in his critical summary commentary on the *Madhyamakāvatara* (the *dBu ma la 'jug pa'i dkyus kyi sa bcad pa dang gzhung so so'i dka' ba'i gnas la dpyad pa lTa ba ngan sel*). If the claim is that self-consciousness is truly established based on the memory argument then this is refuted by the refutation of the four sorts of production—from self, other, both or neither. That is, there is no way that memory could really be the result of sensation given the refutation of causality.[21] But if the claim is that self-consciousness exists conventionally in all mental acts then there is uncertainty of pervasion. It is like when one establishes that there is fire in a certain place and then, using the logical mark of smoke, wants to prove that there is fire else-

[21] *dBu ma la 'jug pa'i dkyus kyi sa bcad pa dang gzhung so so'i dka' ba'i gnas la dpyad pa lTa ba ngan sel* p. 62b.

where. It has yet to be shown that wherever there is smoke there is fire. Likewise it has yet to be shown that wherever there is memory there was self-consciousness.[22] Candrakīrti gives as examples, in order [327] to show uncertainty of pervasion, according to Go ram pa bSod nams ge, the fact that one cannot prove that a magnifying glass was used just because one sees fire, and so on.[23] Conventionally memory certainly occurs as a result of sensing the object previously, even without sensing the consciousness itself.

But Go ram pa bSod nams seng ge's subsequent discussion shows how he failed to realise the distinction, implicit in Tsong kha pa's discussion, between reflexive consciousness of itself and reflective consciousness of self. For he takes Candrakīrti's analysis of how it is possible to say in everyday parlance '*I* saw blue' as a demonstration of how self-consciousness occurs conventionally. Conventionally self-consciousness does occur, he says, since there is memory directed to the object, arising from sensation of the object, and memory of oneself arising from sensation of oneself.[24] In other words, contrary to Tsong kha pa's position above, Go ram pa bSod nams seng ge wants to

---

22 *Ibid.*: rang rig bsgrub pa la khyab pa ma nges te / gzhi gzhan gyi steng du me gzhan sngar tshad mas grub na phyis du ba'i rtags las gzhi 'ga' zhig tu mi grub pa 'thad pa bzhin du / sngar spyir rang rig tshad mas grub na / dran pa'i rtags las de sgrub pa 'thad kyang / phyir rgol gyi ngor sngar rang rig spyi ldog nas ma grub pa da lta dran pa'i rtags kyis mi 'grub pa'i phyir...

23 *Ibid.*, continuation of above: dang dran pa tha snyad pa'i rtags kyis rang rig sgrub pa'i khyab pa ma nges pa'i dpe ni chu tsam mthong ba las nor bu chu shel lam / me tsam mthong ba las nor bu me shel mi 'grub pa bzhin zhes gsungs so /.

24 *Ibid.* p. 62d: gzhung 'dis rang lugs la myong dran gzhan du med pa'i rgyu mtshan gyis yul myong las yul dran skye ba dang / rang myong las rang dran skye ba dran pas tha snyad du rang rig zhal gyis bzhes par grub bo /.

maintain that while we can't infer from memory self-consciousness, memory of the objective part 'seeing blue' or 'blue' is sufficient to establish memory without postulating its constant accompaniment by self-awareness, nevertheless in that it is possible for me to direct an additional awareness to the fact that '*I* saw blue', the subjective part, so self-consciousness is an everyday conventional possibility. The fact that inference from memory to self-consciousness is uncertain doesn't necessitate that self-consciousness never occurs, or that memory may not serve to reveal it. Thus Candrakīrti's choice of examples, the fact that fire *can* be produced by a magnifying glass, although it can also be produced by rubbing two sticks together, shows that he didn't want to refute the possibility of the conventional occurrence of self-consciousness. Otherwise he would have shown not uncertainty of pervasion but rather contradictory pervasion, examples where the occurrence of the one is never accompanied by the occurence of the other.[25]

[328] But let us just note that Go ram pa bSod nams seng ge's argument rests here on the ambiguity of 'self-consciousness', for the very position of Śāntarakṣita, for example, requires that self-consciousness

---

[25] *Ibid.* p. 62b, continuation of n.23 above: de'i don yang dran pa tha snyad pa de yin na rang rig las byung bas ma khyab ste / rang myong med par yul myong ba las kyang dran pa tha snyad pa skye ba yod pa'i phyir / dper na chu shel med kyang char la sogs pa dang / me shel med kyang gtsub shing sogs las chu dang me 'byung ba'i phyir zhes pa'i don te / dpe 'dis kyang rang rig tha snyad du khas mi len pa ma yin te / gzhan du na rang rig [62c] tha snyad pa sgrub pa la dran pa tha snyad pa rtags su bkod pa khyab pa 'gal bar gsungs dgos pa las / khyab pa ma nges par gsungs pa'i phyir ro / dpe las kyang shes te / chu shel dang me shel las chu dang me skye ba srid kyang chu dang me yin na de gnyis las skye bas ma khyab pa dper bkod 'dug pa'i phyir ro /.

rakṣita, for example, requires that self-consciousness in the sense of reflexive awareness distinguishes consciousness from dead objects through its universal presence in consciousness. It is the very mode of being of consciousness, it is what consciousness must be, there is no question of its being present at some times and not at others. If consciousness isn't self-conscious then it is unconscious. It is known through memory because in memory we remember blue and we remember sensing blue, as Tsong kha pa explained. The example of remembering '*I* saw blue' is a misleading alternative variant of this, but it is a variant which led Go ram pa bSod nams seng ge into identifying the possibility of a conventional awareness of self in memory with a mere possibility of reflexive self-consciousness. But Śāntarakṣita could simply reply that the possibility of directing the attention to the subject in a reflective awareness presupposes the constant occurrence of a reflexive self-consciousness, but is not the same as this self-consciousness.

I want finally to indicate one aspect of Mi bskyod rdo rje's impatient critique of Go ram pa bSod nams seng ge's position which raises broadly philosophical problems, without going so far as to suggest even an attempt at their solution.

Mi bskyod rdo rje points out, correctly, that for Candrakīrti reflexive self-consciousness represents a theoretical tenet of certain Sautrāntikas and Cittamātrins.[26] It isn't a matter of everyday, pre-critical, pre-reflexive concern, it isn't a tenet of what philosophers have sometimes rather vaguely called

---

[26] *Dwags brgyud grub pa'i shing rta* p. 457: gzung 'dis rang rig ces mdo sems kyi bstan bcos la grags pa'i mtshon bya'i ming de 'jig rten spyi la tha snyad du ma grags pas /.

'commonsense',[27] and as such there is no question for Candrakīrti of the conventional existence of self-consciousness. It either really, truly, ultimately exists, or it is simply an erroneous tenet, it doesn't exist even conventionally. For Mi bskyod rdo rje Candrakīrti's conventional truth is simply, and only, what is held to be true in pre-critical, non-philosophical worldly commerce.[28] [329] And in wordly commerce people consider themselves just to experience sensations, and then to remember them later.[29] It is sufficient conventionally to talk of sensation and memory as it is of act and effect,[30] but this is certainly not to be examined critically in order to seek for an explanation or founding of the world.[31] When examined critically it is simply the case that all conventions, all 'commonsense' collapses and is seen to be ultimately unfounded.[32] For Mi bskyod rdo rje it is true in the strongest sense, and in a way that it is not true for

---

[27] *Ibid.*, continuation of above: de 'jig rten pas tha snyad du'ang byas pa min gyi /.

[28] For Mi bskyod rdo rje on the two truths see the *Dwags brgyud grub pa'i shing rta* on *Madhyamakāvatāra* 9:23-30, pp. 274 ff. This lengthy section includes an extensive critical discussion of various Tibetan views on the two *satyas*.

[29] *Ibid.* p. 457, continuation of n.27 above: rang rig ces pa'i mtshon bya ming de gang la gdags pa'i gzhi shes myong tsam de dang / de phyis dran tsam 'jig rten pas tha snyad du brjod pa yod pas.

[30] *Ibid.* p. 458: las 'bras dang myong dran tsam tha snyad kyi gzhir rung bas de dag ma dpyad pa'i tha snyad kyis tha snyad de dag 'jig rten na rnam par bzhag go zhes gsal bar bshad pa'i phyir /.

[31] *Ibid.* pp. 457-458:...rang rig rnams ma grub pas de dag 'jig rten gyi tha snyad du tha snyad byed ched du de ltar sgrub pa 'jig rten na'ang don med pa'i phyir ro /

[32] *Ibid.* pp. 457 ff.

Tsong kha pa, that the Madhyamaka holds no positions, it has no explanations.

Now, the problem for the philosopher which I want to suggest arises out of this part of Mi bskyod rdo rje's critique of Go ram pa bSod nams seng ge is this: To what extent is self-consciousness a philosophical *explanation* of everyday experience, and to what extent is it a *presupposition* of such experience? This question cannot be disposed of by pointing to the fact that some philosophers deny self-consciousness and refute those who maintain its existence. For one can still ask of those philosophers who adhere to self-consciousness whether they consider themselves to be engaged in a project of revealing a presupposition of everyday experience, that is, a fundamental structure of experience such that experience *is* experience, a phenomenological investigation, if you like, or whether they consider themselves to be explaining everyday experience, perhaps as some phenomenalists have explained that the everyday world is a construct out of sense data, which form the immediate given of experience. On the former model the philosopher is, in this instance, simply making clear dimensions of everyday experience which may not be clearly articulated by the 'man in the street' but which the man in the street can willingly assent to as being a necessary dimension of, or prerequisite for, his everyday experience.

I'm not sure how one would settle which of these is the case as regards self-consciousness. One relevant point in deciding may rest on whether we can think of an everyday context where, in answer to the question [330] whether someone really knows something or other he would reply, 'Oh yes, certainly I do, for I am conscious and even vividly conscious of doing so'. The case is from Gilbert Ryle, and Ryle maintains that this in fact never occurs.[33] Self-consciousness is not part of everyday experience. But all this seems to indicate is that in normal, everyday activity people don't operate on the level of sophistication which involves uncovering the presuppositions of experience. The contemporary Indian philosopher J.N. Mohanty has claimed that immediate self-consciousness uniquely occupies neither a practical nor a theoretical mode, or, in terms of the previous discussion, it is neither part of familiar, everyday commonsense activity, nor is it simply deduced in reflection, in this case philosophical reflection. Rather it transcends this distinction and yet it accompanies all our awarenesses.[34] If so, then it doesn't follow, in spite of Mi bskyod rdo rje, that to claim that self-consciousness exists is to make a purely theoretical, or, as I have put it, explanatory claim. In postulating self-consciousness it is claimed that it is undeniably present in everyday conscious acts, its postulation uncovers descriptively a presupposition of all experience. For those who deny self-consciousness its postulation is said to be unnecessary to experience, but in both cases the issue has an immediacy not borne by abstract metaphysical *explanations* of the world.

[33] See *The Concept of Mind* p. 155.

[34] See his paper 'Modes of givenness' in *Phenomenology and Ontology* p. 11. Cf. also Mohanty's critique of Ryle in 'Gilbert Ryle's criticisms of the concept of consciousness', *ibid.* pp. 161-169.

BIBLIOGRAPHY

Unless otherwise noted, all Cone Tibetan bsTan 'gyur texts are from the microfiche edition produced by The Institute for Advanced Studies of World Religions, New York, and all Derge bsTan 'gyur texts are from the Taipei edition:

Barber, A.W. (ed.). 1991. *The Tibetan Tripitaka.* Taipei Edition: SMC Publishing.

Abhyankar, K.V., and Shukla, J.M. 1986. *A Dictionary of Sanskrit Grammar.* Baroda: Oriental Institute.

Anonymous. *Bodhisattvacaryāvatāravivṛttipañjikā.* Cone mDo 'grel 26, folio 287a ff. Derge vol. 36, *La* pp. 576 ff. Full commentary version of next text.

Anonymous. *Bodhisattvacaryāvatāravivṛtti.* Cone mDo 'grel 27, folio 177b ff. Derge vol. 36, *Sha* pp. 355 ff. Commentary to chapters 9 and 10.

Aristotle. 1941. *De Anima.* In *The Basic Works of Aristotle,* edited by Richard McKeon. New York: Random House.

Atiśa. *Satyadvayāvatāra.* Peking edition P. 5298, mDo 'grel 29, folio 70a ff.

Bowes, P. 1971. *Consciousness and Freedom.* London: Methuen.

Brentano F. 1973. *Psychology from an Empirical Standpoint.* Edited by Oscar Kraus. English edition edited by Linda L McAlister. Trans. by Antos C. Rancurello, D.B. Terrell and Linda McAlister. London: Routledge and Kegan Paul.

Bu ston. 1971. *Byang chub sems dpa'i spyod pa la 'jug pa'i 'grel pa Byang chub kyi sems gsal bar byed pa Zla ba'i 'od zer.* Included in Lokesh Chandra (ed.), *The Collected Works of Bu-ston*: part 19 (*Dza*). Sata-Pitaka Series vol. 59. New Delhi: International Academy of Indian Culture.

Cabezón, J. 1992. *A Dose of Emptiness: An annotated translation of the sTong thun chen mo of mKhas grub dGe legs dpal bzang.* Albany, N.Y.: SUNY Press.

Candrakīrti. 1978. *Madhyamakāvatārakārikā.* In *mNgon rtogs rgyan dang dBu ma 'jug pa mDzod rtsa ba bcas.* Sarnath: Legs bshad gter mdzod par khang.

Candrakīrti. *Madhyamakāvatārabhāṣya.* Cone mDo 'grel 23, folio 217a ff.

Candrakīrti. 1984. *Madhyamkāvatāra par Candrakīrti.* Version of previous text (*Madhyamakāvatārabhāṣya*) edited by Louis de la Vallée Poussin. Bibliotheca Buddhica IX. Taiwanese reprint; originally published 1907-12.

Dalai Lama, Fourteenth. 1988. *Transcendent Wisdom.* Ithaca, N.Y.: Snow Lion.

Dalai Lama, Fourteenth. 1994. *A Flash of Lightning in the Dark of Night.* Translated by the Padmakara Translation Group. Boston: Shambhala.

Descartes, R. 1965. *Discourse on Method and Other Writings.* Translated by F.E. Sutcliffe. London: Penguin.

Dharmakīrti. 1968. *Pramāṇavārttika of Acharya Dharmakirtti with the commentary 'Vritti' of Acharya Manorathanandin.* Edited by Swami Dwarikadas Shastri. Varanasi: Bauddha Bharati.

Dharmakīrti. 1992. *Nyāyabindu, with the Nyāyabinduṭīkā of Dharmottara.* Edited by Th. Stcherbatsky. Bibliotheca Buddhica VII. Delhi: Motilal Banarsidass. Originally published 1918; Tibetan text (edited by Th. Stcherbatsky) published by the same publishers in the same series as Bibliotheca Buddhica VIII. Originally published 1904.

Dudjom Rinpoche, Jikdrel Yeshe Dorje. 1991. *The Nyingma School of Tibetan Buddhism: Its Fundamentals and History.* Translated by Gyurme Dorje with the collaboration of Matthew Kapstein. Boston: Wisdom.

Ejima, Yasunori. 1978. Contents note to the *sDe dge Tibetan Tripiṭaka bsTan 'gyur preserved in the Faculty of Letters, University of Tokyo.* Tokyo: Sekai Seiten Kanko Kyokai, for the Faculty of Letters, University of Tokyo.

Go ram pa bSod nams seng ge. 1969. *dBu ma la 'jug pa'i dkyus kyi sa bcad pa dang gzhung so so'i dka' ba'i gnas la dpyad pa lTa ba ngan sel.* Contained in *Sa skya pa'i bka' 'bum*, compiled by bSod nams rgya mtsho, vol. 13: *Go ram pa bSod nams seng ge'i bka' 'bum*. Tokyo: Toyo-Bunko.

Gomez, L.O., and and Silk, J.A. (eds.). 1989. *Studies in the Literature of the Great Vehicle: Three Mahāyāna Buddhist Texts*. Ann Arbor: Centre for South and Southeast Asian Studies, University of Michigan.

rGyal tshab rje. 1973. *Byang chub sems dpa'i spyod pa la 'jug pa'i rnam bshad rGyal sras 'jug ngogs*. Sarnath: Pleasure of Elegant Sayings Printing Press.

Gyatso, Geshe Kelsang. 1993. *Understanding the Mind*. London: Tharpa Publications.

Hattori, M. 1968. *Dinnāga on Perception*. Cambridge, Mass.: Harvard University Press.

Hookham, S.K. 1991. *The Buddha Within: Tathagatagarbha According to the Shentong Interpretation of the Ratnagotravibhaga*. Albany, N.Y.: State University of New York Press.

Hopkins, J. 1980. *Compassion in Tibetan Buddhism*. London: Rider.

Hopkins, J. 1983. *Meditation on Emptiness*. London: Wisdom.

Ichigo, M. 1989. 'Śāntarakṣita's *Madhyamakālaṃkāra*'. In Gomez and Silk (1989), *Studies in the Literature of the Great Vehicle*.

Kajiyama, Y. 1989 [reprint]. *An Introduction to Buddhist Philosophy: An Annotated Translation of the Tarkabhāṣā of Mokṣākaragupta*. In *Studies in Buddhist*

Philosophy (Selected Papers), edited by Katsumi Mimaki et al. Kyoto: Rinsen Book Co.

Kamalaśīla. *Madhyamakālaṃkārapañjikā*. Cone mDo 'grel 28, folio 83b ff. Derge vol. 36, *Sa* pp. 167 ff.

Kant, I. 1968. *Immanuel Kant's Critique of Pure Reason*. Translated by Norman Kemp Smith. London: Macmillan. Reprint of 1933 [second] edition.

Kapstein, M. 1988. 'Mi-pham's theory of interpretation'. In D.S. Lopez, Jr. (ed.), *Buddhist Hermeneutics* (Kuroda Institute Studies in East Asian Buddhism 6). Honolulu: University of Hawaii Press.

Karmay, S.G. 1988. *The Great Perfection*. Leiden: E.J. Brill.

mKhas grub rje. 1972. *Stoṅ thun chen mo of mKhas-grub dge-legs-dpal-bzaṅ and Other Texts on Madhyamika Philosophy*. Edited by Lha-mkhar yoṅs-dzin bstan pa rgyal mtshan. New Delhi: Madhyamika Text Series.

Khenchen Kunzang Palden and Minyak Kunzang Sönam. 1993. *Wisdom: Two Buddhist Commentaries*. Translated by the Padmakara Translation Group. Peyzac-le-Moustier: Editions Padmakara.

Klein, A. 1986. *Knowledge and Liberation*. Ithaca, N.Y.: Snow Lion.

Klein, A. 1991. *Knowing, Naming and Negation*. Ithaca, N.Y.: Snow Lion.

Kun bzang dpal ldan. 1989. *Byang chub sems dpa'i spyod pa la 'jug pa'i tshig 'grel 'Jam dbyangs bla ma'i zhal lung bdud rtsi'i thig pa.* Delhi: Konchhog Lhadrepa.

bLo bzang rab gsal, Pa ri. 1969. *'Ju lan ga bur chu rgyun.* Published in India.

Matilal, B.K. 1986. *Perception: An Essay on Classical Indian Theories of Knowledge.* Oxford: Oxford University Press.

Mi bskyod rdo rje. 1975. *dBu ma la 'jug pa'i rnam bshad dpal ldan dus gsum mkhyen pa'i zhal lung Dwags brgyud grub pa'i shing rta.* Published in India by the rGyal ba Karma pa.

Mi pham. 1973. *dBu ma'i lta khrid zab mo.* Tibetan text contained in *Lama Mipham: Calm and Clear.* Translated from the Tibetan with commentary by Tarthang Tulku. Emeryville: Dharma Publishing.

Mi pham. 1975a. *Spyod 'jug shes rab kyi le'u'i tshig don go sla bar rnam par bshad pa Nor bu ke ta ka.* Contained in the *Collected Writings of 'Jam mgon 'ju Mi pham rgya mtsho,* vol. 13. Gangtog: Ngagyur Nyingmay Sungrab Series.

Mi pham. 1975b. *Sher 'grel brgal lan nyin byed snang ba.* Contained in the *Collected Writings of 'Jam mgon 'ju Mi pham rgya mtsho,* vol. 13. Gangtog: Ngagyur Nyingmay Sungrab Series.

Mi pham. 1976a. *dBu ma rgyan gyi rnam bshad 'Jam dbyangs bla ma dgyes pa'i zhal lung.* Contained in the *Collected Writings of 'Jam mgon 'ju Mi pham rgya mtsho,* vol. 12. Gangtog: Ngagyur Nyingmay Sungrab Series.

Mi pham. 1976a(ii). *dBu ma rgyan gyi rnam bshad 'Jam dbyangs bla ma dgyes pa'i zhal lung.* Published in India by the rGyal ba Karma pa.

Mi pham. 1976b. *bDe gshegs snying po'i stong thun chen mo Seng ge'i nga ro.* Contained in the *Collected Writings of 'Jam mgon 'ju Mi pham rgya mtsho,* vol. 3. Gangtog: Ngagyur Nyingmay Sungrab Series.

Mi pham. 1976c. *Don dam par nges pa shes rab ral gri mchan bcas.* Contained in the *Collected Writings of 'Jam mgon 'ju Mi pham rgya mtsho,* vol. 3. Gangtog: Ngagyur Nyingmay Sungrab Series.

Mi pham. 1979. *dBu ma la 'jug pa'i 'grel ba Zla ba'i zhal lung dri med shel phreng.* Contained in the *Collected Writings of 'Jam mgon 'ju Mi pham rgya mtsho,* vol. 1. Gangtog: Ngagyur Nyingmay Sungrab Series.

Mohanty, J.N. 1970. *Phenomenology and Ontology.* The Hague: Martinus Nijhoff.

Mokṣākaragupta. 1985. *Bauddha Tarkabhāṣā of Mokṣākargupta.* Edited and translated by B.N. Singh. Varanasi: Asha Prakashan. For another translation see Kajiyama.

Newland, G. 1992. *The Two Truths.* Ithaca, N.Y.: Snow Lion.

Pabongka Rinpoche. 1991. *Liberation in the Palm of your Hand.* Translated by Michael Richards. Boston: Wisdom Publications.

Padma rgyal mtshan [Loling Khensur Pema Gyaltsen] 1984/5. *Zab don gdams pa'i mig 'byed gser gyi thur ma.* Mundgod: Drepung Loseling Library Society. Two volumes.

Prajñākaramati. *Bodhicaryāvatārapañjikā.* Edited by P.L. Vaidya. See under Śāntideva. Tibetan in Cone mDo 'grel vol. 26, folio 39a ff. Derge vol. 36, *La* pp. 82 ff.

Red mda' ba gZhon nu blo gros. 1983. *dBu ma la 'jug pa'i rnam bshad De kho na nyid gsal ba'i sgron ma.* Sarnath: Sakyapa Students' Union.

Ruegg, D.S. 1966. *The Life of Bu ston Rin po che.* Rome: Instituto Intaliano per il Medio ed Estremo Oriente.

Ruegg, D.S. 1981. 'On the thesis and assertion in the Madhyamaka/dBu ma'. In Ernst Steinkellner and Helmut Tauscher [eds.], *Contributions on Tibetan and Buddhist Religion and Philosophy: Proceedings of the Csoma de Körös Symposium 1981,* Volume 2. Wien: Arbeitskreis für Tibetische und Buddhistische Studien Universität Wien.

Ruegg, D.S. 1991. 'On *pramāṇa* theory in Tsoṅ kha pa's Madhyamaka philosophy'. In Ernst Steinkellner [ed.], *Studies in the Buddhist Epistemological Tradition.* Wien: Verlag der Österreichischen Akademie der Wissenschaften.

Ryle, G. 1973. *The Concept of Mind.* London: Penguin. Originally published in 1949.

Sa bzang mati paṇchen. 1975. *Byang chub sems dpa'i spyod pa la 'jug pa'i rnam bshad gZhung don rab gsal snang ba*. New Delhi. Distributed by the Tibetan Bonpo Monastic Centre, Dolanji, H.P., India.

Saito, A. 1993. *A Study of Akṣayamati (= Śantideva)'s Bodhisattvacaryāvatāra as found in the Tibetan Manuscripts from Tun-huang*. A Report of the Grant-in-Aid for Scientific Research. Miye University: Faculty of Humanities.

Śāntarakṣita. 1976. *Madhyamakālaṃkāra*. In *dBu ma rgyan gyi rtsa ba dang dBu ma rgyan gyi zin bris dBu ma rgyan gyi brjed byang*. Sarnath, India. See also Ichigo (1989).

Śāntarakṣita. 1968. *Tattvasaṅgraha of Acārya Shāntarakṣita with the Commentary "Pañjikā" of Shri Kamalashīla*. Edited by Swami Dwarikadas Shastri. Varanasi: Bauddha Bharati. Two volumes.

Śāntarakṣita. *Madhyamakālaṃkāravṛtti*. Derge vol. 36, *Sa* pp. 112 ff.

Śāntideva. 1960. *Bodhicaryāvatāra of Śāntideva with the commentary Pañjikā of Prajñākaramati*. Edited by P.L. Vaidya. Darbhanga: Mithila Institute.

Śāntideva. 1982. *Byang chub sems dpa'i spyod pa la 'jug pa'i rtsa ba dang 'grel pa Legs par bshad pa'i rgya mtsho*. Sarnath: Sakya Students' Union. Contains the root text and also the commentary by rGyal sras Thogs med (see below).

Sartre, J.-P. 1966. *Being and Nothingness*. Translated by Hazel E. Barnes. New York: Washington Square.

Sartre, J.-P. 1957. *The Transcendence of the Ego.* Translated by Forrest Williams and Robert Kirkpatrick. New York: Noonday Press.

Shah, N.J. 1967. *Akalaṅka's Criticism of Dharmakīrti's Philosophy.* Ahmedabad: L.D. Institute of Indology.

bSod nams rgyal mtshan, bLa ma dam pa. 1973. *Byang chub sems dpa'i spyod pa la 'jug pa rnam par bshad pa dGongs pa nges par gsal ba.* New Delhi.

bSod nams rtse mo. 1968. *Byang chub sems dpa'i spyod pa la 'jug pa'i 'grel pa.* Contained in the *Sa skya pa'i bka' 'bum,* vol. 2. Tokyo: Toyo-Bunko.

Sparham, G. (translator), in collaboration with Shotaro Iida. 1993. *Ocean of Eloquence: Tsong kha pa's Commentary on the Yogācāra Doctrine of Mind.* Albany, N. Y.: State University of New York Press.

Strawson, P.F. 1966. *The Bounds of Sense.* London: Methuen.

Thogs med, rGyal sras dNgul chu. 1982. *Byang chub sems dpa'i spyod pa la 'jug pa'i 'grel pa Legs par bshad pa'i rgya mtsho.* Sarnath: Sakya Students Union.

Thub bstan chos kyi grags pa (= Mi nyag Kun bzang bsod nams). 1990a. *Spyod 'jug shes rab le'u'i gzhung 'grel Zab mo rten 'byung gi de kho na nyid gsal ba'i sgron me.* Contained in the *Spyod 'jug gi 'grel bshad rGyal sras yon tan bum bzang.* pp. 585-679. Beijing: Krung go'i bod kyi shes rig dpe skrun khang.

Thub bstan chos kyi grags pa (= Mi nyag Kun bzang bsod nams). 1990b. *Spyod 'jug shes rab le'u'i spyi don rim par phye ba Zab mo rten 'byung gi de kho na nyid yang gsal sgron me.* Contained in the *Spyod 'jug gi 'grel bshad rGyal sras yon tan bum bzang*: pp. 681-880. Beijing: Krung go'i bod kyi shes rig dpe skrun khang.

Thurman, R.A.F. 1984. *Tsong Khapa's Speech of Gold in the* Essence of True Eloquence. Princeton, N. J.: Princeton University Press.

Tshul khrims rgya mtsho (Ven. Khenpo Tsultrim Gyamtso Rimpoche). 1986. *Progressive Stages of Meditation on Emptiness.* Translated by S. Hookham. Oxford: Longchen Foundation.

Tsong kha pa. 1956. *sPyod 'jug shes rab le'u'i ṭikkā bLo gsal ba.* In the *bTsong kha pa bKa' 'bum* published with the Japanese reprint of the Peking edition of the Tibetan Tripitaka: vol. 153. Tokyo-Kyoto: Suzuki Research Foundation.

Tsong kha pa. 1970. *rTsa ba shes rab kyi dka' gnas chen po brgyad kyi bshad pa.* Sarnath: Pleasure of Elegant Sayings Printing Press.

Tsong kha pa. 1973a. *dBu ma dgongs pa rab gsal.* Sarnath: Pleasure of Elegant Sayings Printing Press.

Tsong kha pa. 1973b. *Drang nges legs bshad snying po.* Sarnath: Pleasure of Elegant Sayings Printing Press.

Tsong kha pa. 1991. *Drang nges legs bshad snying po: The Essence of Eloquent Speech on the Definitive and Interpretable.* Edited by Geshes Palden Drakpa and Damdul Namgyal. Mundgod: SOKU Publications.

Van der Kuijp, Leonard W.J. 1983. *Contributions to the Development of Tibetan Buddhist Epistemology: from the eleventh to the thirteenth century*. Wiesbaden: Franz Steiner Verlag.

Verhagen, P.C. 1994. *A History of Sanskrit Grammatical Literature in Tibet*. Leiden: E.J. Brill.

Vetter, T. 1966. *Dharmakīrti's Pramāṇaviniścaya 1. Kapitel*. Wien: Österreichische Akademie der Wissenschaften.

Vibhūticandra. *Bodhicaryāvatāratātparyapañjikā Viśeṣadyotanī*. Cone mDo 27, folio 192b ff. Derge vol. 36, *Sha* pp. 384 ff.

Vinītadeva. 1971. *Vinītadeva's Nyāyabinduṭīkā*. Sanskrit text reconstructed from the Tibetan and translated by Mrinalkanti Gangopadhyaya. Calcutta: Indian Studies Past and Present.

Williams, P. 1981. 'On the Abhidharma ontology'. *Journal of Indian Philosophy* 9: 227-257.

Williams, P. 1983. 'On *rang rig*'. In Ernst Steinkellner and Helmut Tauscher [eds.], *Contributions on Tibetan and Buddhist Religion and Philosophy: Proceedings of the Csoma de Körös Symposium 1981*, Volume 2: pp. 321-32. Wien: Arbeitskreis für Tibetische und Buddhistische Studien Universität Wien.

Williams, P. 1983b. 'A note on some aspects of Mi bskyod rdo rje's critique of dGe lugs pa Madhyamaka'. *Journal of Indian Philosophy* 11: 125-45.

Williams, P. 1985. 'rMa bya pa Byang chub brtson 'grus on Madhyamaka method'. *Journal of Indian Philosophy* 13: 205-25.

Williams, P. 1989. *Mahāyāna Buddhism: The doctrinal foundations*. London: Routledge.

Williams, P. 1992a. 'Non-conceptuality, critical reasoning and religious experience. Some Tibetan Buddhist discussions'. In Michael McGhee [ed.], *Philosophy, Religion and the Spiritual Life*. Philosophy Supplement 32. Cambridge: Cambridge University Press.

Williams, P. 1992b. 'On *prakṛtinirvāṇa/prakṛtinirvṛta* in the *Bodhicaryāvatāra:* A study in the Indo-Tibetan commentarial tradition'. *Asiatische Studien/Études Asiatiques* XLVI:I: 516-550.

Williams, P. 1994. 'An argument for Cittamātra—reflections on *Bodhicaryāvatāra* 9:28 (Tib. 27) cd'. In *Tibetan Studies*, edited by Per Kvaerne: pp. 965-80. Oslo: The Institute for Comparative Research in Human Culture.

Williams, P. Forthcoming. 'Identifying the object of negation: *Bodhicaryāvatāra* 9:140 (Tib. 139) in context'. In P. Williams, *Studies in the Philosophy of the Bodhicaryāvatāra.*

Wittgenstein, L. 1968. *Philosophical Investigations.* Translated by G.E.M. Anscombe. Oxford: Blackwell.

INDEX